ON THE
CANAL

ON THE CANAL

The Marines of L-3-5 on Guadalcanal, 1942

Ore J. Marion
with Thomas Cuddihy and Edward Cuddihy

STACKPOLE
BOOKS

Copyright © 2004 by Stackpole Books

Published by
STACKPOLE BOOKS
5067 Ritter Road
Mechanicsburg, PA 17055
www.stackpolebooks.com

All rights reserved, including the right to reproduce this book or portions thereof in any form or by any means, electronic or mechanical, including photocopying, recording, or by any information storage and retrieval system, without permission in writing from the publisher. All inquiries should be addressed to Stackpole Books, 5067 Ritter Road, Mechanicsburg, Pennsylvania 17055.

Printed in the United States of America

10 9 8 7 6 5 4 3 2 1

FIRST EDITION

Library of Congress Cataloging-in-Publication Data

Marion, Ore J.
   On the Canal : the Marines of L-3-5 on Guadalcanal, 1942 / by Ore J. Marion with Thomas Cuddihy and Edward Cuddihy.— 1st ed.
     p. cm. — (Stackpole Military history series)
  Includes index.
  ISBN 0-8117-3149-9
  1. Marion, Ore J. 2. United States. Marine Corps. Regiment, 5th. Battalion, 3rd. Company L. 3. Guadalcanal, Battle of, Solomon Islands, 1942–1943. 4. World War, 1939–1945—Personal narratives, American. 5. World War, 1939-1945—Regimental histories—United States. 6. Marines—United States—Biography. I. Cuddihy, Thomas. II. Cuddihy, Edward. III. Title. IV. Series.
  D767.98 .M34 2004
  940.54'265933'092—dc22

                                                            2003024145

Table of Contents

Introduction by Thomas Cuddihy 1

Chapter 1: Late July–Early August 1942 17

Chapter 2: Our Journey to Guadalcanal 53

Chapter 3: The Second Half of August 1942 71

Chapter 4: September 1942 109

Chapter 5: October 1942 147

Chapter 6: November and Early December 1942 . . . 187

Chapter 7: Three Guadalcanals 221

Chapter 8: The Cobbers 261

Epilogue: A Note on Iwo Jima 289

Postscript by Thomas Cuddihy 297

A Guadalcanal Glossary 299

Index 309

Introduction by Thomas Cuddihy

THE MEN OF L-3-5
This is a true story of men at war. The time is August through December 1942, and the place is Guadalcanal. The men are United States Marines, most of them serving with L Company, 3rd Battalion, 5th Marine Regiment—for short, L-3-5.

On the Canal is not an official or even semiofficial military history. It is a personal account of events and experiences remembered by several good and brave men who served their country with honor on the front line of battle, but mostly as remembered by M. Sgt. Ore J. Marion, USMC (Retired). Their stories are harrowing, profane, funny, irreverent, heartbreaking, down-to-earth, and deeply human. That is what makes this book different from—though no less significant than—World War II official histories. Some details related in the following pages are, as in other books of this kind, at odds with the accounts in Washington's official archives. Warfare is a messy business, and no account of any battle is ever going to be perfectly accurate. Whether we are accredited historians, frontline warriors, or ordinary writers and editors, we simply do our best to put down the facts as we know them and try to get the story nearly right.

Many of this book's stories first appeared in different, much-abridged form in *Guadalcanal Echoes*, a quarterly newspaper edited and written by veterans of that historic campaign. This book's chief narrator, Ore J. Marion, frequently contributed to *Echoes* over the years, and his accounts were also cited in several widely published battle histories. In August 1942, when the marines first landed on Guadalcanal, he was a corporal and one of L-3-5's squad leaders. By the time the 5th Marines were taken off the Canal, Marion was a sergeant and the ranking NCO of a battered, severely understrength, but still formidable platoon of fighting men.

Among the other marine veterans of L-3-5 who have contributed to this story, either directly or indirectly, are Richard "Yogi" Milana, Curtis "Speedy" Spach, Art Boston, and Ernest Snowden. Each of these men, like others who figure in the account, saw parts of the Guadalcanal campaign from his own perspective—and whether you're in a war zone or sitting at home in your backyard, all perspectives are limited. After approximately sixty years, some of these marines' memories are unavoidably hazy, and in a few cases, minor details will seem to conflict with finer points in their buddies' accounts. If, by chance, a professional historian happens some day to pick up this book, read a chapter or two, and perhaps scoff at a few details that are at variance with the "official records," I can only remind him that these guys were there at ground zero. Few if any of the historians were anywhere near the Solomon Islands in 1942. Many weren't yet born. I would further remind him of something once said by Ivan Illich, the Austrian philosopher and sociologist who died in 2002: "Historians who rely on previously published material perpetuate falsehoods." Henry Ford put it more bluntly: "History is mostly bunk." Ford was mistaken on several points, including his pre–World War II judgment of the Axis Powers, but his opinion about history is generally agreed to have some merit. In any case, nits can be picked, and inconsistencies in war stories like this one are unavoidable. But they are also unimportant in view of the book's larger purpose.

That purpose is simple: to bring you, the reader, close to scenes of combat and unremitting danger so you can share something of the World War II fighting man's emotions—his fears, his sense of humor in the face of ugly realities, and his overpowering feelings of duty, pride, and loyalty. That loyalty was first directed toward his buddy in the next foxhole, and then extended to the Marine Corps as a whole, and to the nation, which the corps has always served with honor.

Heroic flourishes and patriotic jargon are markedly absent from this story. But the sense of humanity is here in large measure. So are the world-famous marines' spirit of "can-do" and their loyalty, the inspiration for their well-known motto, *Semper Fi*. This is not a story of superheroes, but of guys who did a job for their country, then came home, earned a living, raised families, grew old, and never wanted or needed to be known as anyone other than your neighbor who lives down the street. The word *hero* has always embarrassed these men because they think it exaggerates their acts. From their point of view, they were simply obeying orders and doing their duty. Today, more than a half century after their victory, time is depleting their ranks. We won't embarrass them with words like *hero*, but we will insist that their generation gave the United States a measure of glory that we hope will be remembered for as long as this nation prevails.

GUADALCANAL: AN OVERVIEW AND BACKGROUND OF THE CAMPAIGN

In addition to the island's land campaign, several significant naval and air engagements occurred in the Guadalcanal war zone. The naval engagements were, in a sense, a microcosm of the larger war in the Pacific, since they began with an American near-disaster, and then gave way to later victory. Although historically important, the Guadalcanal naval and air engagements are outside the scope of this book, and so this summary touches on them only in passing.

In retrospect, it appears that at first, both the Japanese and the Americans perceived the World War II campaign on Guadalcanal as a minor engagement at the periphery of the Pacific theater. But gradually, without either antagonist fully intending it, the Guadalcanal confrontation grew to become a pivotal battle. During the six-month period from August 7, 1942, to February 8, 1943, Guadalcanal became a crucible in which the will of one nation was forged while its opponent's fortunes showed the first signs of faltering. Japanese defeat at Guadalcanal marked the end of that nation's territorial expansion and the beginning of the end for Japan's imperial designs. The lion's share of credit for this accomplishment goes to the approximately eleven thousand U.S. Marines of the 1st Division who made the initial August 7 landing under the command of Lt. Gen. Alexander A. Vandegrift. Another 1st Division unit landed on the tiny adjacent island of Tulagi, met with fierce Japanese resistance, but secured the island within a few days. Reinforcements began arriving on Guadalcanal in late September, as both U.S. and Japanese forces strove to keep pace with one another. After a heroic and successful defense of the island's air base, Vandegrift's force was finally relieved in December by a strong, well-supplied U.S. Army unit, the Americal Division commanded by Maj. Gen. Alexander Patch. The army then mopped up what remained of Japanese resistance, deprived the Japanese of a vital air base, and secured that base for American use.

THE ISLAND'S TERRAIN AND ITS STRATEGIC IMPORTANCE

Guadalcanal is a jungle island, roughly ninety miles long and varying between twenty-five and thirty miles in width. For comparison purposes, you might think of it as being about the same size from west to east as the full length of New York's Long Island, from the East River, just across from Manhattan, to Montauk Point. However, from north to south, Guadalcanal is roughly twice as wide as Long Island. It is part of the South Pacific's Solomon chain, which lies just south of the equator and northeast of the Australian continent. At the time of World War II, Guadalcanal's coastline was home to a small population of Melanesian natives who lived in scattered villages, all within sight of the sea. In addition, there were a few Christian missionaries and a temporarily abandoned coconut palm plantation owned by Lever Brothers, Ltd. Visible to the south, inland from the island's north beaches, were intermittent stretches of grassy plain.

Covering the rest of the island, and constituting most of its area, were—as there are today—steeply rising networks of rugged highlands and naked coral ridges protruding above irregular patterns of thickly grown jungle valleys. The island's high point within the combat area, Mount Austen, was situated several miles inland, between the Lunga and Matanikau Rivers. From the top of Mount Austen, an observer can look down on the patchwork of jungle and ridges and see virtually the entire area where the Guadalcanal campaign was fought. Today some of the island's jungle has been cleared by encroaching civilization, but in the 1940s, it was virtually uninhabitable by humans.

Except for a few domesticated cattle—which the marines called caribou—tended by the island's natives and confined to the grasslands, the rest of Guadalcanal was home only to a variety of insects and wild animals: flies, malaria-carrying mosquitoes, lizards, land crabs, snakes, and ugly gray rats that nested high in the coconut trees and came down by the hundreds at nightfall to forage wherever they might find food, even if it meant in a marine's sweaty foxhole. Then there were the island's many small rivers, some containing man-eating alligators. Put simply, Guadalcanal was hostile territory for both the Japanese and the Americans. Why did it become the site of a major battle?

By mid-1942, the Pacific theater's only important land battle was taking place some 600 miles to Guadalcanal's west, on New Guinea, where British, Australian, and U.S. Army troops held off a Japanese invasion in what became a protracted stalemate campaign. Japan's intention there was to expand and consolidate its control of western Pacific territory, and ultimately to cut off contact between Australia and its United States ally, thus knocking Australia out of the war. While vying for control of New Guinea—which is just north of Australia—the Japanese already had important naval and air bases at Truk in the Caroline Islands and at Rabaul on New Britain. Guadalcanal is only 565 miles southeast of Rabaul, which placed it well within range of Japan's land-based planes. Japanese strategists decided that the time was ripe to expand their area of control by establishing a military outpost and a new airfield to their southeast, on the island of Guadalcanal.

They began building the airfield on one of the island's few usable sites, a stretch of grassy plain on the northern coast, within sight of the ocean and near the point where the Lunga River empties into the sea. The Japanese airfield was still in its early stage of construction, occupied by only a small military contingent supervising hired Korean workers, when the Americans saw the need to act, primarily to protect Australia and New Zealand from impending attack. The marines' mission was to take both Guadalcanal and the tiny adjacent island of Tulagi. The naval and air bombardment preceding the marines' landing on Guadalcanal sent the Japanese scurrying westward from their construction site and out of the adjoining native village of Kukum, which they'd been using as a supply base. They consolidated as best they could at points to the west, along the island's coastline.

THE GUADALCANAL CAMPAIGN IN BRIEF
The campaign began on the morning of August 7, 1942, on a relatively quiet note. Following a naval and air bombardment of the beach, the marines landed unopposed on the island's north-central coast—a spot designated as Beach Red. By contrast, the invasion on tiny, neighboring Tulagi led to a short but fierce battle, which was over within days. Guadalcanal presented the marines with an entirely different situation. On August 8, D-Day plus one, the marines occupied Guadalcanal's abandoned airfield. They encountered no land-based resistance and only sporadic harassment from Japanese planes. Within a few weeks, a detachment of U.S. Navy construction engineers—known as Seabees—picked up work on the airfield where the Japanese had left off. The field became an American base, albeit a rudimentary one, and was named Henderson Field in honor of a marine pilot who'd been killed two months earlier at the battle of Midway. Subsequently, the airfield was expanded to include two smaller runways. Fighter Strip One was located east of the main airfield and near the Ilu River. Fighter Strip Two, completed late in the campaign, was built to

the northwest of the main field, across the Lunga River near the village of Kukum.

Naturally, the Japanese wanted their airfield back. U.S. warships off Guadalcanal gave the marines ostensible protection while their transports unloaded supplies. But on the night of August 8, a Japanese naval striking force attacked the U.S. fleet and inflicted severe damage, sinking several American ships. That was the battle of Savo Island. Vice Adm. Frank J. Fletcher, fearing a decisive naval loss—especially of precious aircraft carriers—withdrew his task force from the area, leaving the marines stranded. More than half of their supplies vanished with the fleeing transport ships. The marines were able to maintain their foothold on the island only because the Japanese land force on Guadalcanal was momentarily too small and too scattered to constitute a major threat. At the outset, neither side had accurate estimates of its enemy's strength or positions on the island. The marines established and held an area on the northern coast, its perimeter extending less than five miles along the beach, with the airfield at its approximate center. The irregular southern perimeter extended, at most, a few thousand yards inland from the shore and parallel to it, traversing the island's mix of high, bare coral ridges and jungle no-man's-land.

Initial marine patrols made probes from the western perimeter and, with the help of native scouts, detected the presence of a small concentration of Japanese a few miles farther west, at the Matanikau River. Believing that the Japanese unit wanted to surrender, a small detachment of 5th Marines and a group from Division Intelligence Section (G-2), led by the 1st Division's intelligence officer, Lt. Col. Frank Goettge, went out to find them. On August 12, Goettge and his group were ambushed and massacred at the Matanikau. Several Americans survived the firefight, only to be summarily executed by their Japanese captors. A few Americans managed to escape and eventually made it back to the marine-held perimeter, where they reported the atrocity. The confused intentions of both American and Japanese combatants in that encounter remain clouded to the present day. In any case, the Goettge disaster taught the marines to be more cautious in future dealings with their enemy. What's more, the perception that the Japanese killed prisoners inspired most of the marines to hate their enemy and strengthened their resolve to fight them to the death. On both sides, Guadalcanal became a "take-no-prisoners" war.

With any American naval threat now some distance away, the Japanese began to reinforce their shaky position on the island by sending in more troops and supplies from their bases at Truk and Rabaul. The regular flow of Japanese ships that ferried troop reinforcements to Guadalcanal became what the marines called the "Tokyo Express." The Japanese assumption was that the marine contingent could be overwhelmed in short order, after which the Japanese could make their air base operational, as originally intended. The assumption was reasonable, since the marines were isolated, undersupplied, underfed, and had only enough men to defend a small part of the island effectively. However, the Japanese were in for a surprise.

The Japanese launched their first important land assault on August 19 under the command of Lt. Col. Kiyoano Ichiki. He came ashore stealthily with nearly a thousand men at Taivu Point, which is well to the east of what was then American-held ground. The marines learned of the Japanese landing only after the fact from native scouts. Aware that an attack was imminent, the marines had dug in and were waiting along the Ilu River, also known as Alligator Creek. On August 21, Ichiki's force staged a night attack, making a direct assault on the marines' eastern perimeter in what is known to military historians as the battle of the Tenaru River. (Many marine maps were mislabeled, confusing the nearby Ilu and Tenaru Rivers.) The 1st and 2nd Battalions of the 1st Marine Regiment were well dug in. They held their position and methodically annihilated their attackers, whose notion of battle tactics was to launch one reckless banzai charge after another. The tactic had often worked against an incompetent Chinese Army on the Asian mainland, but the U.S. Marines, though understaffed and inadequately supplied, were rigorously trained fighters. They killed nearly 90 percent of the Japanese attackers, including Ichiki himself. Scarcely 100 Japanese survivors straggled back to Taivu Point.

In addition to being an American victory, the battle of the Tenaru River taught the marines a useful lesson. It was the first of several firefights in which they discovered that many Japanese field commanders suffered from a fatal delusion that became known among the wiser Japanese military leadership as "victory fever." Many Japanese seemed to believe that their simple presence on a field of battle, combined with their ferocious determination, was enough to cow an enemy and ensure Japanese victory. "Victory fever," in its disregard for more sophisticated battle tactics, was a dangerous flaw, a delusion that failed to distinguish between a competent and an incompetent enemy. Colonel Ichiki's disaster demonstrated its results.

General Vandegrift's overriding fear, and a reasonable one, was that the Japanese would make a direct seaborne frontal assault on the marine-held section of beach to recapture the airfield. Thus marine units were positioned along virtually all the roughly nine thousand yards of beach that formed their northern perimeter. Despite Vandegrift's concern, such an attack never materialized. Instead, the Japanese made more cautious troop landings at points along the beach where they were able to evade immediate detection and direct opposition. Some landings were to the east, but most were to the west of the marines' position. From there, the Japanese and the Americans took turns making landborne thrusts at each other's strongholds.

The weeks that followed the battle of the Tenaru River saw continued Japanese reinforcements to the island, with troop landings and consolidation of positions around Cape Esperance, at the island's northwest tip, a considerable distance from the marines' position. Additional Japanese landings followed at Tasafaronga, Kokumbona, and Point Cruz—locations that, while nearer to the airfield, were still the better part of a day's march to the marines' western perimeter. Meanwhile, because of Japanese naval dominance in adjacent waters, the marines received only unreliable and inadequate visits from American supply ships. Despite severe supply problems, Henderson field was soon in condition to allow some U.S. carrier-based planes to land and establish a small, ragged military air command. The first planes arrived on August 21. They came to include a handful of Grumman F4F "Wildcat" fighters; Douglas SBD "Dauntless" single-engine dive bombers; and slow-flying Bell P400 "Airacobra" planes, used mainly to strafe and harass Japanese ground forces.

Many small-scale land skirmishes followed the Tenaru River battle. Casualties mounted on both sides. Though often fierce and bloody, these firefights had only marginal strategic importance. One noteworthy engagement, now known as the first battle of the Matanikau, took place on August 19, when several companies of the 5th Marines probed westward from their main line of resistance (or MLR) in an attempt to gauge Japanese troop strength west of the Matanikau River. A firefight ensued, and L Company—in which Ore Marion was then a corporal and squad leader—wiped out a Japanese unit. Though the battle gained no additional territory for the marines, it was nevertheless a clear victory. Before L Company returned to the MLR by Higgins boats, its members discovered the remains of the Goettge Patrol, partially buried in beach sand near the mouth of the Matanikau. Sixty years later, that discovery has yet to be officially acknowledged by the U.S. Department of the Navy, though it has subsequently been recorded by several reputable military historians.

During the entire Guadalcanal campaign, the only real goal of the Japanese was the recapture of Henderson Field. Their troop placements between Cape Esperance and the Matanikau River served only as staging areas for intended attacks on the airfield. Additional landings at Taivu Point, well to the east of the marines' position, were intended to serve the same purpose. Meanwhile, the marine defense perimeter around Henderson Field remained intact, which allowed the

Introduction

marines to make frequent probes outside their perimeter to harass and discourage Japanese advances.

A constant and more serious menace to Vandegrift's force was the shelling from Japanese ships. There were, however, increased ship-to-ship engagements between the U.S. and Japanese navies, with losses taken by both sides. Because of the many ships sunk in this region—an expanse of sea between Guadalcanal and the nearby islands of Savo and Tulagi—the area acquired a nickname that persists to this day: Ironbottom Sound. Less serious than Japanese shelling from the sea, but potentially demoralizing to the land-based marines, were the almost daily bombing and strafing raids by Japanese planes and random intermittent bombardment by a long-range Japanese field artillery piece, which the marines nicknamed Pistol Pete.

Meanwhile, both Japanese and American land troops suffered from a common enemy—a combination of the jungle island's hostile environment and the chronic malnutrition caused by supply difficulties on both sides. Thousands of casualties resulted not from battle, but from malaria, dysentery, and a debilitating skin condition called jungle rot. Many Japanese troops and U.S. Marines in the field were chronically sick with persistent low-grade fever, which plagued them even as they engaged each other in combat.

A second massive Japanese military offensive in mid-September, called the battle of Bloody Ridge, nearly captured Henderson Field but failed. This was probably the single most decisive battle of the Guadalcanal campaign. A third attack on Henderson Field occurred October 22–25. Both the September and October attacks took the form of furtive Japanese advances into the jungle to the south of the marines' perimeter, followed by a succession of intensely fought northward thrusts toward the airfield. But to reach the airfield from the jungle, the Japanese first had to surmount an irregularly shaped piece of high ground defended by the marines—a geographic landmark that soon took the name Bloody Ridge.

That high point on the terrain—also called Edson's Ridge, after Col. Merritt A. Edson, one of the leaders of its marine defenders—stood above a jungle-filled slope on the American southern defense perimeter. The ridge served as a kind of natural fortress, a wall protecting Henderson Field, which lay below it on its seaward side. Because the ridge directly overlooked Henderson Field and General Vandegrift's command post, the Americans would have been checkmated if it had fallen. The Japanese would have overrun the airfield, and Guadalcanal would have been lost.

The September 13–14 assault on the ridge was initiated by more than two thousand Japanese troops, commanded by Maj. Gen. Kayotaki Kawaguchi. Like the Ichiki unit that had met disaster in August, Kawaguchi's force landed east of the marine position at Taivu Point. Instead of proceeding directly along the shoreline, however, Kawaguchi led his troops into the jungle highlands, circling to the south of the marines' MLR. From there, he charged Bloody Ridge in a head-on collision with Marine Raider and 1st Parachute Battalions, led by Col. Merritt A. Edson. While Kawaguchi's force assaulted Bloody Ridge, a smaller Japanese force, led by Col. Akinosuku Oka, approached the marine position from the west, advancing along the coast toward the marines' western perimeter. Oka's force engaged the 3rd Battalion, 5th Marines' L Company along the western MLR, attacking at points both near the beach and inland at a smaller ridge, which the Japanese called Tora Ridge. The marines who defended that ridge called it simply L Company Ridge. Meanwhile, the Japanese main thrust at Bloody Ridge continued to rage.

The marine defenders at Bloody Ridge suffered nearly 150 casualties, including 40 killed, but they succeeded in repulsing a series of three ferocious banzai attacks. Meanwhile, L Company successfully defended the western perimeter, taking relatively light casualties despite fierce fighting. Kawaguchi's and Oka's losses were catastrophic. Kawaguchi suffered an estimated 1,000 killed, and his blunted army was compelled to retreat westward toward Kokumbona. In the numerically smaller but equally significant western perimeter engagement, Oka's detachment was routed and forced to retreat by L Company, which inflicted heavy losses on the Japanese. The battered Japanese were unable to regroup for a second assault against the marines' MLR until late in the following month.

Following Bloody Ridge, a series of Japanese troop reinforcements arrived by sea and consolidated at points along the coast to the west of the marines' position, mainly concentrating in areas between Kokumbona and the Matanikau River. During October, several engagements were fought in the vicinity of the Matanikau River, including an ill-conceived Japanese thrust led by light tanks. Fighting was often fierce, but the Japanese thrusts were blunted in every instance by tenacious marine defenders. The second battle of the Matanikau occurred September 24–26, when several marine units merged into the so-called Puller Group commanded by Col. Louis "Chesty" Puller. It met stiff Japanese resistance and suffered 160 wounded and killed in a battle whose outcome was indecisive. A third Matanikau battle of October 7–9 included the author's L Company and was another hard-fought encounter. The marines eventually gained a tactical advantage, but their attack was called off by General Vandegrift, who received intelligence indicating an impending major Japanese landing on the island.

A final Japanese attempt to assault Henderson Field commenced on the rainy evening of October 24, the main thrust made by the Sendai Unit under the command of Kawaguchi. Smaller units were led by Maj. Gen. Yumio Nasu and Colonel Oka. Again the Japanese suffered defeat. At least one and perhaps several overly optimistic Japanese radio reports were sent back to Rabaul, claiming that the airfield had been captured. In fact, the Japanese offensive was spent. The marines' southern perimeter had been penetrated, but the Japanese infiltrators were too few and too badly scattered to organize an effective attack. Even so, for several days, they constituted a lethal threat to individual marine units, until, one by one, the Japanese were wiped out.

At the same time, the attack by Colonel Oka's 4th Infantry Regiment, which engaged American forces in the vicinity of the Matanikau River, was ill coordinated with the Sendai Unit's main thrust. Oka's unit also met with defeat and took heavy casualties. For the Japanese, the October offensive was their final one on the island, and a clear failure. Not only did they fail to gain their objective, but they lost at least two thousand killed in action and many more wounded. Several of the Japanese Army's most important field commanders, including General Nasu, numbered among the dead.

By the end of October, the remaining Japanese on the island were compelled by attrition to shift from an offensive to a defensive war. A November 13–15 naval engagement in waters off Guadalcanal was costly to the United States, resulting in the loss of several warships, including the heavy cruiser USS *Atlanta*. However, that sea engagement proved strategically disastrous to the Japanese. Though tactically a stalemate, the battle prevented the Japanese from landing still another powerful new invasion army. It also made Japan's high command aware of the futility of attempting further large-scale landings on the island.

But where the Japanese landing had failed, a similar American invasion force succeeded. The Americal Division of the U.S. Army arrived and consolidated in October and November, commanded by Maj. Gen. Alexander Patch. Well equipped and supplied, the Americal Division relieved the weary, battle-scarred marines, allowing the 1st Marine Division to leave the island in early December after having waged a successful campaign. On December 18, the Americal Division launched a full-scale land offensive against what remained of Japanese opposition. The American offensive lasted through January 1943 and encountered many pockets of stiff Japanese resistance. However, the outcome was never in doubt. On February 8, Patch's headquarters declared Guadalcanal secure.

Thomas Cuddihy

August — December 1942

South Pacific Ocean

Florida Islands
Savo Tulagi
Malaita
Iron Bottom Sound
Indispensible Strait
Area of Detail
GUADALCANAL

Iron Bottom Sound

KOLI POINT
MARINE LANDING SPOT
LUNGA POINT
To Kokumbona
POINT CRUZ
GOETTGE BURIAL SITE
Kukum
FIGHTER STRIP 2
HENDERSON FIELD
FIGHTER STRIP 1
BEACH RED
Matanikau
1-LOG BRIDGE
Matanikau River
Lunga River
Alligator Creek
Ilu River
Tenaru River
L COMPANY RIDGE
BLOODY RIDGE
MAIN LINE OF RESISTANCE
MOUNT AUSTIN

—N—

2 MILES

JOHN WEIBEL, DERBY, NY

CHAPTER 1

Late July–Early August 1942

THE KORO ISLAND FIASCO

At the end of July 1942, Koro Island was a South Pacific tropical paradise, as I'm told it still is today. Back then, I was Cpl. Ore J. Marion, a squad leader in the 1st Platoon of L Company, 3rd Battalion, 5th Marine Regiment—or L-3-5—and we were about to invade the Fiji island of Koro. We were not going into combat, but engaging in practice amphibious landings, making a brief stop on our way from Wellington, New Zealand, to a real invasion at a place that turned out to be Guadalcanal. We didn't know it yet, but we were just over a week away from fighting one of the pivotal campaigns of World War II.

We arrived in the Fiji Islands aboard the transport ship USS *Fuller*, and on the morning of July 28, we climbed down the *Fuller*'s cargo nets and boarded the Higgins boats that were about to storm peaceful Koro Island. The 1st Platoon's Higgins boat was approximately at the center of the first wave, and my position as port-side Lewis gunner in the bow gave me a fine view in all directions. That was an advantage the rest of the platoon didn't enjoy. Their orders were to keep their heads below the gunwale, a perfect place for anybody who enjoys inhaling the landing craft's diesel fumes.

That day and the next few gave us unnecessary practice in large-scale Higgins boat movements. We spent July 28 to 31 aimlessly riding up to Koro's reef and back to the ship. Koro is one of the smallest of the Fiji Islands. I'd estimate it to be no more than eight or nine miles from one end to the other, and less than three miles wide. I'm guessing here, because L Company saw only a very small part of it. Today's maps show a couple of tiny villages located a safe distance away from where our maneuvers took place. But back then, and from our point of view, the main thing Koro Island *did* have was beaches barricaded by coral reefs.

A junior naval officer was assigned to our boat for the landings. Rumor had it that he held the title of "wave commander," and as he directed the first wave toward Koro Island, those of us who were able to see the beach knew we had a problem on our hands. Even a dummy like me without any training could see that given our heading and the movement of the water, we wouldn't even come close to our designated landing point. Back in '42, a marine officer or staff NCO was considered unqualified to direct any phase of any kind of amphibious operation until it was well ashore. The U.S. Navy was supposed to do the directing. I've often wondered how we survived going ashore without the navy's special assistance.

Our first wave approached the beach about one mile to the right of the designated landing point. The beach was littered with coral and lava rock, which forced the landing craft to stop about fifty yards from the beach's waterline. Had this been the real thing, with enemy gun emplacements on the beach, we'd all have been killed for sure. The platoon went over the side and into the water—then we stumbled, fell, and tripped in surf and coral. Somehow we made it to the beach.

I vividly remember arriving on that beach, because there at the berm line was a small grove of lemon trees. I picked a couple of the lemons and ate them like oranges, much to the annoyance of salivating troopers nearby. For most people, lemons are too sour to eat that way, but to this day, I find them great thirst quenchers, especially after strenuous exercise. And anybody who has ever stumbled through fifty yards of surf on slippery coral and lava will tell you that they've just experienced a bout of strenuous exercise. We hiked along the shoreline until we reached the place where we *should* have landed. From there, we boarded our Higgins boats and returned to our ships.

On the second day, we went ashore again, and this time we were dropped to the *left* of the designated landing point. Positioned behind us a short distance out at sea, two of our destroyers gave us live covering fire from what I estimated to be three-inch or five-inch guns. The trouble is, one of the destroyers didn't get the word to cease fire when we got to the beach. We had to hug the sand at the waterline and pray a little. The Higgins boats backed off, and it took a lot of semaphoring from several coxswains to convince the destroyer that the moment had arrived for them to cease fire. Somehow we made it back to our transport ship, and we chalked up the incident as just another day's work. The following day, we made our final practice landing, and thanks to the navy, that turned out to be the biggest screwup of them all.

Like many another experienced marine, my twenty-year active career included several adventures that made me doubt the IQs of the top brass in the U.S. Navy. That final Koro Island landing was one of them. After the Guadalcanal invasion, the newspaper headlines might have read, "Everyone went to the amphibious landing but the first wave missed the boat." That's damn near what happened. We almost missed the Guadalcanal landing, because barely one week before D-Day, we found ourselves stranded on Koro Island. That could have spelled disaster for the Guadalcanal campaign.

On our final Koro Island landing, we went ashore at almost the correct spot, but after that, everything went wrong. As we reboarded our landing craft and began heading back to sea to be picked up by our transports, we suddenly faced deep trouble. The entire fleet was taking off at full speed, and our view of the U.S. Navy was smoke and ships' sterns disappearing on the horizon. Then all that was left was smokestacks. Those bastards are taking off on us, I thought. We didn't know what was happening, but we knew it wasn't part of our landing operation. We looked at each other, thinking, What the hell's up? It was late afternoon, getting near dusk. Our Higgins boats were in a V formation, chasing the fleet—*and not catching up*. My platoon's boat led the hapless formation, and one of our sailors started signaling a destroyer by semaphore: "What's going on?"

No response. It was getting near dark, and we were being abandoned in the wrong part of that unimaginably huge body of water called the Pacific Ocean. Worse yet, though we didn't know it, we were the marines scheduled to be the first wave to land on Guadalcanal—the ones slated to make the first offensive landing against the Japanese in World War II.

Frantic, our sailor signaled again, asking for information and advice. We were a long way from shore by now, and the only vessel in sight was the rear-guard destroyer, now about a mile ahead of us. Finally a sailor appeared on the destroyer's fantail and started signaling. It was getting harder to see, but we were able to make out his flags. His message told us to return to the beach. He kept signaling, breaking worse news yet: "Jap fleet in the vicinity."

"Holy Christ!" we said to each other. "We're stranded in the middle of the ocean, it's damn near dark, Koro Island is behind us, over the horizon and out of sight, and the goddamn Japanese Navy is coming after us!"

Our Higgins boat's sailor signaled the destroyer: "How do we get back to the beach? Give us an azimuth."

We waited a painfully long time, and after what seemed like a week, we got an answer consisting of an azimuth, the approximate number of miles back to the beach, and "Good luck."

Yeah, good luck. Daylight gave out completely as we received that final message. The destroyer vanished into the night. This was our first experience of abandonment by our own navy. We didn't know it then, but it wouldn't be our last.

At a signal from our boat, the other Higgins boats moved in close with engines idling. The situation was explained from boat to boat, and the destroyer's directions were passed from coxswain to coxswain. The boats formed a single file, each close to the boat ahead of it, with our boat in the lead. It was a moonless night, and by now it was dark as hell.

We went on for what seemed like hours, not daring to use our running lights—not with the Japanese Navy lurking somewhere out there. Every once in a while, the boats would stop and the crews would check to be sure the formation hadn't lost any of the craft. We traveled strictly by compass. Thank Christ that the sailors manning the Higgins boats knew their business—as it turns out, these operators were coastguardsmen.

Our column of boats traveled for about an hour in total darkness. Then word was passed, engines were cut off, and everyone fell silent. We listened for the sound of surf. There was none. For all we could tell, Koro Island had just sunk to the bottom of the Pacific. We started up again, and it might have been a half hour later when one of the guys called out. Again the engines were cut, and we all held our breath and listened. *There it was!* The sound of surf. Maybe we were going to survive this disaster after all.

One of the Higgins boats found a passage through the reef and made it to the beach. The rest of us followed. We disembarked, then helped beach the boats before we prepared to settle down for the night. L Company of the first wave of marines had just made it back to Koro Island. We were a hell of a long way from Guadalcanal, but the Japanese Navy hadn't gotten us, and we were still in one piece. We were merely abandoned by our own navy.

We didn't have our field packs with us, because we hadn't planned to spend any more time on this beach than it would take to land and then go back to the *Fuller*. No packs meant no supplies, but we made the best of the situation. We built small fires on the beach to keep warm, and that's how we spent the night. With morning, some of the men explored the area and returned with arms full of yams, fruit, a few chickens, and a couple of small pigs. Breakfast was beckoning. Best damn chow we'd had since leaving Wellington, New Zealand!

We waited on the beach. We waited some more. By now it was the middle of the afternoon, and we were still waiting. Then, far off on the horizon, the tiny images of ships started to appear. The U.S. Navy was returning. We responded by backing the Higgins boats off the beach, and soon we were aboard them, heading out toward the fleet. We eventually caught up with the *Fuller*, but even while L Company was climbing the transport's cargo net, the fleet continued moving. We hadn't been worth stopping for, but at least the navy decided to give us a break and slow down.

Back aboard our ship, nobody from the navy bothered to tell the marines why they'd bugged off on us. At the time, it didn't bother us as much as it should have. Most of us were young, still kids, and we didn't always know enough to realize when we were being slighted. We were just the dumb troops who were going to land on Guadalcanal and help change the course of World War II in the Pacific.

Not long after we made the real landing—the D-Day landing on the Canal—we would become expendable again. And then we'd drop down one more notch: This group of young, expendable marines would once again be abandoned!

The Koro Island incident has an ironic postscript. Years later, when talking about it with sailor friends, several of them corrected my story. One of them was my brother Jim, who was a sailor aboard the battleship *North Carolina*. "That was no Jap task force approaching our fleet," one of them told me, and the others agreed. They insisted it was the U.S. battleship *North Carolina* and her battle group, moving in to join us for the landing operation. This isn't official. It's only what I heard from a couple of the U.S. Navy's ordinary seamen. Even so, I'm inclined to take their word for it.

While we went through our comedy of errors on Koro Island, my parents, relatives, and friends back in Buffalo didn't have any idea where I was, only that I was with my marine unit somewhere in the South Pacific. When they picked up their copy of the *Buffalo Evening News* on July 27, they read:

ALLIED, JAP TROOPS
STAGE FIRST BATTLE
ON NEW GUINEA SOIL

Nipponese Strike Back with Raid
On Darwin; Townsville also is Target*
(copyright 1942, the *Buffalo Evening News*)

Back on Koro Island and aboard the *Fuller*, we didn't know anything about New Guinea. At the time, I'm not sure I knew where New Guinea was located, or that it even existed. We were too busy getting ready for our own coming battle.

APPROACHING OUR DESTINATION
After the naval screwup that nearly left L Company and our Higgins boats abandoned in the Fiji Islands, the four days that followed on the USS *Fuller* were uneventful. On D-Day minus one, we were briefed on our destination—an island in the Solomon chain called Guadalcanal—and were told what little was known about it. Details came mainly from civilians who had operated coconut palm plantations along the coast before evacuating when the Solomons turned into a war zone. Our officers had maps, but we later found out that the maps were inaccurate in many details. We were told that the Japanese had an engineering party and construction crew on the island and were building an airfield. That much was correct. Our mission was to take that field away from them. The Japanese had a military unit supporting the construction crew, but we were told that its strength was unknown. It turned out that our operations planner overestimated Japanese military strength on the Canal at the beginning of August, but in any case, we were given to understand that we wouldn't have much cause for worry when we landed. Famous last words.

---

*This and all other quotes that follow from the *Buffalo Evening News* are reprinted here with permission from the *Buffalo News*.

I have a vivid recollection of something that happened on the evening of August 6. My unit, aboard the USS *Fuller*, was approaching Guadalcanal, and we knew that when morning came, we were going to make our landing. Having gotten all my gear and equipment ready for the next day, I was lying in my canvas bunk in close quarters below deck, reading whatever I was able to get my hands on that day, when a good buddy, Francis R. "Chink" McAllan, came over to talk with me. I could tell he was upset about something and wanted to get it off his chest. I put down my book, and he started telling me what was bothering him. A little earlier that evening, right after chow, Chink's closest friend, Sgt. William Steen, had quietly cornered him and handed him a sealed envelope.

"What's this?" McAllan had asked.

"It's a letter," Steen said. "To my wife."

Both Steen and McAllan were from Portland, Maine. Steen had gotten special leave just before we'd left stateside and had married a hometown girl. Now Steen was giving Chink the letter he'd just written to her.

"I've got a strange feeling," Steen told him. "I don't think I'm going to make it through the Guadalcanal operation."

At first Chink tried to scoff, but seeing that Steen was serious, he grew distressed.

"Look, Chink," Steen said. "if anybody's going to make it through this war, you will. After the Guadalcanal operation, please mail this letter to my wife."

Now Chink was telling me Steen's story. "Why me?" Chink asked. "Why did he choose *me* to take this responsibility?"

"What's the big deal, Chink," I said. "Just stuff the envelope in your field pack, and when the operation's over, you can give it back to him. By then you can both laugh about it."

But Chink was really distraught.

D-DAY, AUGUST 7

We had reveille before dawn the morning of August 7, our fleet now anchored in waters between Guadalcanal and Tulagi. The navy gave us a good breakfast. That means there was a

D-Day on Guadalcanal. NATIONAL ARCHIVES

piece of meat with it. They'd feed you some good chow and push you off the ship, feeling like they did their duty. Soon after chow, we mustered on deck at our assigned stations. The sun was up by now and the morning sky was clear, the weather calm. We heard distant booms as our cruisers began shelling the beach. Several of our planes came overhead, I'm guessing from a carrier located somewhere beyond our horizon. They flew directly over us on their way to the island, where they dropped bombs along the beach. At about that time, we were scrambling down our ship's cargo nets and into our Higgins boats. We were the 1st Platoon of L Company, commanded by Capt. Lyman D. Spurlock, in the 3rd Battalion, 5th Marine Regiment.

Our platoon leader was Lt. John "Flash" Flaherty, a Yale graduate from a wealthy and prominent family. He was also a fine marine who got his commission as second lieutenant in the corps the day he graduated from college. There were other good marines like him, young men from prominent families who believed it was their solemn duty to serve their country whenever the need arose. Also assigned to our Higgins boat was Sgt. "Wild Bill" Kulchycki, a tough, likable veteran of military skirmishes in several parts of the world before World War II, a typical specimen of the Old Breed. He had also survived more than a couple saloon brawls and thought of himself as an educated man, having earned his Ph.D. in beer. But when the chips were down, we trusted Kulchycki, and he deserved our trust. He'd told us several times, "You know me, men. I'm Wild Bill, and I done fought me a couple of wars. You pay attention and stay with me, and I'm gonna get you back home to your momma." For most of us, he succeeded.

Our Higgins boat fully loaded, its diesel engine changed pitch, and we began moving away from the *Fuller*. It was midmorning, a little before 0900 hours, and the sea was calm, the air windless, the sky bright, visibility unlimited. I had a better view than most. As I had during the Koro Island maneuvers, I was up in one of the boat's two machine-gun turrets, manning one of the Lewis guns. The other Lewis gun was manned by my

Unloading heavy equipment from the USS *Alchiba* on August 7, 1942. By the time this photo was taken, the men of L-3-5 had already landed at Beach Red. NATIONAL ARCHIVES

good buddy Pvt. Harry "Stinky" Denham. Our Higgins boat circled slowly, waiting for the other boats that would form our invasion wave. L Company would be part of the first wave. When all the first-wave boats were ready, our coxswains maneuvered them into formation, and we began moving toward the beach, several thousand yards ahead. As we got closer to shore, our cruisers ceased fire, and our destroyers, with their smaller, shorter-range guns, took their turn firing over our heads, shelling the shore. Once in a while there would be a short lull in the firing, and in the far distance to our rear, we'd hear muffled booms from the invasion of Tulagi and Gavutu, which by now was well under way. At about six hundred yards out, Stinky Denham and I, along with the Lewis gunners on the rest of the first-wave boats, began spraying the beach with machine-gun fire. By then our destroyers had stopped firing. Our machine-gun fire was indiscriminate, since we had no special targets. The general idea was to soften up the beach in case of any enemy presence there.

Most of the other men on the boat were crouched low, heads below the top of the gunwale. That was standard operating procedure. The Higgins boat's diesel engine throbbed steadily, pushing us toward our landing site, which was designated on our maps as Beach Red 1. Looking to starboard, then to port, I had a good view of the other boats in the first wave. More Higgins boats were behind us—enough of them to land nearly eleven thousand marines.

There was no sign of activity on the island. By now I had a clear view of the strip of sand beach and a structure of some kind that stood on the beach—a large hut. Behind it at the berm line, there was tropical foliage, palm trees, and what looked like thick jungle growth. If the enemy was back there, they'd be watching us approach and getting ready for us. But we kept getting closer, and nothing appeared to move on the beach. The island's silence was ominous. Were the Japanese waiting for us to hit the beach before they opened fire?

I could make out a big sign on the seaward-facing side of the building on the beach. That outbuilding stood smack in

Landing craft heading toward shore on D-Day. The USS *Hayes* is in the background. U.S. NAVAL HISTORICAL CENTER

the middle of our approach point—and the sign read Lever Brothers, Ltd. Lever Brothers? On the beach of a remote jungle island held by the enemy? It was like a joke without a punch line. What the hell were the Lever Brothers doing in the middle of our combat zone? We didn't take any chances. We were well within range and didn't know who or what might be inside the building, so I trained my gun on the hut, and several others did the same. As I fired, I moved my gun from left to right and back again to get a crossfire effect with the other gunners. We poured maybe a hundred rounds into that shack but didn't get a single round of return fire. Not from the shack, and not from anywhere else.

At about a hundred yards from the beach, we ceased firing. I quickly cleared the Lewis gun and dropped down from my gunner's position and to the stern, where I slipped on my light pack and grabbed my Springfield '03 rifle. Just about then, the boat scraped bottom at the shoreline, and I heard Sergeant Kulchycki's voice: *"Go!"*

We went over the side, and I was right behind our platoon sergeant, Sgt. Quentin Shumate—practically on his heels. Rolling out of the boat on the opposite side, our platoon leader, Lt. John "Flash" Flaherty, was the first from our company on the beach, with Sgt. "Wild Bill" Kulchycki directly behind him. Surf was low, and the first wave of boats had all come ashore in a comparatively straight line. My squad was over the side, directly behind me, all of us now keeping our correct distance apart, the way we'd been trained. Again, exactly as we were trained, I stopped, and the rest of my squad spread out. We hit the deck, prepared to lay down a base of fire if the situation called for it.

We'd been well trained, and we felt ready. Nothing came from the jungle brush just a few yards ahead. Nothing came from the Lever Brothers hut, now bullet-riddled and looking as though it had probably been deserted before our arrival. Everything was quiet—which left us with a strange feeling. Where were the Japanese?

By the time we got up on the dry sand, we figured there were no Japs around, because they'd be shooting at us. There were plenty of spots close enough that they could have picked a few of us off.

At a time like this, all your senses wake up and are on full-blast. You hear everything. You see everything. There's a rush that's hard to describe. You've been practicing this for two years. You're ready for anything, and now, here you are. You just don't know what to expect. What you were taught to expect was Japs. And there weren't any. But you don't relax. You never relax your guard.

Immediately we were up again, the way we'd practiced a thousand times during training exercises. You run. You get off the beach as fast as you can, and you head for your first objective.

We crossed the sand beach, which was about twenty-five yards deep at our landing point. My squad reassembled just past the berm line, where the edge of jungle foliage gave us some natural cover. We'd never checked inside the shack, and I don't think any of the other squads did either. But we were on the alert. An infantryman's first moments in a combat situation are like being born into a brand new life. You find yourself looking around, seeing, hearing, and smelling things in a way you never have before. The self-preservation drive instantly sharpens all your senses and instincts, and the computer in your brain takes in the thousand details around you, storing them all away, so that if you survive, you'll remember these details many years later. Just as I recall them now.

Jungle air everywhere has a distinctive, slightly unsavory smell, a rank, rich odor that makes you think of decay. I'd first noticed it before the war, in 1940–41, when our unit was stationed in Guantánamo and went for maneuvers to some of the Caribbean islands. Guadalcanal's air smelled much the same way—slightly rotten, as the island's heat, humidity, flies, and maggots did their work on fallen coconuts, dead vegetation, shellfish washed ashore, and the land animals that die in the natural course of events. Later, as weeks progressed and we started killing enemy and being killed by them, that faint but pervasive odor of rottenness would grow into something strong and terrible. It would become a gut-wrenching stench. We would live with it day and night. But not yet. On this first day, the jungle's overripe aroma was there, but was slight enough to disregard.

Once we were off the beach, we swung to our right, moving parallel with the coastline and crossed a small, shallow river that barely got our boots wet. It was the Ilu River, which we marines later nicknamed Alligator Creek. Two weeks later, two other marine units—not ours—would win an important victory at this spot in the famous battle of the Tenaru, in which the 1st and 2nd Battalions, 1st Marine Regiment, would annihilate a Japanese attack force led by Col. Kiyoano Ichiki. On that night, August 21, and from our own defense position, we would hear the distant, steady rattle of gunfire but wouldn't know what was going on until the following morning, when it was over. But I'm getting ahead of myself.

Our maps weren't very reliable. In fact, I never *saw* a map of Guadalcanal until long after I left the island, and I'm not even certain that our platoon leader, Lieutenant Flaherty, saw one. Guadalcanal has dozens of streams, creeks, and rivers, all of them flowing in a roughly northerly direction from the interior highlands, then emptying into the ocean. Our company crossed the Ilu and advanced through a large area overgrown with tall, thick grass called kanai. That's where we stayed for the rest of the day and through that first night, keeping alert for opposition that didn't materialize.

While we were digging in on shore, we saw several two-engine Jap bombers, code-named "Betty," appear over the water, low in the sky, then drop bombs on our ships in the bay. There was a lot of commotion with the noise of the aircraft, some antiaircraft fire, small boats shitting and getting, guys shouting. Right in front of us, we could see one of our transport ships, the *George Elliot*, get hit. A bomb went directly down into its hold and caused heavy damage. We knew there would

Japanese "Betty" bombers dodge flak while attacking U.S. ships off Guadalcanal, August 8. Although the 1st Marine Division was ashore, Japanese raids hindered the landing of vital supplies.
NATIONAL ARCHIVES

be mangled bodies down there, some of them dead. We were already getting pretty used to death.

The bombers were answered by AA guns from several of our ships, and we saw one or two enemy planes knocked out of the sky, trailing black smoke, and with pieces falling off them before they crashed into the water. The *Elliott* moved away, smoking and limping toward Tulagi, where it beached. The Japanese bombers made just a single pass over our ships, then disappeared, but they'd thrown a scare into the U.S. Navy. It wasn't long before our fleet began easing away, and by the time dusk approached, our ships were gone. Supplies had been unloaded in haste and not very efficiently. From where we were dug in, we could see them piled in haphazard stacks along the beach. What we didn't know yet was that they were all the supplies we were going to get for a while. Fearing the threat of a major Japanese attack, our ships were moving out on us, still carrying half the supplies—supplies we needed badly. For a second time, we were being abandoned.

Soon it would be nightfall. Our orders were to stay put for the time being and dig in. Sergeant Kulchycki was going from one man to the next, laying out the platoon's positions within our area of responsibility. As an Old China Hand who had joined the corps just after the Nicaragua campaign in the late 1920s, Kulchycki knew how to handle a combat situation. Our own education had hardly begun, but we were smart enough to know it, and to know we'd better listen to him. He was kind of funny, though, working his way back and forth along the line like an old mother hen, pointing out somebody's small mistake at one foxhole, advising how to correct it, giving the next guy a quick word to the wise, then moving on. To use one of Kulchycki's own turns of phrase, he was like a one-armed trombone player with the crabs.

"Dig in a little deeper there, Mac," he'd say. He'd squat down and look out at the area beyond the perimeter. Then he'd extend his arm and swing it in a short arc. "Your field of fire will be from there to there."

He'd move on to the next man, and he'd have more things to say. When he was satisfied, he called all the squad leaders together, and that included me. "I want you to be a hundred percent alert as soon as it gets dark. No smoking in the foxholes, no talking, and everybody maintain fire discipline, just the way you've been trained. We don't want anybody getting trigger-happy. Wait for a command to open fire."

Troops put into a combat zone who have yet to face battle, combined with an order to maintain fire discipline, is what you might call a contradiction in terms. I didn't know that yet, but I'd find out soon enough. We went back to our holes and waited. In the jungle tropics, darkness arrives with a silent crash. I'd seen it before in other parts of the world, but its suddenness still came as a shock. Within minutes, everything around us went from daylight to pitch-blackness. I could not see my hand in front of my face. So we waited. For the Japs or for morning, whichever came first.

I was down in my hole, and nobody was talking now. No unnecessary movement. Like most of the others around me, I'd have loved a cigarette just about then, but the smoking lamp was out and wouldn't be on again until morning. My eyeballs were actually hurting from staring into total blackness. The jungle's night noises always start the moment daylight disappears. Lizards scuttled in the thick kanai grass. A bird screeched in the distance, making an almost human sound, like no bird you'll ever hear back in the States. A rat scurried down from its nest, high in a coconut palm, and started its nightly foraging on the ground. Crickets and other night insects chirped and buzzed.

I crouched in the darkness of my spider hole, not daring to move, or even whisper to a buddy just a few yards away. I had my rifle at the ready, but my index finger rested safely on the outside edge of the trigger guard. Under these conditions, you don't want to keep your finger on the trigger. It's too easy to squeeze off an accidental round and give away your position. The nerve-wracking night sounds underlined the fear in us all that an enemy point man might be just a few yards outside our perimeter, with a squad of Japs creeping up right behind him. That's when I started hearing a new sound—a sound that turned my blood cold. Somebody was out there. I was hearing steady, shuffling footsteps in the grass, and they were coming straight at me.

We'd been taught, warned, advised, threatened, indoctrinated—you name it—to hold our fire until we were sure we had a target. But one of our guys crouched somewhere to my left panicked and cranked off a round. Somebody else fired another round. We were nervous and shook, and every one of us was sure that the *step-pause-step* sound in the tall grass was a point man for a squad of Japs.

Sergeant Kulchycki was the first among us to show common sense. He went up and down the line, whispering to each of us: "Hold your fire. Calm down. There's nothing out there but land crabs."

Discipline and training always take over in the corps, and we stopped firing. The only sounds now were the natural ones that always come out from the jungle, and among those, the *step-pause-step* of Guadalcanal's land crabs.

What is a land crab? It's about five inches across, one leg longer than the other, ending in a big claw that's strong enough to snap an eighth-inch twig in two. They had an alarming habit of dropping into a marine's foxhole, just to keep him company. They eat anything that doesn't move, and if you're a combat infantryman who's been killed in action, the crabs will pick out your best parts and eat them too. I still hate those things.

But land crabs were only the first of that night's strange noises. Sergeant Kulchycki and Lieutenant Flaherty shared a foxhole just a few yards from my position, near enough that at one point I could hear the lieutenant whisper to Kulchycki: "Take a break. I'll stay on top of things for a while. You can crap out and get some rest."

Kulchycki apparently agreed, because I didn't hear another word. The next five minutes or so produced only the normal symphony of jungle sounds. Then, suddenly, without preliminaries of any kind, there came a series of god-awful noises—

guttural noises, huffing and groaning sounds, all of them damn near loud enough to be heard halfway to Mount Austen, several miles inland. I was startled. Everybody around me was startled. But it was only Kulchycki sound asleep and snoring. The rasping noise was steady by now, like an old steam-powered band saw, with every other tooth broken, trying to cut through a pine knot. Then, suddenly, came choking, gagging, spitting, and abrupt vocal detonations that no words can adequately describe.

"Sarge, Sarge!" Lieutenant Flaherty started yelling. "Jesus Christ, Sarge!"

One of our warriors panicked and squeezed off a round. Down the line, another frightened marine fired a shot. So much for our fire discipline.

By now I was out of my hole, and so were the other junior NCOs. We were crawling left and right, from one hole to the next, hissing orders at the scared warriors: "Calm down. Play it cool. Hold your goddamn fire!"

Gradually, up and down the perimeter, the rifle fire ceased, the yelling stopped, and the situation returned to normal. Nearly normal. From where I was positioned, I could hear Sergeant Kulchycki, now wide awake, muttering a string of wonderfully colorful curses and four-letter words. The air around him would have turned blue if it wasn't already so black.

It wasn't until the following morning that the rest of us found out what had happened. An inquisitive lizard, never before hearing so strange a noise on Guadalcanal, stopped by for a look-see at the sleeping sergeant. The lizard had the misfortune of getting too close. Like a Hoover vacuum cleaner with a faulty motor, Kulchycki had inhaled several inches of hapless lizard into his mouth and clamped teeth together, hard. Thus the choking, coughing, spitting, and swearing.

We had no idea how many Japanese were on the island, or how well armed they were. We were bivouacked little more than a few thousand yards away from the airfield they'd been constructing. They could be lurking in the deep shadows just outside our perimeter, preparing a *banzai* attack. All we knew for certain was that they were here with us on this strange jungle island, and they wanted to kill us if they could.

Adding to our ignorance about anything that might be happening around us was our total lack of radio communication. We had to rely on our eyes and ears, and on runners to communicate from one unit to another. It was the middle of the twentieth century, but communication at company level and below was on a par with the armies of the ancient Greeks and Romans.

Just before dark, one of our neighboring platoons got orders to establish a security outpost about twenty or twenty-five yards to the front of the perimeter. The detail went to Sgt. William Steen, who selected four men to go with him. Before they moved out, he told the rest of his platoon that he'd be back to the perimeter as soon as he got his men dug in. He led his men out and they vanished almost immediately into the dense, tall kanai grass that grew everywhere around us. After establishing the forward outpost, Steen headed back toward the perimeter alone. By now darkness was total, and what little visibility the night sky might have given us was nullified by the kanai grass.

Several men in Steen's platoon heard the sound of somebody thrashing through the grass, coming in their direction. Their nerves were on edge. Nobody had a clue as to where the Japanese were, or whether they'd located our position. A voice came to the platoon through the darkness, low but clear.

"OK, men. It's me."

A shot rang out as Sergeant Steen spoke. One of his men, frightened and trigger-happy, had squeezed off a round from his rifle. It hit Steen in the chest. Within seconds, the men got him back behind the line, but it was no good. He was bleeding profusely, and within three minutes, he was dead.

Later that night, the man who had shot Steen cracked up. Corpsmen took the man away, and nobody in our unit ever heard from him or about him again. The company had taken two casualties, and we had yet to encounter our first Jap. Steen's premonition that he wasn't going to survive the Guadalcanal campaign turned out to be tragically accurate, but his good buddy Chink McAllan had that letter to Steen's wife in his field pack.

We were on the Canal for three days before my family and friends read about it in the hometown newspaper. My parents wouldn't have known that *I* was there, only that the Americans had landed. Even then, the news services got the story wrong, attributing the American invasion of the Solomons to the army. Or maybe it was MacArthur himself sending out what today is called misinformation. Anyway, the marines had made the landing, but we weren't mentioned in this August 10 story:

**U.S. Soldiers Force Landing
On Jap-Held Solomon Isles**

**M'ARTHUR'S TROOPS
JOIN NAVY, AIR CORPS
IN ASSAULT ON
ENEMY**

**U.S. Cruiser Sunk and 2 Damaged,
Two Destroyers and Transport Hit
By Defenders of Area**
(copyright 1942, the *Buffalo Evening News*)

At this point, Guadalcanal and Tulagi weren't yet specified as the islands in the Solomons where we'd made the "assault." We were there, all right, but to tell the truth, it often felt more like the Japanese were assaulting *us*.

THE AIRFIELD

August 8, D-Day plus one, at about 0800, our company moved out from the position we'd established on our first night. We headed for the airfield, which we knew was located just beyond the Ilu River. We progressed across the island's tropical grassy plain, with the 2nd Platoon acting as point, and with flank guards moving along both sides of the main body of marines.

Henderson Field as seen from a USS *Saratoga* aircraft. This airstrip, pocked with bomb craters, was the focus of the entire Guadalcanal campaign. NATIONAL ARCHIVES

Late July–Early August 1942

We still hadn't encountered any enemy. After about forty-five minutes, word was passed back from point that the airfield was in sight.

Now our platoon took its turn at point, and the 2nd Platoon fell back with the main body of troops. The flank guards changed, too, coming from the 3rd Platoon. Changing point and flanks at regular intervals was standard procedure. My squad took point for our platoon, and there, straight ahead of us was the Jap airfield's runway. My two point men were Hap Poloshian and either Stanley Zega or Curly Woods, all three of them good men, and to my knowledge, we were the first Americans to set foot on what would soon be called Henderson Field. We occupied the airfield without incident, and with no sign that Japanese troops were in the area.

My squad was on the runway, which was good news, but we also were wide open, and that was bad news. The rest of L Company's 1st Platoon came in behind us. I positioned myself directly behind my two points, but I kept the squad well spread out because of our potentially vulnerable position. Suddenly somebody hollered, "Cover! Cover!"

The next thing I heard came from the sky—the drone of approaching aircraft. Cover, hell! Where do you find cover on a goddamned, wide-open airstrip? All we could do was hit the deck and hug the ground.

At best, I caught maybe a glimpse of Japanese float planes at about the same moment they cut their engines and came gliding toward us. I say maybe a glimpse, because they were coming at us with the morning sun directly behind them. Bullets started pinging around us, and the only thing we could do was answer blindly with small-arms fire while we hugged the dirt. Then the aircraft engines roared back to life, and the planes were gone. We picked ourselves up, shaken by the ordeal, but nobody had been hit. No casualties. It was our first experience with enemy fire, and this time we were lucky.

That incident was our first encounter with a standard Japanese trick, and we knew we'd have to learn how to deal with it. And learn fast. This was no time to cry for momma, and no time for pissing and moaning from the ranks. We were there to fight a war for the U.S. of A., and if we were going to survive, we'd have to learn how to cope.

It was August 29 before the folks back home read that we had captured a Japanese airfield. I don't know who the "eyewitness" was in the *Buffalo Evening News* story below, but the Japanese we killed on the Canal weren't in any caverns. The quantity of captured supplies noted was also overrated, but the story's main point was correct. We had taken the airfield, and it was ours for keeps.

EYEWITNESS SEES MARINES KILL JAPS IN ISLAND CAVERNS
Stars and Stripes Wave Over 7 Solomon Islands, First Reconquered Territory

. . . The Marines have taken the Japanese airbase on Guadalcanal which was 85 per cent completed. They captured intact base installations, scores of huge fuel trucks and great quantities of stores, food, fuel oil and medical supplies.

(copyright 1942, the *Buffalo Evening News*)

With the marines now established on the airfield, L Company moved on, crossing the Lunga River and heading for a beach position beyond the river's west bank. General Vandegrift's command post was about to be located in the area adjacent to the airfield, but we had a different assignment. If nothing else, the visit by Japanese aircraft had made it clear that they wanted their airfield back. It was our job to make sure they didn't get it.

KUKUM VILLAGE

From the river's west bank, L Company swung around and headed back in the direction of the beach. We were about to enter Kukum, a small village of native huts situated just above the beach and not much more than a hundred yards or so west of where the Lunga River empties into the sea. In short order, our scouts held up our parade, passing word back to us that they were on the outskirts of Kukum. They'd heard what sounded like a running motor, and they wanted some of us to go up with them and verify the source of the noise. I took my squad up ahead, and we found that the noise came from behind a six-foot-high boxlike structure. From where we stood, it looked like a refrigerator or a freezer.

Clearly, it had been left behind by the Japs, which meant it might be booby-trapped. Following standard safety procedure, we requested a length of rope, and word was passed back to the platoon. When the rope reached us, the scouts took it to the box and tied one end to a kind of door handle. They backed off slowly with the rope, and then pulled from a safe distance. No explosion, and no problem of any kind. In fact, the news was good. The door swung open, and lo and behold, we were gazing at a cooler full of ice-cold Asahi beer, imperial-size quarts. But now we were getting word to move forward. Sgt. Wild Bill Kulchycki appeared.

"What's the holdup?" he asked. Then he saw the beer.

I've already mentioned that old Bill was a connoisseur of beer. Quicker than I can describe it, he took a sample from the cooler, cracked open the bottle, and took a long pull. He lowered his bottle and let out a sigh of pleasure.

"Each man take one bottle and move out," he said. We followed the sergeant's orders. I followed his orders twice.

Kukum consisted of little more than a few huts and two larger wooden shacks, apparently built by the Japanese. One was a crude warehouse, and the other was used as a mess hall. Inside the mess hall, we saw a long table with rice bowls, the rice still uneaten. The U.S. Navy's early morning shelling the day before must have scared the Japanese away from their breakfast. We didn't stay for more than a quick look. We kept moving out of Kukum, down to the beach, then west along the shore for not much more than another hundred yards. There we established our position for the rest of that day and the following morning.

So there we were, sitting under coconut trees on the berm line and looking out to sea. The day was hot, nearly a hundred degrees, so we did what came naturally, which was to drink our ice-cold beer. Situated in our area was a gun emplacement with a five-inch gun and plenty of ammo inside its parapet. Two of our guys had been seagoing, becoming familiar with artillery, and now they were looking this gun over. They concluded that it was American made and guessed it had probably been captured by the Japanese when they'd taken Wake Island, then shipped here for shore defense.

Several others from my squad joined the original two guys examining the gun, and pretty soon they were operating the mechanism that raised it up and down. Next they began moving it laterally. A guy named Jerry told us that at one time he'd served aboard ship and had been on a five-inch gun crew. By this time, one of the riflemen in my squad, Yogi Milana, was tracking, and Larry Gerkin, my BAR man, was being shown how to set time on the ammo. Everybody was drinking his beer and feeling happy. No officers were around.

Suddenly, from out of nowhere, a Jap submarine broke through the water's surface close to shore. There was no mistaking it, and and its gun crew was rushing out on deck. They swung their deck gun, aiming it toward us as though they owned the damn place and knew we were drinking up their beer.

Jerry, our original artillery "expert," assembled his makeshift crew and got them tracking the gun. The sub was moving very slowly on the water and was easy to track. Larry Gerkin had just loaded a point-detonating armor-piercing round. From my vantage point at the base of a coconut palm tree, I clearly saw that the Jap gun crew was in action, too. By now they had their gun pointed at us. If we'd been on the Canal longer and had time to develop some battle sense, we could have forgotten about that five-inch gun and picked off the Jap sailors with our Springfield '03s, as the sub was only a few hundred yards offshore.

"They'd better hit that fucker with their first round," I remarked to our platoon sergeant, as we watched our guys preparing to fire. Meanwhile, they continued tracking the sub. Jerry was on elevation. He kept calling out the range and other information. Suddenly he called out, "Stand by to fire!" Then, *"Fire!"*

Boom! The gun went off, and we watched. They missed the sub by two or three hundred yards long and a hundred yards wide. The Japs had been waiting for that. The moment after our gun went off, the Jap crew fired two quick rounds, then hurried off deck as the sub started submerging. We each took cover as best we could. Both Japanese rounds hit our beach, exploding near us, but miraculously not hurting any of us. Were we frightened? Hell, yes—but we calmed down again after about five minutes.

About then, a jeep came bouncing down to the beach and braked to a stop. In it was the regimental commander, Col. Leroy Hunt, and was he pissed off! He wanted to know what the hell we were firing that gun at. Where the hell were our CO and platoon leader? Who the hell knew? He yelled for a while, threatening to put us all in jail, but under those conditions, that was part of his job. Nobody was about to go to jail, or get court-martialed, or anything else. The beer bottles had been stashed out of sight, the gun crew wasn't anywhere near the parapet, and the sub was gone.

A very important problem never addressed during the entire Guadalcanal campaign was the fact that marine units had no real system of communication with other units. With rare exceptions, we had no radios or anything else to pass on information regarding what we did or did not see. To let the company command post know that a sub had just surfaced, we'd have had to send a runner, and that would take time. If the company commander or a flanking platoon had any input, or advice, or remarks to offer, a runner would have to relay that information, too. That would take more time. It was our training and our experience that took over whenever a firefight or any other unexpected situation developed.

Backtracking a little, Yogi Milana, who was part of the gun crew that day, recalls the submarine incident a little differently.

> Several of us were examining the abandoned Japanese antiaircraft gun situated in our area of the beach. The sights were smashed, but we could still move and point the gun, and there was a lot of ammunition. That's when the Japanese submarine appeared offshore. It was much farther out than Ore's estimate. I used to do a lot of ocean fishing, and I came to understand that anyone looking at a ship or any other object across a body of water, and having no other references, generally comes up with a poor estimate of the ship's distance. I figured that the sub was maybe a mile offshore—which was beyond the range of our rifles.
>
> The gun crew on the sub started firing toward us, and we fired back. Some of our shells were designed to explode on direct contact. Others had timing mechanisms. Five of us manned the gun, including Jerry, Larry Gerkin, a guy named Motsinger, and me. Jerry loaded the gun with a timed shell, closed the breach, and we fired. The shell exploded way past the sub, as Ore said. What he didn't say is that we fired several more shells, cutting back on the timing mechanism with each shot. Finally, when we'd gotten one down to about eight seconds, the shot burst right above the sub. I'll swear we saw some of the Japanese gun crew blown off the deck. We lowered the elevation slightly, but before we could fire another shell, the sub disappeared below the surface. We weren't credited for the encounter, which went to the 11th Marines.

About twenty minutes after the submarine disappeared, fifteen or twenty Japanese two-engine bombers came over and dumped their load of bombs on the bastards who had stolen their cold beer—us! That was the beginning of four months of daily bombing, shelling, and anything else the Japs could throw at us. We didn't take any casualties from that bombing. But it did leave us shook up, with our nerves on edge and maybe a little jerky. Anyway, no one was wounded.

The really bad news came that night, though it took a while before we found out about it—and learned how serious it was. Far out at sea, we heard the fireworks and saw flashes as naval artillery shells lit up the night sky. We didn't know it, but from our beach, we were witnessing the battle of Savo Island, in which the U.S. Navy took a beating. It might have been the next day that our own navy's brass met on a ship and received word of an additional approaching Japanese task force. They weren't about to take any chances with our own ships. Once again, the U.S. Navy was making plans to abandon us.

THE RIFLE GRENADE

It was on D-Day plus two that one or more Japanese, observing us from a distant inland high point, decided to take a few shots at us. The rifle fire came from somewhere up on a ridge. The 1st Platoon, L Company, was moving west along the shore toward what would become our permanent position on the MLR. We were nearing our destination when those rounds of rifle fire came winging into our area. We all hit the deck and lay flat for a few minutes, waiting, expecting more rifle fire. There wasn't any more, but we took our time getting up. One thing you never want to do is present yourself as a potential target to an enemy rifleman, especially when you can't see him. Lt. Flash Flaherty happened to be on the ground near me, and I don't recall whether it was his idea or mine, but we decided that this was a good time to try out one of our new rifle grenades.

We were first introduced to the rifle grenades in Wellington, New Zealand, just before we shipped out for combat. We'd been told that this model was a Belgian invention. A gunnery sergeant held a brief class session and showed us how to use them, but they were nearly as new to him as they were to us.

Now, lying in the dirt, Flash Flaherty and I were doing our best to recall how to fire one of those grenades at the suspected enemy position. Between us, we recalled that what we had to do was attach a special wire piece on an '03 rifle by extending the wire from the rifle's rear sight to its front sight. Next, we'd have to put what the instructor sergeant had called a trombone attachment on the end of the rifle barrel. The rifle grenade itself was a fat thing that fit into the attachment.

Flaherty pointed at the ridge. "The Jap fired at us from there," he said.

I agreed. If the Jap was alone, or with just a few men, they would have sized up the strength of our unit and by now would be moving away from us fast. But just in case anyone was dumb enough to remain up on that ridge, we decided now to take a shot at him.

"You ever shoot one of these grenades before?" Flash asked me.

"Hell no," I said. "We can try it, though."

Every squad had one man who carried the equipment to fire this new Belgian rifle grenade. We located the guy in my squad, rigged up his rifle, and put the trombone launcher attachment on the barrel. This was going to be an experiment, a learning experience. We did remember being told that we couldn't launch a grenade with a normal bullet. The live bullet would go right through the launcher and wreck it. We had to put a blank cartridge into the rifle's firing chamber. Somebody elected me to shoot the thing—or maybe I elected myself. So, there I was, peeking up from the ground, sighting my target. I pointed to a large boulder up on the ridge, some seventy-five yards distant and above us. "That'll be my aiming point," I said.

"Okay," Flash said. "Go ahead."

I jammed the rifle stock tight against my shoulder, raised myself up off the ground to a kneeling position, and squeezed the trigger. The rifle went *bang!* and the recoil jarred it loose from my grip. The rifle smacked me hard in the jaw. With that, I went down on my face while the little bluebirds started going *tweet, tweet, tweet* around my head. I might have been out for about ten seconds before I shook myself back to consciousness.

"Did I hit it?" I asked. "Did I hit it?"

"Yeah, yeah," Flash said, not sounding enthusiastic. "But it didn't blow. The damn thing didn't explode."

"What do you mean? I *fired* the damn thing!"

"I don't know," he said. "All I know is it didn't explode."

"But I hit it, didn't I? I hit the target? It came down on the target?"

"Yeah, you hit it," Flash said. "The damn thing just didn't work."

We tried to figure out why the rifle grenade hadn't exploded and finally decided that maybe it was a dud. We didn't have time to do much speculating, because by now it was clear that the enemy had vanished, and we still had to dig in at the spot that would become our permanent position. A day or two later, we ran into a guy from another unit who really understood how the new style grenade was supposed to work. We explained our misfortune to him, and he asked us, "Did you pull the firing pin out?"

"Pin? What pin?" we said.

The pin. The goddamn pin! We should have figured out that a rifle grenade would have a safety pin to pull, the same as a hand grenade. I got smacked in the jaw for nothing. That, I have to admit, was deeply embarrassing, both to me and to Flash. We didn't talk about it much after that day.

OUR GENERAL SITUATION

We never gave it much thought, nor were we ever too concerned about it, but the Japs on Guadalcanal kept a much closer watch over our ground activities than we did over theirs. At least, that was the case while we were contained within the small perimeter around Henderson Field between August and December 1942.

In addition, the Japanese must have had some type of communication system that was at least as good as ours—and ours was one step above nothing. L Company, 3rd Battalion, 5th Marines, was dug in on a line that extended from the beach, across a coconut grove, and up an incline to its high point on a coral ridge that formed part of the south line of defense. Looking south from our ridge was looking toward the island's interior, a series of highlands surrounded by thick jungle. On the ridge, our line of defense turned left and connected with our neighboring company, also from the 5th Marines.

Shortly after our line of defense was established, those of us in rifle companies spent our days performing five basic tasks. First was going out on small-group patrols. Second was working on our defense positions, making our foxholes—or spider holes—more comfortable and deeper. Third was scrounging for materials, including barbed wire and anything else to make our lives safer. Fourth was performing work details in the area to our rear. Fifth was cleaning our weapons and manning our defense line.

Most of the time, the Japs managed to sneak observers close enough to our line to keep track of what we were doing. They probably watched us on a regular basis, getting familiar with us to a point where they might have had nicknames for us—maybe *Sko-she-san*, which means "Little Guy," or *Taux-e-san-okie*, which means "Big Guy." Many years have passed, and my Japanese is slipping, so readers are welcome to correct me here.

On one occasion, we started digging a well in the center of our coconut grove, because the water we were getting from our rear was being transported in cans previously used to hold oil or gasoline. That was a simple case of poor logistics, which left our water supply undrinkable. Digging a well in the sandy soil was a slow, tedious job, made slower by the fact that we had to do it between our normal, official job routines. Well digging was not considered an official company project. One day, when we were about halfway though the job, the once- or twice-daily flight of Jap bombers that normally came over to bomb either the airfield or Kukum dropped their bombs short. They left a line of bomb craters that strung right through our area. Lucky for us, we didn't take any casualties, and the bombs also missed our partially dug well.

The incident meant nothing to me at the time, but thinking about it years later, I decided that our half-dug well had been their intended target. Probably a Japanese ground observer had told his commander that *On-o-nay*, or "Old Round-eye," was digging some kind of hole at specified grid coordinates, and it probably deserves a special plaster job from the bombers.

On another occasion, much later, we went to work building what we thought would be a super-duper, one-of-a-kind air-raid bunker. Several hours after we completed that project, the air-raid siren sounded, and about six bombers came over. They dropped all of their bombs, plus a couple of empty, screaming bottles, right into our area. The empty bottles were the Japanese version of psychological warfare. As they fell through the air, the bottles gave off a screaming whistle, which could sound pretty scary. One five-hundred-pound bomb scored a direct hit and finished off our brand-new bunker. That hit told us that one of their observers had been watching us from a point where we couldn't see him. He probably didn't know what we were building, but just to be safe, he passed word up through command, and they decided to knock it out.

Then there was that infamous lone Jap field artillery piece that marines all over the Canal came to know and hate, Pistol Pete. Random incoming rounds from Pistol Pete were a harassment, and not great for our morale, but they seldom caused serious damage. A half dozen or so of us would be sitting in a group, clowning around, skylarking, trading stories, and suddenly a round from Pistol Pete would come in. You might hear it whistle over your head if it was long. Or maybe it would be short. You never see the one that gets you. But in either case, it was no big deal. Except a few minutes later, a second round would come in, and we knew for sure that its deflection and range had been corrected. If the first round had come in long, the second would come in short. Or vice versa. The first among us to notice the correction would holler, "It's a bracket!"

We would dive into our holes like a bunch of ground squirrels. And we knew that in this case, a Jap observer was somewhere out in the jungle, watching us, observing the location of Pistol Pete's shell bursts, then signaling the information back to the gun crew. He had some mode of communication—maybe a telephone, maybe a radio—and was instructing the gun crew and helping them zero in on the target, which happened to be us.

By itself, this might not sound like a big deal, but on the Canal, it was an advantage that the Japs had and we didn't. When we moved forward on a platoon patrol or on a squad or small-group patrol, we had no way of communicating with our main force to our rear. Headquarters' attitude was "Good luck. See you when you get back."

We were being watched, and most of us riflemen manning perimeter positions seldom gave the situation a minute's thought. Walking around on our main and only line of defense, knowing that we were probably being observed, and not being particularly concerned about it tells you what it takes to be a frontline fighter. The main ingredients that make a good warrior are youth, lack of fear, stupidity, and patriotism, in roughly equal amounts. That was us.

CHAPTER 2

Our Journey to Guadalcanal

There we were, yours truly and thousands more marines like me, stuck on a miserable jungle island, half starved, abandoned by our own navy, and being shot at, bombed, and shelled by the Japs. How did we get here? How did it all start? What were the circumstances that sent each of us into the United States Marine Corps? My L Company cobbers and I were one hell of a long way from home—and sometimes our chances of ever seeing home again didn't look very good. Like every other fighting man who ever went into combat in any war, we thought a lot about home.

Sometimes when I remember the sight of thirty scared marines huddled in a Higgins boat, or eight cobbers moving low through dense jungle, bucket helmets on their heads and Springfield '03s ready, or just recall the look of a lone shirtless buddy sitting next to his spider hole looking skyward at Jap bombers on their way to a target, I remind myself who was fighting this war.

Kids were fighting this war. Kids.

MY FAMILY AND CHILDHOOD

I was born in a very small Pennsylvania town called Austin, a few miles south of the New York State line and about halfway between Pittsburgh and Buffalo. Austin is so small that some Pennsylvania maps don't even show it. I first saw the light of day in July 1921, the fifth of nine Marion children. Both my parents originally came from the Abruzzi region of Italy, high up in the Apennine Mountains, about a hundred kilometers east of Rome. The family name Marion was originally Mariani.

My mother was Annunziata, so named because she was born on the feast of the Annunciation in March 1892. After she came to America, she called herself Nancy. She arrived in America soon after she and my father were married. My father, Perry Marion, was a good-looking guy who attracted the eye of many a young lady, but he had eyes only for his Nancy. Unlike many Italian immigrants of her generation, Mama learned proper grammatical English from a teacher, and she disapproved of some Italians who came to America, enjoyed the good things America has to offer, but never took the trouble to learn proper English. She had her standards and she held to them, but she was also a woman with a very warm heart.

We marines who went to Guadalcanal were children of the Great Depression. Mostly poor and hungry, and a little underfed, we were street smart. I like to say either "street smart" or "hill smart," depending on where someone came from. Yogi Milana was street smart, Brooklyn style, and had a couple years of college on top of it. Others, like Ernie Snowden and Speedy Spach, were country boys from Kentucky and North Carolina, and they demonstrated their own style of smarts. But in any case, we knew how to think on our feet and find our way in and out of a tight hole pretty damned fast. Some people say we were survivors.

I was street smart, getting most of my education on South Park Avenue in Buffalo, New York, where my family moved when I was seven. Most of my friends didn't go to high school. This was a time before the squadrons of yellow school buses that now take kids from their front door to school every day. We kids couldn't afford the carfare and the things you needed to go to school. Some of us were fortunate enough to be able to walk to high school. We Marions were relatively fortunate. I completed three years of high school and my older brother, Jim, stuck it out and graduated, but most of my generation's kids in the neighborhood didn't make it. We were all working to help at home. I had one good shirt to my name, one decent pair of trousers, and one pair of shoes. We would stuff cardboard in our shoes to keep the water out when we wore through our soles. Our whole generation was that way. It didn't matter if you had a potato on the dinner table in South Buffalo or a bowl of potato soup out in Kansas. Some days you were hungry. We had smarts all right, but they were different smarts from the kind kids have today.

JOINING THE MARINES

Coming of age at the tail end of the 1930s, when jobs and money were still scarce and my career prospects as a civilian were less than encouraging, I joined the marines. When we thought about joining the armed services, we didn't think about career training or talk over our opportunities with guidance counselors. No, it was more like three guys standing on the street corner and finally deciding: "This is shit. Let's see if we can join the service." There was a lot of talk of war in the late 1930s, so the service was on everybody's mind.

It was very hard to join the service in 1939–40. That would change dramatically in a year or so, but in '39 and '40, there were only about seventeen thousand men in the Marine Corps, and in the Buffalo district, the quota for a month was three recruits. I was very fortunate, or maybe unfortunate.

The food at boot camp was crappy compared with the food in the military today. They used to give you what you might call cheap meat, like spare ribs and liver. But to us kids from the cities along the East Coast or from the hills, it was a feast. I ate it with both hands. It beat the potato or small bowl of pasta I'd have for supper at home by one helluva long shot. This was food. Besides, you got your original issue of clothes, although you paid for anything you lost or needed after that out of your salary. I weighed about 128 pounds when I joined the marines. I got paid $20.80 a month, plus a place to sleep and all I could eat three times a day. Not bad! They'd take a few dimes out of your pay for the Old Sailors' Home, and you'd still have enough to buy some tobacco and paper and roll your own cigarettes.

We were so accustomed to doing what we were told—or at least pretending to do what we were told—that the harshness of Marine Corps boot camp was not much of a shock to any of us. NCOs barked orders at us, and as crazy as they might have sounded, we carried them out. In that era, when your father told you to do something, you didn't question it. You did it. And he wasn't about to negotiate with you over following directions. If the priest over at Holy Family Church told you to do it, if the cop from the precinct told you to do it, you just did it. So a marine NCO was no shock to our sensibilities.

A little later on, if we complained among ourselves, we complained because we knew there was a war in our future, we knew we'd be fighting the Japanese, and we knew the corps didn't have the tools we needed to carry on a war. Before Pearl Harbor, the appropriations for the military were sadly inadequate. Even after Pearl, we went into combat with ammunition, hand grenades, and small arms of World War I vintage. Our rifles were '03s, and that '03 stands for the year the military first purchased them from the Springfield arms factory: 1903. But at the same time, the army was getting new rifles, M-1 Garands, while we still were firing World War I Springfields.

The corps preached at us every day that it was inevitable that our country was going to war with Japan. Not Germany. It was always the Japanese. We would be sent to fight the Japanese, and everything we were learning, everything we were enduring, was to help ensure that we would come back alive from that war. Too many of us didn't. But for all of us who did, and for all of us who lived to see a new life, with television, international travel, flights into space, and the dawn of the twenty-first century, we owe some of it to the attitudes passed on to us from the marines of the Old Breed.

In 1940, there was very little grumbling. There was even an offense called "silent contempt," which meant you gave your superior a dirty look and your expression told him you thought he was a jackass. Silent contempt was worth three days in the brig with "piss and punk." There were a lot of quiet "fuck hims," but they were *very* quiet. After boot camp, when I was first assigned to Indian Head, Maryland, near D.C., I didn't get liberty for more than two weeks. Finally, when I got up enough nerve to ask for twelve hours so I could go over and see Washington, I was told that my services could not be spared. Ore Marion was so goddamned important to the well-being of the United States Marine Corps that he couldn't get a few hours' liberty to see the nation's capital.

Yes, we were kids, no smarter or stronger, no wiser or more worldly than the generations of kids who preceded us, or those who have followed us to this day. But we were kids with exactly the set of character traits needed in 1941.

PREWAR YEARS IN THE CORPS

I joined the corps on April 25, 1940, and was sent directly to Parris Island. Boot camp at Parris Island, South Carolina, was tough in those days, but it was no trouble for me, or for most of the guys who came into the corps with me. The only time I had a problem was when we went to the rifle range. Our coach turned out to be a big-mouth rebel boot corporal who sized me up and asked, "Where yooo from, boy?"

"Buffalo, sir."

"That's in New York, ain't it?"

"Yes, sir."

"An' you a Dago, ain't chew?"

"Sir, I'm Italian descent."

"A Dago from New York. That's the worst mix for a Moreen."

He went on and on like that, and I had no choice but to listen to it. He saw to it that my time on the rifle range became two weeks of hell, but much to that idiot corporal's surprise, I qualified. I never saw him again after boot camp. During my twenty years in the corps, I stayed on the lookout for that son of a bitch, but he saved me the trouble of knocking him on his ass, either by getting himself killed in the war or by leaving the corps. Much later, when it became my turn to exert some leadership, I thought of him as the first among a handful of NCOs and officers who taught me how *not* to teach or treat my men. His kind was a minority in the corps, but it takes only one to make a marine's life miserable.

Ore J. Marion shortly after completing boot camp at Parris Island in 1940. ESTATE OF ORE J. MARION

After boot camp, my first duty station was at the Naval Powder Factory at Indian Head, Maryland, about twenty miles south of D.C. At that time, that was its official name: the Naval Powder Factory. Its official name is now Indian Head Division, Naval Surface Warfare Center. There were about twenty-five men at that post, and the single purpose of our being there was guard duty, day after day after day—*and* night. Our typical watches would be four hours on and four hours off, followed by four more hours on and eight hours off. That, in turn, would be followed by four more on and sixteen hours off. That completed the cycle, which would be repeated over and over again without a break. In other words, no time for liberty. Hours off duty gave us just enough time to wash our clothes, press uniforms, shine our shoes and leather belt, and quietly repeat to ourselves: "I love the corps." Try to fall asleep and they would make us fall out for close-order drill, or "dive-bomb" and police the area outside, picking up cigarette butts and trash. I kept myself, my clothes, and my gear squared away and looking good, and in short order I was standing watch at the post's main gate.

After three months, I decided it was time for a change in routine. I asked for and got a transfer to Dahlgren, Virginia, across the Potomac. You had to be on the ball to get assigned to Dahlgren. The marine detachment there consisted of only eighteen men and a platoon sergeant who was officer-in-charge. Dahlgren was where the navy tested all of its big ships' guns. At that time, they were also assembling and adjusting the top-secret Norden bombsight, which became an important fixture on U.S. bombers during World War II. After three months' duty at Dahlgren, a certain young lady of my acquaintance from off post threatened to get me into the kind of trouble I didn't need. I told the sergeant about it, and he suggested that my safest course was to get myself transferred out of Dahlgren. One phone call to D.C. was all that was needed. Two days later, I was on my way to the Fleet Marines in Guantánamo, Cuba. That's where I joined L Company, 3rd Battalion,

5th Marine Regiment. I didn't know it then, but that put me on the road to Guadalcanal.

I joined L Company at the beginning of December 1940, just a little over a year before Pearl Harbor. At that time, L Company's strength was only about thirty-five men, with a cadre of maybe two or three officers and one corpsman. We were the Raggedy-Ass Marines, dressed up with campaign hats, field clothes that were part Marine Corps and part navy, leggings, high-top dress shoes, and model '03 .30-caliber Springfield rifles.

Most of the sergeants in the Fleet Marine 5th were old-timers. When military historians refer to the Marines' "Old Breed," these are the men they are talking about. A few of them who had fought in France during World War I were still active. All of them had fought in places like Haiti (which they pronounced *Hay-tie*), Nicaragua, and San Domingo (today the Dominican Republic), and some had even exchanged potshots with the Japs in China. It was these men, the famous Old Breed, who trained us at Guantánamo. It was from them that we learned many good maneuvers, tactics, and tricks—battle savvy—that would save many of our lives during the following years, when we were pitted against the Japanese in the Pacific. Pretty soon, we were teaching the same tricks to new recruits who were coming into the marines with the growing threat of war. They were the kids we had to train and then lead into combat.

By the end of December 1940, marine reserve units were being called to active duty. For L Company, that meant raising our strength from thirty-five to fifty men. The corps repeatedly tried to get us better and newer equipment but those efforts produced few results. The navy's battleship admirals and their other top brass fought the corps tooth and nail for every piece of equipment they were forced to give us. As they saw it, they could win any war at any time they pleased with the big guns on their battleships and cruisers. The events of World War II demonstrated time after time that they seldom hit anything with those guns. Anybody who thinks I'm overstating the case should keep in mind that the navy never won a major World War II sea battle with surface vessels until the very end, by which time the Japs had no seapower or airpower left. The big sea battles that our navy won, starting with the Coral Sea and Midway, have to be credited to our navy and marine pilots, and to the planes they flew from the decks of our carriers.

Our training at Guantánamo gave all of us the opportunity to familiarize ourselves with every weapon our unit carried—weapons that we used later on the Canal. They included the '03 Springfield rifle, the BAR (Browning Automatic Rifle), VB rifle grenades, and water-cooled .30-caliber machine guns. We didn't fire them, mind you. Firing weapons cost money, and in 1940, the Navy Department wasn't about to let us expend their resources. That .30-caliber ball ammunition cost 3 cents a round in those days. We'd been taught that we were professionals whose primary function was to eliminate all enemies of the United States in the most expeditious manner, and at the lowest cost to the taxpayer.

While we were in Cuba, my gunnery sergeant and an old veteran of *Hay-tie* made scouts out of me and one of my best buddies, Harry Denham, who was better known in the platoon as "Stinky." Stinky Denham and I had a special talent for driving the gunny nuts, but we also learned a lot from him. It was combat knowledge that became valuable to us later when we went to war.

GETTING READY FOR WAR

Before the United States entered World War II, we marines had no choice other than to take part in the political games our leaders were playing. France was under Nazi occupation, and by mid-1941, the Vichy French had several small warships anchored at Martinique and in Dakar, Africa. Apparently, somebody in Washington saw those ships as a threat to the U.S.A. We—that is, the 5th Marines—were sent down to Martinique twice, on old battleships that were held together with not a hell of a lot more than paper clips and chewing gum. Our ships would approach the harbor and signal to the Vichy French, "Come out and fight." They'd signal back, "Up yours!" or the French equivalent.

Aboard ship, we ran practice drills, the intention at least in theory being that we would use whaleboats and an odd assortment of motor launches to land on the Martinique dock. We were carrying our '03 Springfield rifles and attired in campaign hats, leggings, khaki shirts and trousers, and dress high-top shoes—polished, no less—and were augmented and guided by several bluejackets. The idea seemed to be that at the sight of us, the French would panic and run like hell. We went to Dakar once with the same drill, and they weren't impressed either. Following those futile gestures, we were sent ashore on liberty, where the French champagne and women were—one cheaper than the other—and then we sailed back to Norfolk. From there, we returned to our base at New River. At that time, the 6th Marine Regiment, previously based in San Diego, was transported through the Panama Canal then up the coast to Norfolk, where it took over our supply and ammo ships, and sailed north to occupy Iceland.

Four or five months before Pearl Harbor, the 5th Marine Regiment intensified rifle company training to the point where each company would leave our tent camp at 0730 on Monday mornings, go out into the boondocks, train, and not return until midmorning on Fridays. During that period, we graduated from tent camp to fiber huts. The Friday routine didn't vary: (1) clean weapons and gear; (2) shave and shower; (3) undergo inspection of all weapons, including crew-served ones; (4) go to chow; and then (5) go on liberty, usually at about 1300 hours, and be free through the rest of the weekend.

During that period just before the war, the 5th Marine Regiment was commanded by Col. Bobby Blake, a World War I veteran. Colonel Blake was fifty or so, tall and handsome, clean-cut, a father of a man. I don't know many details about his career, but I do know that he'd been stationed at posts and

L-3-5's company street at New River (now Camp Lejeune), North Carolina, in 1941. Back then, tents were standard living quarters, and the only permanent structures in company areas were mess halls and latrines. ESTATE OF ORE J. MARION

on ships around the world, had been in France during World War I, and had later participated in the so-called Banana Wars that erupted throughout the Caribbean and Central America. At the time he commanded the 5th Marines, a rifle company consisted of fifty to sixty enlisted men, including NCOs, and maybe four officers. Combined into the 5th Marine Regiment, these companies played what I believe was the most important role in Marine Corps history.

When the war broke out, the 1st and the 7th Regiments were reactivated with men from the 5th Regiment, augmented with new recruits. When the 1st Raider Battalion was formed in 1941 at Quantico, it consisted of the 5th Marines' 1st Battalion, later augmented with raw recruits who'd had only three weeks of training at Parris Island. When the 1st Parachute Battalion was formed in 1941, many of the men came from the 5th Marines. The same was true of the Tank Battalion's 1st Scouts. Most officers in the 1st Raider and 1st Parachute Battalions came from the 5th Marines.

By now we were getting replacements at New River, and we were training day and night to get our new warriors ready for combat. We *knew* we were going to war, because we were told as much at least ten times a day. What's more, we knew we were going to war against Japan, because the Old China Hands in our outfit were telling us as much and were teaching us everything they knew about the Japs. But unless we were actually out in the field on training exercises, we never talked about our training, and we never talked about war. We just didn't give a damn, because we knew we'd have to do more than talk about it later—when the war actually came. The men I associated with in L Company—including Willie Shoemaker, Pete Rogers, Stinky Denham, George O'Dell, Larry "Hardrock" Gerkin, Chink McAllan, Hank Klemicki, Joe Barnes, Ben Selvitelle, Speedy Spach, and Art Boston—talked about everything and anything *but* war. We didn't worry about it and we didn't give a damn about it. We knew it was coming, we knew we were good, and there was no reason for us to brag about how we were going to fight the war when it came. We just didn't talk about it.

COLONEL BLAKE'S SPEECH

On Friday, December 5, 1941, liberty call sounded first for the NCOs. The rest of us fell out in the company street, and the first sergeant instructed the senior PFC to march the men to the parade ground, where he was to report to a certain captain. As my own L Company approached the parade ground, I saw Colonel Blake sitting in a jeep. I saw other companies approaching from different directions, arriving at the parade ground from their own company areas. When we were all present—about 150 of us, privates and PFCs, all kids—the captain in charge had us approach the colonel's jeep and stand at ease.

Colonel Blake stood up in his jeep and motioned for us to come right up around him. He didn't have a microphone, so he raised his voice a little. But he didn't have to shout. He started talking to us "gravel crunchers." Many years have passed since that afternoon, but I still vividly recall the scene.

"Men, you have been training hard these past several months, and I'm happy and proud of your progress. When I've finished speaking, I want you to go on liberty, relax, and have a good time. Because when you return, you must become even more serious. You must prepare to become the future leaders and teachers in the corps.

"In a few days, this country will be at war. And within a very short time, the corps will more than triple in size. The training and direction of those new recruits will be your responsibility. You are the future staff NCOs of the corps. The present staff NCOs will soon be the senior staff NCOs, and a large number among them will become commissioned officers."

We "gravel crunchers" looked at each other with amazement, and we probably all were thinking the same thing: *"Me, a staff NCO in the corps?* The Old Man must have been out in the North Carolina sun too long!"

Colonel Blake continued: "What the corps does and how well it succeeds in the coming war depends on you. We will give orders, but it will be each one of you men who trains, moves, and directs your platoon. You are the men who will see that our orders are executed. The honor of the corps and the honor of our country will depend on you." He was looking at each one of us. "Enjoy your liberty now, but when you return on Monday, be prepared for increased responsibility. Be prepared to teach as you've been taught. The corps is depending on you. Good luck. I have all the confidence in the world in you. Dismissed."

That was it. Either the Old Man was suffering from sunstroke or he knew something—maybe simply intuited something based on his long experience in the corps. Two days later, the Japanese bombed Pearl Harbor, and within a very few weeks, we in the 5th Marine Regiment were training raw recruits, turning them into fine marines. Those kids—only a little younger than we were—looked to us for advice. We had to set the standards and lead them by example. So we trained our new warriors, went with them to New Zealand, and from there to Guadalcanal. And from Guadalcanal, those one-time recruits went on to become NCOs who led squads and sections to other battlefields, on Bougainville, Peleliu, Iwo Jima, Okinawa, and several other ferociously contested Pacific islands on our road to Tokyo Bay.

A FEW GOOD MEN
Today the Marine Corps uses a fitting slogan: "A few good men." Back in 1941, when America entered World War II, many good men from all over the country came into the corps. The country needed them, and these kids recognized the need and responded. I've been calling them kids because that's how they started out: as good kids. Facing war, we all grew up in a hurry and became men—damned *good* men. In my opinion, L Company, 3rd Battalion, 5th Marines, got some of the best of them, and to this day, I try to keep in touch with many who are still alive. Several of these good men have reminded me of incidents that I'd half forgotten, in part helping me tell L Company's story.

Arthur J. Boston of Sanford, Maine

I was sixteen when the Japanese bombed Pearl Harbor, and I had to wait about four weeks before I turned seventeen. I was planning on joining the Marine Corps, but my mother and father were opposed. Back then, my parents had to sign for me to go in when I turned seventeen. My brother-in-law came to my rescue. He said to my mother, "They won't take him in the marines. You've got to be six-foot-something. What they'll do, they'll put him in the 'sub-marines.' He'll just pick up trash around the barracks, and he'll never see combat."

She said okay, she'd sign for that, but my father didn't want me to go. I told him, "You know, Dad, those Japanese, what they've done over in China—I wouldn't want to see them coming down the street here in Sanford. I want to fight them in Tokyo. Right in their own country."

He thought a while and then said, "I suppose you're right. Okay. I'll sign for you."

Richard "Yogi" Milana of Hernando, Florida

I was born and grew up in Brooklyn, New York, and was a student at Brooklyn College when the United States entered World War II. I left school for the duration of the war and joined the marines. After boot camp at Parris Island, I was assigned to Company L-3-5 at Camp Lejeune, North Carolina.

Toward the end of May 1942, we went to Norfolk, Virginia, and embarked on the transport ship *Wakefield*. The cruise to the Panama Canal was delightfully sunny. Rather than sleep in the crowded room I'd been assigned to share with seven other marines, I was able to sleep on the deck. The nights were magnificent displays of shooting stars. When we entered the Pacific Ocean, we picked up a naval escort. After a few more days, we were on our own, sailing down the coast of South America, our destination being New Zealand. During the crossing, we hit a violent storm, which delighted the ship's captain because no Japanese submarines could operate in that weather.

We stayed with that storm for almost two weeks. At times, the sea swells reached almost eighty feet, and most of the marines and sailors became seasick—but not me. I had no money, so I washed another marine's clothes for $1.25. Then I got into a small poker game, had fantastic luck, and accumulated about $90. Soon after that, I entered a higher-stakes game, the players including many sergeants. Lady Luck stayed with me and I won over $2,000. During the passage westward toward New Zealand, we had to take turns on submarine watch duty, but I no longer drew submarine watch because the sergeants wanted me to keep playing cards in hopes of relieving me of some of my winnings. However, I kept on winning, and in one deal I even pulled a royal flush.

We were on strict censorship, and our letters home couldn't hint at where we were headed. The Japanese were hitting the Aleutians at that time, according to news broadcasts that came through to us, and we were issued fur caps with face guards. That turned out to be a false alarm, because our ship kept its course for New Zealand.

At my earliest opportunity after we'd disembarked in Wellington, I went to a bank and was able to send about $3,000 in poker winnings home. Some secret destination *that* turned out to be, now that my parents knew where I was. We spent a few weeks in July at a camp outside a town called Paekakariki, about twenty-five miles north of Wellington. After that, we were ordered back to the docks at Wellington.

We shipped out to the Fiji Islands for a practice invasion. From there, we headed for Guadalcanal. On the evening of August 6, we were assembled on deck and informed of the invasion the next day. Then our group sang songs, accompanied by one marine who played a guitar and by me on my harmonica. We managed to get a few hours' sleep that night, then before dawn, we went down the nets, over the ship's side, and into Higgins boats. We were right on schedule, headed for the Canal.

Ernest Snowden from Clay City, Kentucky

I was born in Powell County, a couple miles from Clay City, on August 28, 1924, the son of Bryan and Fannie Tipton Snowden. I had four brothers and three sisters. I went to school in Darlingville, Kentucky. My first day in high school was September 1, 1939, the day Hitler invaded Poland and started World War II. I quit before finishing high school and went to work.

On December 7, 1941, when the Japanese bombed Pearl Harbor, I was seventeen and a half years old. Not long after that, I went to Lexington so I could join the navy, but the navy office was closed when I got there. A marine recruiting officer was there, and he told me to come on over and talk with him. I did, and ended up signing with the marines. I had no idea I would wind up on Guadalcanal.

CHAPTER 3

The Second Half of August 1942

ABANDONED, WE DID THE IMPOSSIBLE
On August 7, 1992, to mark the fiftieth anniversary of Guadalcanal's D-Day, the *New York Times* printed a pertinent, right-on-the-mark article by the historian and writer William Manchester. Manchester arrived on the Canal in 1942 as a marine corporal, and though he makes a point of saying that he didn't see combat on Guadalcanal, he did experience his share of fighting in a later bloody campaign: Okinawa. I hope that as an old marine, Manchester won't mind if this old marine borrows some of his eloquent words on the subject of our ordeal on Guadalcanal:

> At 1:43 A.M. on Sunday, Aug. 9, a powerful Japanese fleet roared down from New Britain, sank four of the five Allied cruisers [the U.S. ships *Quincy, Vincennes,* and *Astoria,* and the Australian ship, *Canberra*] and crippled the fifth. Our remaining warships and troopships departed, taking everything the Marines needed with them. Maj. Gen. Alexander A. Vandegrift, the Marine commander, immediately put all hands on half rations.
>
> That first naval victory gave the Japanese command of the waters around the island, and they began landing reinforcements every night. Our prospects were dim. Gen. Douglas MacArthur thought our survival was "open to the gravest doubts." The Army Air Corps

refused to send aircraft there; the crews of merchantmen bearing food, ammo and supplies for us refused to sail there; the senior admiral in the Solomons refused to strengthen the force there. The Marines were written off—doomed.

I don't recall the date of this event, but all of us in Company L-3-5 were dug in at our area of responsibility. I was one of the guys in the 1st Platoon who noticed Captain Spurlock, our company commander, and the three lieutenants who led the platoons as they returned from some other part of our sector. Lieutenant Flaherty, my own platoon leader, was one of them. We assumed they were coming back from a briefing with higher command, maybe at battalion level, possibly at regimental level. There had been a lot of those briefings lately, so we didn't give it much thought until maybe a half hour later. That's when Flaherty sent a runner our way. He wanted the platoon sergeant and the three squad leaders to muster at his foxhole for a short meeting.

Again, this wasn't unusual. As ordered, we got together with the lieutenant. The five of us sat on the ground in the open daylight in a fifteen-foot circle and listened to Flaherty. He was six feet tall when he stood, but thin like the rest of us. They called him "Flash" Flaherty because he'd scored a touchdown against Harvard. That made him a college football hero, but he was okay anyway. The lieutenant started speaking in generalizations, covering all kinds of things but not going into much detail about anything. I was starting to think that the meeting didn't have much point. Then he tossed a question at us, keeping his voice casual.

"I'd like an opinion from all of you," he said. "Suppose we had to leave this island. I don't mean just our platoon, or even the entire company. I mean every marine who's now on the island. How do we do it? Let's get some opinions. What do you guys think would be the best way to go about it?"

Whoa! What the hell did he just say? What was being suggested here? We looked at each other, then back at him.

One of the squad leaders spoke up. "Hell, lieutenant. We're getting off this island the same way we came here—on navy transports."

Flaherty didn't answer right away. He looked at us, and then he looked off toward the sea. "What if there *are* no transports to take us off? What do we do then?"

"What the hell do you mean, no transports?" I chimed in. "We stay here and we fight those bastards until the navy *takes* us off. That's what we do!"

"Okay," he said. "But what happens while we're waiting for those ships you're talking about? What do we do about chow? What do we use for supplies? What do we do about arms?"

"What the hell," one of the other squad leaders grumbled. "What chow? We don't have any now."

"What's the big deal?" somebody else said. "Maybe we make rafts, then we drift out to one of the other islands around here."

"Oh yeah!" I broke in. "Go to another island, then sit there like these Japs were doing here. Sit on our ass and wait for a miracle. The hell with that. The navy brought us here, and it's up to them to take us off!"

"Right!" somebody else said. "Meantime, we'll fight these bastards whichever way we can, goddamn it."

The lieutenant was listening to us, but there was something else he wanted to say. "Maybe before we leave, we dump mustard gas on the field. Dump it on all the island's other low-lying areas. That way, the Japs can't use the airfield. And they can't try building another one on some other flat location. We could make the island useless to them for the duration of the war."

"Hell," another squad leader remarked, "somebody dumps mustard gas on this island, they gotta dump that gas on us, too. 'Cause we ain't going nowheres until our damn U.S. Navy takes us off this damn place!"

"Yeah!" the rest of us said. "We're not going anywhere. We stay here and fight!" That was the end of the discussion. Without any one of us having to say another word, it was clear that the lieutenant agreed, the sergeant agreed, and all three of us

Raising the colors on Guadalcanal, August 1942.
U.S. NAVAL HISTORICAL CENTER

raggedy-ass squad leaders agreed. And that's exactly what happened. During the rest of the campaign, I never heard another word about leaving from anybody. We were the marines, and we weren't going anywhere.

OUR PLACE IN HISTORY

> **cob-ber** \'käb-ər\ *n.* [origin unknown]
> *Austral* (1895): BUDDY
> —from *Merriam Webster's*
> *Ninth New Collegiate Dictionary*

We picked up the word *cobber* when we were in New Zealand, just before going off to battle on Guadalcanal, and somehow it stuck. For us, a cobber is a guy who went through hell with us and became like a blood brother, especially on Guadalcanal. To this day, we marine veterans of the South Pacific theater use the word *cobber* with affection and reserve it for very special friends, especially those who went to battle with us.

By the time we raggedy-ass marines dug ourselves in on Guadalcanal, we had learned a great deal about life for our young years (I was old, at twenty-one), but the scope of the war and our role in it—what has now become known as our place in history—was not a thought we had spent even a moment dwelling on. When we landed on this island, we knew where we were in relation to Japan. We had been thoroughly schooled on that on the ship after we left New Zealand, on our way to the Canal. But even the thought of landing on the Japanese mainland—a savage task we were fortunate enough never to have to face in wartime—was still three years away. We never even considered that Japanese forces might someday invade the United States mainland. That was preposterous. We were in a war and we were going to win it. We were sure of that.

When we cobbers sat next to our spider holes on a tropical evening, waiting for a Jap ship to lob a shell or two at us, we had plenty of advice for Roosevelt. We didn't know what MacArthur was doing, or what the Allies were doing against the Nazis on the other side of the world. But we had plenty of advice just the same. There was so much we didn't know about fighting a war on these islands. And to make it worse, neither did the top echelon giving us our orders. Here we were with mosquitoes as big as moths, carrying deadly malaria, and we had no nets and no medicine to speak of. We had no modern communications. We had nothing to treat jungle rot. Our weaponry was antiquated. I never once saw a map of Guadalcanal during our four months on that island. By the time I became a platoon leader, I didn't need a map. Shit, yes, we had advice for President Roosevelt: Get us some chow and some ammunition and we'll kick their asses back to Tokyo. We talked about everything; everything, that is, except death. At our age, we were sure that only the other guys would die.

We usually thought the infantry was doing okay. But we knew our navy was getting the shit kicked out of it. No one told us. We just needed to look out over the waters of Ironbottom Sound to see it. And we knew that six or eight of our planes would come in and go out. And then there would be five and then four and then three. And one day a few planes would go out and none would come back. And all the while, the Jap bombers just kept coming. We never knew the big scheme of things, but we knew exactly why we were on Guadalcanal. The goddamned United States Navy would not come back and get us off!

Even when most of us were sick, and hungrier and thirstier than we had ever been on the worst days back home, surrender was not a consideration for the cobbers. We had an inkling of what the Japs had done to prisoners on Bataan. When I read after the war that Admiral Ghormley had been told he could leave us on the island to surrender if he felt it was best, and that it would not be held against him, I was so goddamned mad I couldn't speak. That one time when it was suggested we might have to build rafts and drift off into the Pacific, we all said, "No fucking way are we going to get pushed off this island."

The other thing we never considered was going home. In today's army, with today's communications and transportation, if you get a little Hollywood wound, a big airplane and a crew swoop in to pick you up and evacuate you to a hospital and eventually home. To be evacuated from the Canal, when that was possible, you had to be considered "nonoperational" for a year. A guy with a compound fracture would be back in three months on crutches. It was an attitude. When you were sick and had a temperature of 105, you said, I joined the marines when I was young and healthy, and I'm staying in the marines until I'm old and healthy again.

After the Guadalcanal campaign was over for us and we were in Australia, we had a better idea of what was going on in the world. Down in Australia, they were very liberal with their information. War news was on the radio and in the papers. Later still, it became clear to us that we'd be invading the Japanese mainland. Even when we were training in Hawaii to land on Okinawa and the atomic bomb was dropped, we didn't have a very good notion of what that was. But we heard it was a pretty big one, and the training all but came to an end.

So much for making our place in history. I would have to say that if it was on the list at all, it was way down near the bottom. It was nowhere near as important as getting some decent chow, and pushing the Japs into the sea. And in our scheme of things, it wouldn't have compared with saving our lives or winning a war. It was not a concept that struck a chord with a bunch of wet, smelly, and hungry Marines on an island nowhere in the Pacific Ocean.

FOOD

For us marines hanging on to the small perimeter around Henderson Field, the immediate result of our abandonment by the U.S. Navy was a shortage of everything. It wasn't long before we started running out of all the things you need to fight a military campaign—and for that matter, running out of just about everything you need to keep yourself alive: ammunition, general supplies, medical supplies, and not least of all, food. You didn't need a Ph.D. to figure out we were in trouble.

Our food rations were woefully short, and one of the things that saved us was the fact that we'd been able to augment our stateside chow, when we had it, with food left by the Japs in the Kukum warehouse. That had been the supply depot for the Japanese and Koreans when they were constructing the airstrip that we captured on August 8. But now, for us marines abandoned by our supply ships, stuck in our spider holes, and guarding our defense perimeter, our rations became one or two mess-kit spoonfuls of rice, sometimes twice a day, sometimes once a day, and on a few days, none at all. It went on that way for quite a while.

Many years later, I was reminiscing at a military reunion with several buddies from Company L-3-5. When someone mentioned the Japanese rice, another guy added, "Yeah, how 'bout those maggots!"

I reminded them how at first we picked the maggots out of the rice and ended up with only half a spoonful.

"Yeah," somebody agreed. "Then after a while, we got smart and left the maggots in. Used a pinch of dirt to simulate pepper, and the taste was just fine!"

"Fine" might be exaggerating a little. Thank the Lord we were hungry, young, and foolish, in that order. Besides, our corpsman told us that those maggots contained protein, along with many other things that were good for us. By that time, we were happy to hear that *something* on the Canal was good for us, even if it had to be maggots.

Rice wasn't our only run-in with maggots. Most of us living in jungle conditions came down with tropical ulcers on our bodies. Sometimes we'd wake up in the morning to find maggots nibbling away at our ulcers, cuts, and scratches—and the doctor told us that was good for us, too. Man! How lucky we were to have maggots with us on the Canal!

For many years after Guadalcanal, facing a meal that included rice was hard for me to do. Whenever anybody mentioned rice, my mind's eye came up with a vision of rice crawling with maggots. That was one of several unpleasant things we had to deal with on the Canal. I've never been a fussy eater, but that Guadalcanal memory taught me to dislike rice with a passion, and to keep right on disliking it for many years afterward.

FIRST BATTLE AT THE MATANIKAU

August 18 and 19 were two tough days for L Company. At about 1000 hours on the eighteenth, we left our position where we were defending our sector of perimeter and moved west toward the village of Matanikau, three and a half or four miles along the coast and across the Matanikau River. Our purpose was to attack an enemy unit that was known to be west of the Matanikau. Capt. Lyman D. Spurlock led L Company, accompanied by Lt. Col. William J. Whaling, the scout and patrol specialist from G-3, along with Marine Gunner Bill Rust and Sergeants Monk Arndt and Frank Few, the last three attached to L Company for this mission.

Arndt and Few were two of only three survivors of the August 12 patrol, which was the first patrol to the Matanikau. Every student of the Pacific war will recognize that as the Goettge Patrol, which had been ambushed and its members slaughtered by Japanese who had used the white flag of surrender to ensnare the Americans. That encounter became a clear signal to us from the Japs that the Pacific war was to be a "take-no-prisoners" struggle. We learned from them in a big hurry and fought back in kind.

Backtracking to about five days earlier, my good buddy Art Boston of L Company's 3rd Platoon recalls being in a defense position out on the beach at the time the Goettge Patrol was being ambushed. That would have been the night of August 12–13. Of course, neither Art nor anybody else in L Company knew exactly what was happening at the time.

> When I was down on the beach that night, I saw tracer bullets in the distance, flying through the air. Pfc. Reno

Roy was with me on the beach watch. I said to him, "Those boys are in deep trouble down there. Look at those tracer bullets."

Sure enough, next morning at daybreak, we saw this person in the distance and coming toward us, coming up along the beach. From a distance, he looked like a Japanese. But he didn't have a rifle or bayonet. All he had was a pair of shorts. Reno was going to start shooting at him, but I said, "Wait a minute. Don't shoot now, Reno. He can't hurt us. Look at him. He ain't got nothing on except that pair of shorts. I'm sure he ain't hiding a weapon or anything in there."

So we let him get close enough so we could make him out and we found out that he was Sergeant Few. I believe he was an Indian. He had those slanted eyes, which at first made us think he was Japanese. He told us he'd been wounded—hit in the shoulder and somewhere else. He said that the captain told him, "If anybody can get through this, sergeant, you'll be the one to do it."

He did somehow break through. And Reno and I were the first to see him as he made it back.

The Goettge Patrol massacre made August 12 a grim day for the marines, but back home in Buffalo, family and friends were getting more upbeat news. And at last, the press was correctly crediting the marines, not the army, with the Solomon Islands invasion. Here, in part, is the August 12 *Buffalo Evening News* story.

Marines Enlarge Foothold on Solomons
Allies Back Up
Landing With
Extensive Raid

[Today's War Sumary]

The Second Half of August 1942

> ... Sea-borne American invasion forces, officially described as trained in "new twists to the business of killing Japs," battled the enemy in fierce hand-to-hand fighting in the Solomon Island jungles 900 miles northeast of Australia today, and the Navy in Washington declared: "The Marines have opened the door to an Allied offensive in the South Pacific."
> (copyright 1942, the *Buffalo Evening News*)

My family still didn't know that I was with the invasion force, nor did any of the parents of the guys in my unit.

Five days after the Goettge Patrol incident, L Company was a major part of the combat patrol assigned to flush out the Japanese in the vicinity of the Matanikau, where Goettge and his men had been slaughtered. B Company, led by Capt. William Hawkins, was also on this mission and maintained a holding position on the east bank of the Matanikau. A third company, I Company, was supposed to advance on the Japanese from the beach between Point Cruz and Kokumbona after coming in on Higgins boats. But I and B Companies never joined the attack, for reasons to be explained later.

The terrain was rough—in some places nearly impassable—and our advance was slow. The lead scouts had moved some distance ahead of us to locate a proposed area where we planned to bivouac at nightfall. The scouts ran into several Japanese who were out ahead of their own unit. My platoon was behind our company's 2nd Platoon Headquarters Section, led by Lt. George Mead. One of that platoon's riflemen was Pfc. Ernest Snowden.

> We marched all day and caught a few Japs wandering out there in the grass and killed them. That evening we climbed a hill just above the village of Matanikau and set up a defense line so we could stay the night. Three of our boys had a radio with a generator and an

antenna. They sent a message back to the compound, saying that we had arrived at our destination. It was in Morse code, and anyone with a radio could hear it, all over the country. So then, next morning when we woke up, there was a Jap ship in the bay. Somebody said it was a cruiser, and we could see it out there in the bay, moving around. So our other company coming in on Higgins boats couldn't come ashore, with that Jap ship out there, and with the machine guns the Japs had set up on the beach.

I don't recall seeing an enemy ship out on the sound, but there's no question that the Japs were in force on the beach, in and around the little village of Matanikau. And Snowden's correct about that radio message. Looking back on the event, it's clear that everybody from Savo Island to Tulagi who had receiving equipment must have heard our radio being cranked up. If the Japs hadn't already known we were coming, they certainly knew it now. Snowden continues:

Lt. George Mead and Platoon Sgt. John Branic led our 2nd Platoon down the steep terrain toward the village. With us was the platoon guide, a runner, and the platoon corpsman, who for this operation was "Doc" Little. The squad leaders were Corporals Miglen, Carver, and Quentin Shumate. My fellow squad members were J. W. Smith, Timothy E. Muck, Eugene Ballentine, Thomas F. Simon, and other good marines. I asked Ore Marion years later why he believed the 2nd Platoon Headquarters section was leading the charge. He said things were so messed up that any unit could have led.

We went down through the brush a piece, and someone was coming up through the brush. Man, they were knocking brush every which way and making a racket, but we couldn't see who they were. Lieutenant Mead challenged them, but we didn't get an answer. They got quiet for a little while. Well, we waited for a minute.

The lieutenant challenged them again; still no answer, so Mead said, "Let it go." So everyone fired on them. If the enemy was there, we didn't go down to check. We just went on down to the village, but on the way down through the brush, the Japs killed Lieutenant Mead.

In the village, we were met by rifle fire from snipers. We had a fellow with us by the name of Somick [Pvt. Boris C. Somick], and he got hit in the back of his head. It wasn't serious, but blood was getting on his blond hair. We found shelter in a shack, and Corpsman Little patched him up. Well, someone—I don't know who—started shooting into the shack. I don't know if it was the Japs shooting or our own bunch, but we had to get out of there. We got outside, and the Japs made a bayonet charge from out of the brush. Someone—I believe it was Cpl. Willie C. Shoemaker—set up a defense line. I jumped behind a log and lay down beside Corpsman Little. A Jap sniper in a tree shot Little through the head and killed him. One of our boys shot the sniper in the tree. He didn't fall out, but we knew we got him when his shooting stopped. The Japs made a bayonet charge from out of the brush at the line Corporal Shoemaker set up, and as they ran past Corporal Miglen they killed him. But we killed all of them in the charge, and after that, things quieted down.

That was Ernest Snowden's experience with the 2nd Platoon. I was a squad leader in the 1st Platoon, which followed behind his unit. Yogi Milana, a rifleman in my squad, experienced something else.

After we'd spent the night behind a knoll above the village, we crawled to the top of the knoll. I saw a Jap climbing a tree that stood near the trail leading into the village. I pointed out the Jap to Eddie Woods, who was lying next to me. From our position, the sun was behind the Jap, making him a perfect silhouette, but he was about 350 yards away from us. "I guess I'd better shoot him," I said.

Ed said that would be some shot.

"I never miss what I aim at," I told him. I fired and the Jap fell backward, and Ed confirmed it. I told him I'd aimed at the Jap's neck, expecting the bullet to drop a few inches as it traveled.

As I was talking, Lieutenant Flaherty ran toward us and shouted, "Who fired that shot?"

I raised my hand. "I did."

"Don't you know this was supposed to be a secret patrol?"

My own recollection is going down the steep jungle trail, the 2nd Platoon directly ahead of us, preparing to lead the attack into the village, which we knew was full of Japs. We could clearly see Lieutenant Mead's platoon ahead of us and below us on the embankment, moving downhill in single file, quiet, well disciplined, everyone alert. Then they disappeared into the foliage ahead of us, and that's when we heard the first small-arms fire. Moments later, Jap machine guns and rifles opened up and poured it on. Then came the heavier sound of our BARs and '03s returning the fire. Next, it was our platoon's turn. We were about to get our first real baptism under fire.

As we approached the edge of the village, I saw the 2nd Platoon's sergeant, John Branic, lying facedown on the trail. He was dead, but we had to keep moving. We entered the village, and immediately I saw Lt. George Mead lying crumpled on the ground. He was dead too.

Marine Gunner Edward Rust, an old veteran of Nicaraguan jungle fighting, was crouched near the ground, directing our platoon squad by squad, instructing each squad leader as we entered the village.

"We have to form a line along here," he told me, pointing from the spot where we were crouched and moving his arm to indicate the beach. "See that fallen log near the tree out on the beach? Put your BAR man behind that log. Move 'em fast because these slope-heads are going to attack us in force. And they're gonna do it real soon."

I looked toward where the Japanese rifle and machine-gun fire was coming from. I saw one of my best friends, Cpl. Charlie Miglen from the 2nd Platoon. He was lying on the ground, his body doubled up. Dead. Several other members of his squad were wounded and being tended to by Corpsman Little. As I was watching, Little jerked backward and dropped instantly to the ground.

Nearly a year later, Nick Sileo recounted the story of his platoon entering the village of Matanikau to a reporter from the *Los Angeles Evening Herald and Express*. The story appeared in that paper on Tuesday, July 27, 1943.

> I came across the body of a Marine—one of a group ambushed a week or two ago.
>
> All this time my squad is in the lead and I'm last man in our squad. As we get to the village our scouts open fire on seven Japs acting as rear guard. The Japs fire back and run into the jungle to the left.
>
> We continue right into the village. It's deserted. We get to the far edge of the village, where the jungle starts again.
>
> Our squad goes into a staggered column to keep contact and we move in about 25 feet when our scouts spot the Jap line 75 feet ahead. We deploy into a skirmish line and open fire. . . .
>
> My station is the extreme left, and that puts me out on the open beach at the edge of the woods. I can't see the rest of them, but I can hear a lot of shooting back and forth.
>
> I'm crouched below a three-foot knoll, or dune, that runs along the beach and trying to take cover behind a palm leaf from a fallen tree when out of nowhere all at

once I see these six Japs jump out of the jungle, screaming and yelling and come running zig-zag down the beach right at me....

Anybody who says he wouldn't be scared is a liar and I'll tell him so. I was scared like in a nightmare, couldn't move for a second.

Back in training camp I barely passed in marksmanship and here were six Japs to my one Springfield....

Then the miracle happens. Somehow I get the gun to my shoulder and the first shot hits three of the Japs and all three go down, the leading one not 20 feet away from me....

The other three Japs take off back up this ridge and I take off, too—into the jungle to find the BAR man. I can't see a Marine anywhere....

Then I see the three Japs who tried to get me crouched up ahead in the jungle, and without thinking, I open fire....

That's where I should have remembered Sergeant York. Remember the story of the turkeys and how you should always shoot at the turkey farthest away? Sure. I'd seen the movie.

But at that moment I wasn't thinking of movies and I made the mistake of firing at the closest Jap first. I get him and then the second one, but the last Jap got away and it almost costs me my life....

I fire after the last Jap but miss him, and then the other 20 Japs up ahead open up on me. They know now where I'm hiding.

My rifle is empty and I haven't time to reload. I jump out on the beach and take cover behind the sand ridge. I see a bush 30 feet away and run for it, zig-zagging. Ten feet from it they nail me....

The first shot gets me in the right groin, fracturing the pelvis bone, and as I start down, a bullet creases my chest on the left side, paralyzing my left arm.

It doesn't knock me out, but I drop my rifle in the sand and sprawl on my left side, and lying there half dazed, I suddenly see this last Jap I'd missed coming down the beach after me. He comes up to me and shoves his rifle in my face. (If he had a bayonet I wouldn't be telling this.) I put up my right hand to ward off the shot. . . .

The next thing I remember is lying on my face with my right hand under my chin and I can see blood spurting up and I think it's from my throat.

I pull my right hand away and then I see most of the bleeding is from my right thumb, which is shot off. My throat is lacerated from several fragments of the explosive bullet—(later they removed the explosive cap lodged in my neck)—but it's my hand that worries me.

I know I've got to stop that bleeding, but I can't move off my left arm. It feels dead. Finally I roll over but it's no good because the left arm is too numb to use from the elbow down. There's no way I can stop the bleeding. . . .

Meantime, the platoon counter-attacks, and the first marine I see I call, and he yells for a corpsman. . . .

The corpsman is Second Class Pharmacist Mate Arnold and, without thinking of himself, he comes out on that open beach and gives me first aid with bullets flying all over the place.

(He got a Silver Star for this, but I'd give him all the medals in the world!)

He kneels down and goes to work on me and stops most of the bleeding. I remember the captain coming up later and the platoon leader and even the colonel, to take a look at me. (I know they didn't think they'd ever see me again.)

Pretty soon the Higgins boats come up to the beach and they put me on a stretcher and load me on a boat with three others who are dead. I hear one of the corpsmen say, pointing at me, "Is he dead, too?" So I surprise him by saying, "Gimme a cigarette!"

The only facts I can add to Nick Sileo's story belong to the good-news category. He survived the war, returned to civilian life, married, fathered children despite the fact that his battle wounds included the loss of one testicle, and lived a long and productive life.

When it was my own squad's turn to form a defense line, as Gunner Rust had ordered, I turned to my squad and ordered my BAR man, Pfc. Lawrence E. "Hardrock" Gerkin, to move out with his assistant, Pvt. John Case. I indicated the beach. "Get behind that log," I told them.

Without a second's hesitation, Case took off running, but kept low. He'd taken about five fast paces when he went down, hard and fast, as though somebody had belted him across the legs with a baseball bat. He'd been hit in both legs by enemy machine-gun fire. A corpsman reached him before long, and later he was evacuated safely.

I repeated the order to Hardrock. "Move out when you can, Gerk, and make for that log near the water."

Hardrock took off, dashing, carrying his BAR, dodging a new spray of incoming enemy rounds, and by some miracle made it to the log. It lay out in the open on the beach sand, and I watched Gerkin duck out of sight behind it, his field pack still visible above and behind the log.

I managed to deploy the rest of my squad, positioning them so that they formed a line of defense that extended inland from the beach to the middle of the village, a distance of maybe thirty yards. Then it was my turn to find a sheltered position from where I could direct the squad. I chose a palm tree down near the beach, and I took off toward it like a shot out of hell, bullets flying all around me. As I dove behind the tree, I landed in a pile of coconut husks, and instantly a million tiny ants came scurrying out of the husks, attacking every part of my body. They were biting like hell, and at that moment they seemed even worse than the Japanese gunfire. Like a crazy man, I dashed out from behind the tree and into the water, getting rid of the ants. A few seconds later, I was behind another tree, now close to Gerkin. I could still see the field pack on his back, sticking up from behind the log. The Japs saw it too. It attracted a fresh volley of enemy machine-gun fire, the bullets stitching a pattern across the top of the log, throwing hundreds of wood chips and sawdust into the air.

Splinters flew up into Gerk's face. By now he had pulled back the BAR's actuator, the bolt was open, and suddenly the gun was filled with wood chips and splinters. They were everywhere, jamming the gun and getting into Larry's eyes.

He began hollering. "I can't see! I can't see a thing! And my gun's jammed! My gun's jammed!"

"Are you hit?" I called.

"No, but I got all that tree bark in my eyes. I can't see!"

He wasn't hit. That was the important thing. "Okay," I said. "Get your BAR ready, and when the bastards come at us, I'll tell you which direction to fire."

"But my gun's jammed!" he said again. "And I can't see! What the hell am I supposed to do?"

"Damn you, Gerk!" I yelled. "You've fieldstripped that gun a thousand times in practice, and you've done it blindfolded. You can do it again, right here and now, Gerk. Your eyes will clear up quick, so don't worry."

"I'm trying!" he yelled. "I'm trying!"

Gerkin knew and loved his Browning automatic rifle the way a mother knows and loves her baby. He had fieldstripped it blindfolded a thousand times, and he'd lugged that smokepole halfway around the world. I knew he could do it. Meanwhile, I had other things to worry about. Japanese rounds were still coming in, and two men in my squad had received minor wounds. I had to check on them. Maybe three or four minutes passed when I yelled back at Hardrock.

"Can you see, Gerk? Can you see?"

"Yeah—I think I can see a little bit."

"How about the BAR?"

"It's cleaned," he said. "It's okay."

That might have been the Jap machine gunner's signal to open up on Gerk one more time. Two or three bullets went through his field pack, but he yelled at me, "I'm okay! I'm okay!"

"Okay, good," I said. "Try to keep your eyes clear. The Japs are going to come charging down the pathway straight in front of us. When they do, let 'em have it."

That's about the time George Miller got hit. Yogi Milana, who was right beside Hap Poloshian, remembers how it happened.

> I ran into the village and got down into a firing position. George Miller and Hap Poloshian were on either side of me. A shot rang out, and the bullet hit Miller's helmet, penetrating it, making a racket, spinning around inside his helmet, then coming out and lodging in his back. It wasn't a deep wound. I could see the bullet, so he was lucky. The Jap who'd shot at us kept firing at us, and I finally spotted him. He was behind a tree. I aimed my rifle and shot at the tree's base, but I didn't get him because the tree protected him. I had one clip of armor-piercing bullets that were supposed to be able to penetrate thirty-six inches of wood, so I reloaded my rifle with that clip. Again I aimed at the base of the tree, then fired. I saw the Jap rise up and fall backward.

We could hear the Japanese giving out a war chant of some kind. Meanwhile, Sgt. Ben Selvitelle had men from his platoon maneuvered so that they were on our right flank, which was farther inland. His unit included a couple of BARs. Suddenly the Japanese made a banzai charge, coming out from the underbrush, rushing down the path three or four abreast, and firing at us. Gerkin opened up with his BAR, and another kid named Motzinger also fired a BAR. I got off several shots with my rifle, while on our right flank, Selvitelle and his men opened up with everything they had.

Off to one side, I spotted Sergeant Kulchycki, who had been issued a brand new submachine gun, the Reising gun, which was first manufactured at the start of the war. The company that designed it should have stayed with sewing machines, or whatever it was they originally made. Kulchycki fired a short burst at the charging Japanese, and the gun jammed. He dropped to his right knee, switched magazines, sprang up again, and fired another short burst. Again the gun jammed.

Letting out a loud curse, Kulchycki flung the Reising gun at the charging Japs as though it were a boomerang. Before that god-awful gun hit the dirt, Kulchycki had drawn his .45 sidearm from his holster and commenced firing, this time effectively. The rest of us with rifles kept firing steadily. It was all over in a few minutes. We wiped out most of the attacking Japanese, and the few who got away faded off to our right, inland, disappearing into the jungle underbrush. There couldn't have been many survivors. My own platoon suffered several wounded, but nobody was killed.

"Lucky I didn't turn in my .45 like I was ordered when they issued me that damn piece of junk," Kulchycki remarked, gesturing in the direction of his abandoned Reising gun. "Holding that piece of crap in your hands is like holding hot air."

All told, it was one hell of a day—and it wasn't over yet. We were moving around now, looking for Jap stragglers and tending to our wounded. By now Gerkin was up from behind his log, and another of our guys was looking at him intently.

"Larry, what the hell is that slop running down your back?"

Gerkin looked surprised, and then an expression of shock came over his face. "Oh jeez," he kept repeating as he took off his shot-up field pack and pulled out two bullet-riddled cans of rice and potato rations, relics from the World War I era. "Look what those bastards did to my emergency chow."

Food was in short supply on Guadalcanal, and two cans of tasteless World War I rice and potatoes—which under better conditions we often tossed away—would now be like dining at the Waldorf. Those rations seemed as precious as gold. The other guys in the squad looked at Hardrock with disapproving expressions on their faces, as though to say that he'd been hoarding by stashing away that extra chow.

Hardrock looked at the expressions on our faces, and I could see that he was hurt because he knew what we were thinking. "Look, you guys," he said. "You were throwing this crap away back in New Zealand. I thought it was a shame you were throwing food away—and I still do. I put these cans in my pack then, and I've been lugging them every damned day since. I intended to open and share them when things got really rough." Nobody said anything. "So that's my story," he said. "Now you guys can believe me, or you can shut up and go to hell." We all knew that whatever his failings, Larry Hardrock Gerkin never lied. If Gerkin said he intended to share that rice and potatoes, that's exactly what he was going to do. Case closed.

With that, he turned away and went looking for a corpsman to flush out his eyes, which were bloodshot and swollen from the wood chips, their lids half closed. For his brave conduct under battle conditions at the first battle of the Matanikau, Pfc. Lawrence Gerkin was awarded the Bronze Star with Combat "V" for bravery.

The story of Sgt. John Branic, the first marine killed in that Matanikau engagement, isn't a happy one. A few years ago, at home in Buffalo, I got a phone call from a guy on Guadalcanal. Innes was his name. He told me he represented Australia and the United States in the Solomons and was still in the process of seeking out the remains of some of our KIAs. Native islanders had turned in some human bone fragments, a marine belt buckle, and a ring with the initials J. B. inscribed inside. He asked me if I could remember where John Branic's body was the last time I saw it. I told him the exact spot where John was KIA—a ravine just above what was the village of Matanikau in 1942. According to Innes, my description concurred with the location where the natives had found the bone fragments, buckle, and ring. Branic originally came from Pittsburgh, but a

U.S. government search that followed failed to locate anybody in Pittsburgh who knew, or remembered, or was related to Branic. That ruled out any DNA testing of bone fragments. Later I wrote to all the old cobbers, telling them what I'd learned about Sergeant Branic's remains. We all felt bad about having to leave his body in the ravine. I talked about it with Ben Selvitelle, a few years ago not long before Ben died. "What could we have done, Ben?" I said. "I was just a corporal and at that time, you were only a sergeant." In fact, there *wasn't* anything we could have done—but I still feel bad about it.

DISCOVERY OF COLONEL GOETTGE'S REMAINS
For readers unfamiliar with the details of the Goettge Patrol, I'll briefly review the event. When we first landed on the Canal, the 1st Division's intelligence officer, Col. Frank Goettge, was told by a captured prisoner that the fleeing Japanese wanted to surrender. Acting on that report back on August 12, Goettge led a small detachment consisting of men from the division and 5th Regiment Intelligence section. Their mission was to find and bring back the Japanese who Goettge believed wanted to surrender.

Goettge's unit was ambushed by the Japs and massacred at the Matanikau. Several Americans survived the firefight, only to be summarily executed by their Japanese captors. Three marines managed to escape: Sgt. Ernest "Monk" Arndt, Sgt. Frank Few, and Cpl. Joseph Spaulding. Arndt was back with us now at the Matanikau. Sergeant Few had been with us at the outset of our patrol, but as night was falling on August 18, he and Colonel Whaling returned to the MLR.

A question that keeps recurring in various reports regarding our August 18–19 action at the Matanikau is whether or not the remains of the Goettge patrol were ever found. I'm stating here, as I've been quoted in other published accounts of the battle, that I was among those who saw the shallow graves in which Col. Frank Goettge and several others from his ill-fated patrol were partially buried. I believe that every other active member of L Company also saw those bodies.

Following our battle, I was among many marines in L-3-5 standing on the beach near the Matanikau River. We were waiting to be evacuated by Higgins boats and returned to our regular defense perimeter. Other members of my squad included Yogi Milana, Hap Poloshian, and Larry Gerkin. Monk Arndt was also at the scene, and he pointed to the shallow graves and said, "See the arm sticking up, and the riding boot? That's the colonel." By "the colonel," he meant Goettge. The bodies were badly decomposed, and it would have been impossible to recognize their individual features, but Arndt had known Goettge well. He was certain that he was seeing Goettge's remains, and I have no reason to believe he was mistaken. Yogi Milana and Ernest Snowden also recall the discovery. As Snowden describes it:

> After we had done the Japs in, they sent Higgins boats for us. We were going down toward the beach, which is when we walked by the remains of Goettge's patrol. Sand was thrown over the bodies, and their arms and legs were sticking out of the sand. Even though the record says they were never found, we found them because they were lying there. We didn't bother them, but they were there.

THE BATTLE OF THE TENARU RIVER

L Company played no part in the next marine victory, known in the history books as the battle of the Tenaru River. That engagement took place at the far eastern end of our MLR, while we were at our line's far western edge. Throughout the black night of August 21, we heard distant gunfire, but we didn't know its meaning until later.

Colonel Ichiki and his unit of a thousand Japanese troops had staged a series of nighttime banzai attacks against our eastern perimeter, defended by two battalions of the 1st Marine Regiment. Ichiki was convinced that he could blast straight through the American defense line and retake the airfield by morning. He was seriously mistaken. Ichiki's force was virtually annihilated. The battle of the Tenaru River became a morale booster, a decisive American victory at a time when we had seen few victories.

The story, delayed by censors, didn't appear back home in the *Buffalo Evening News* until October 3, but they got it right this time, even though everybody got the name of the river wrong. To this day, it's still called the battle of the Tenaru River, though it took place at the Ilu River, informally known by the marines as Alligator Creek.

BATTLE AT RIVER ADDS NEW HONORS TO MARINE LISTS

(The Navy Department made public today the following account by Sergt. James W. Hurlburt, a Marine Corps combat correspondent . . .)
. . . Tenaru River on Guadalcanal Island took its place today with other great battlegrounds where United States Marines have met the enemy face to face and emerged victorious.
(copyright 1942, the *Buffalo Evening News*)

INEPT LEADERSHIP

The Rev. Harry D. Miller from Ohio, known to many of the old cobbers as Sergeant Miller of M Company, 3rd Battalion, 5th Marines, machine gunner first-class, and also known in the corps as "Punchy" Miller, middleweight boxer, wrote me a letter not long ago that started me thinking about military leadership. "During World War II," Miller wrote, "we unfortunately had a number of unqualified leaders who made blunder after blunder, costing the lives of many of our cobbers. Fortunately, the Japanese had an even greater number of leaders who fit that category."

I agree with Miller. In the military, everything depends on competent leadership, and with my old buddy's remark in mind, I recall several cases in point.

KOKUMBONA ON AUGUST 27–28

Being present and at arm's length from a senior field-grade officer unceremoniously relieved of his command by a superior officer is a very uncomfortable position to be in. That was especially true on a day when the witness to the event—in this case, yours truly—happened to be an enlisted man. It was even more uncomfortable because the enlisted man and the relieved officer recognized each other from different times and places, and they didn't like each other. Not that this individual officer was a great favorite with many in the corps— enlisted men *or* officers.

Anyhow, being in the wrong place became my problem one day in late August, but there was nothing I could do about it. I was a lowly corporal and an infantry squad leader in L-3-5. The field-grade officer, Lt. Col. William E. Maxwell, who at that time was the commander of the 1st Battalion, 5th Marines, also put himself in the wrong place, but there was plenty he could have done about it if he'd been better at his job. He put his battalion in the wrong place, and not long afterward, I arrived at the scene to witness what could have been a catastrophe.

While Maxwell was getting himself and his battalion in trouble, I was about five miles east of his position. I was with my squad, holding our position on the main defense perimeter, and all was quiet. That left us with rare leisure time for clowning around and skylarking—until word came my way from a runner: "Saddle up your squad and move out fast to Kukum Beach." I was told to report to a certain captain. I recognized the captain's name. He was regimental staff, which told me something important was going on.

My five-man squad moved along the beach toward Kukum. From the boat pool, which was some distance ahead, I spotted another marine giving me the arm-pump signal. That meant hurry it up! Double-time!

We jogged the rest of the way, until we were stopped by the captain who'd sent for us. He wasted no time giving me orders: "You're going with Colonel Hunt to Kokumbona. I don't know how long you'll be gone, but you will protect him, and if he establishes a command post, you will protect it at all times." Col. Leroy P. Hunt was our Old Man, commander of the 5th Marine Regiment. He answered directly to General Vandegrift, who commanded the 1st Marine Division, which was the entire Marine Corps operation on the Canal. Colonel Hunt was well liked by the regiment, but as I received my orders, he was looking grim as he waited for us to get the show on the road. Whatever was going on today, it was serious. Kokumbona was a native village on the beach to the west of us, several miles beyond our own western line of defense. The only way to get there with reasonable speed was by boat.

We helped ready a Higgins boat, then gave the word: "Okay, Colonel. All set to go." Colonel Hunt and a lieutenant climbed aboard, the coxswain backed the Higgins boat off the wharf, and we began heading west, parallel to the shore, in the direction of Point Cruz.

We were passing Point Cruz and still moving west, about halfway to our destination, when the lieutenant came to me and quietly gave me the scoop. He told me that the 1st Battalion had gone to Kokumbona earlier that day on orders from General Vandegrift. They had since radioed back confusing reports that included a request for assistance. That, the lieutenant told me, was why we were going to Kokumbona now. Colonel Hunt was personally taking the situation in hand, looking over the 1st Battalion's position so he could make his report. I knew that there was only one man the colonel would be making his report to: General Vandegrift. While the lieutenant spoke to me, I glanced across the Higgins boat toward the normally affable colonel. His expression was stern. He didn't look one bit happy. We had been sitting within fifteen feet of the colonel for thirty minutes or more, and he just stared out across the water, silent. You don't talk to your Old Man unless you're spoken to. He said a few words to his aide, but that was all.

We didn't know what the problem was, but we knew there must be one hell of a problem. When the regimental commander goes out in the field, you know something bad is up.

It was a little before 1800 hours—in civilian terms, nearly six o'clock in the evening—when we approached Kokumbona Beach. The sun would be setting in a little more than an hour, which meant there was still plenty of light for us to see four or five Japs scrambling up the steep embankment that overlooked the beach. Apparently they were trying to get away from the area. I spotted one of the Japs carrying a Nambu light machine gun. I'd placed a man in my squad in one of the Higgins boat's two gun turrets. He manned a BAR, and now he hollered back to me: "Corporal! Do you see them?"

We saw them, all right, and so did Colonel Hunt.

"They're about five hundred yards from us. Do you want me to fire a couple bursts?"

"No. We don't know what the situation is like below them." I had answered him automatically, not thinking to consult the colonel first. Now I turned to the colonel for approval.

"You're right, corporal," he said. "We don't know what the hell is going on."

We heard small-arms fire. We saw the Japanese darting glances over their shoulders, looking toward our boat as they scuttled upward. They made it to the top, hurried into some underbrush, and disappeared. Back down on the beach, the entire 1st Battalion was clustered together, most of the men flat on the sand and in prone positions.

We beached the Higgins boat, and a gunnery sergeant I happened to know hurried to meet us. It was clear that our arrival surprised him. He was wondering who we were and why we were there. Then he recognized Colonel Hunt.

"Sir! What the hell are *you* doing here?"

Colonel Hunt didn't answer the question. He said, "Where's your battalion commander? I want to see him right now!"

The gunny complied, sending a man to get the battalion commander. While we were waiting, the sergeant took it upon himself to make an urgent request. "Sir! Do something with this man before he gets us all killed!"

By "this man," he meant Lt. Col. William E. Maxwell, a man I had known as a no good son of a bitch from way back. We still didn't know what was the matter, but my gut said it was Maxwell. The Old Man listened but didn't respond. We waited, and lucky for us, there was no further gunfire. The momentary mayhem caused by those four or five Japanese had quieted down as soon as they disappeared. Soon enough, the battalion commander approached us, wearing a blank look on his face. It was a face I recognized, because I'd had a couple of personal run-ins with Maxwell long before Guadalcanal and halfway around the world—first at Parris Island, then later in Cuba. I was far from the only marine on that island who had a low opinion of his ability.

Colonel Hunt began chewing Maxwell out. I was standing not more than three feet away from Colonel Hunt when he said, "Maxwell, I'm relieving you of your command. Get on my boat and get the hell out of here right now. And when we get back to the perimeter, I don't want to see you on this island!"

I stood there dumbfounded while the Old Man gave Maxwell hell. Maxwell stood at attention and listened, but he wasn't looking at Hunt. Maxwell had recognized me—one of his many old-time enemies—and I was an old enemy who was only a lowly corporal. Cpl. Ore Marion happened to be witnessing Maxwell's humiliation. Maxwell's steely eyes looked dazed as he glared directly at me, and at no one else. When Colonel Hunt was finished with him, Maxwell walked to the Higgins boat, climbed aboard, and we watched the boat pull away.

The Old Man took over. Maxwell hadn't been gone more than five minutes when one of the company commanders approached Colonel Hunt and told him that all four COs wanted to report and have a talk with him. They were totally pissed off at Maxwell. The Old Man replied, "That's why I'm here. Get them together quick."

There wasn't any more gunfire, which made it possible for Colonel Hunt to confer with the 1st Battalion's company commanders. I heard them tell the colonel that they'd asked Maxwell for permission to move forward off the beach and find out where the original bursts of small-arms fire had come from. Maxwell had said no.

Next, they'd requested permission to send out small patrols, feel out the enemy, and locate the Japanese that way. Maxwell's answer was "No. Stand fast."

Meanwhile, Maxwell had radioed several messages back to Colonel Hunt, requesting reinforcements or, failing that, requesting that his battalion be evacuated in small boats. Hunt got Maxwell's message to General Vandegrift, and Vandegrift's reaction was to get mad and tell Hunt to go to Kokumbona and find out what the hell Maxwell was doing. Several reports published after the war say that Vandegrift had sent a radio message to Maxwell before Colonel Hunt's departure, telling Maxwell he was about to be relieved of command. That may or may not be accurate. What I know is what happened in my presence, including what I heard when Colonel Hunt and the 1st Battalion's company commanders spoke together.

All three captains in command of the battalion's three companies told Colonel Hunt that they were embarrassed because of the poorly handled situation. They apologized, but the Old Man didn't seem to place the blame on them. "It will be dark soon," he told them. "Dig in. Be prepared for the possibility of a nighttime attack, and if all goes well through the night, we'll move out shortly after sunrise."

The company commanders left us then to join their units. My squad located a depression along the berm line and decided it was the safest location for the colonel to spend the night. We dug in around the depression for protection in case of an attack, then we all bedded down for what turned out to be a quiet and uneventful night.

As we were moving out in the morning, one of the company commanders directed Colonel Hunt into the village, then into one of the huts. With my squad, I accompanied him inside. There, spread-eagled on the dirt floor, were the dead bodies of two native girls, both of them not more than ten years old. Bamboo poles had been rammed into their vaginas. Maggots were just starting to take over their bodies, which meant they'd been raped and murdered within the past twenty-four hours. What crossed my mind was the thought that the Japanese soldiers responsible for that atrocity must have been trained by cannibals.

My squad moved out on foot with the 1st Battalion. We returned to our perimeter, arriving at about 1400 hours, and I led my men back to our regular 3rd Battalion defense position. I never saw Colonel Maxwell on the Canal again.

GUADALCANAL IN LATE AUGUST

We knew we had been abandoned, but we were confident that we had the know-how to get ourselves out of the mess we'd been dropped into. I was ordered to move my squad to our recently assigned secondary position on beach defense. It was early in the day, and we'd been told that a Japanese convoy including several loaded transports was headed our way. They were expected shortly after dark, so our orders were to dig in a little deeper and make sure everything was ready to repulse a possible seaborne landing.

My squad's position was on the berm line at the extreme end of our MLR. From there, we had a clear view of the Kukum boat basin—which amounted to a mere six or eight Higgins boats. We dug in a little deeper here, chucked a little sand there, and then stayed put while we watched ten or fifteen two-engine Japanese Betty bombers come overhead to remind us whose territory they thought we were occupying. Several bombs came down nearby, but the Jap planes disappeared, and we were okay. We were soon joined by two machine-gun crews from M Company. They dug in among us with their heavy water-cooled machine guns.

Some young officer I'd never seen before appeared from out of nowhere and told the M Company gunners that new tactics were now being put into effect. "Go down to the middle of the beach and dig two holes," he told them. "As soon as it gets dark, move both of your machine guns into those new positions. Make sure it's dark before you move those guns, because we're probably being watched from a distance by Japanese observers. We don't want the Japs beyond our perimeter to know we're moving our machine guns."

He was probably right about that detail, because the Japs were definitely up on Mount Austen, and their binoculars and telescopes were as good as our own, if not better. But the order he was giving the machine-gun crews was based on poor reasoning, and they knew it, even if he didn't.

One of the M Company crew told him as much. "The incoming tide will swamp us. Not only will it ruin your plan, but it'll ruin our guns and ammunition. Can't we move back as the tide moves in?"

"Your orders are to stay there until tomorrow morning at dawn," the young genius told them.

Another guy from the machine-gun crew persisted. "If the Japs try to make a landing tonight, L Company's BARs and riflemen will be shooting over and directly through our beach positions." He was referring to us, and he was correct, but the young military genius was giving the orders, and nobody was going to change his mind.

A little later, Lieutenant Flaherty came by to check our positions. We told him about the after-dark maneuver that the machine-gun crews were supposed to be making, but he wasn't in a position to do anything to correct it. He smiled, maybe a little puzzled, and said, "That's their business. Let's hope they know what they're doing. We'll just stay with our plan and hope for the best."

As soon as it became dark enough, the M Company crews carried their guns out to their newly dug midbeach positions. I heard one of them muttering, "I hope that stupid bastard knows what he's doing."

Right on schedule, during the middle of the night, the tide started coming in. Lucky for us, there were no Japanese coming in with it. The machine gunners passed word back to us that one of their NCOs would be coming through our lines to go make a final plea to the military strategic geniuses who had conceived the plan. The NCO came through, disappeared into the darkness behind us, only to return shortly after. He was cursing and mumbling, and that was enough to tell us that his plea had fallen on deaf ears. Deaf and dumb. More dumb than deaf.

We were on full alert, 100 percent awake and awaiting a possible Japanese landing. The moon shone bright on the beach, and from back on the berm line we could see clearly that the surf was starting to reach the machine-gun positions. Louder than the sound of surf came the curses and four-letter words from the gun crews. Finally we heard one of M Company's sergeants shout loud and clear: "Fuck the peckerhead who gave this stupid order! I've been in this gun section since 1940 in Cuba, and I've taken care of these guns like they're my children." He shouted to his men: "Get these guns out of this goddamn sand and water, and let's do it now! Move it, men. Save what ammo belts you can, but get the guns to dry ground right away!"

They started moving the guns back, and he continued to shout: "Call this treason if you want, but I'll go to the Naval Prison in Portsmouth before I lose these guns! And fuck the stupid dickhead who gave this order!"

The machine guns had taken seawater damage, and they were out of action for the next couple days, while their crews worked frantically to get them back in operating condition. They asked for help, and my squad lent them a hand. We helped get the heavy canvas ammo belts reloaded, which meant that first we rinsed them in the bay a half dozen times to get the sand out of their weave, then sun-dried them on shrubs, keeping them off the ground until they were thoroughly dry. Meanwhile, we rinsed sand off thousands of rounds of ammo and passed them on to a man who hand-rubbed them with a dry cloth, before passing each round to another man who inserted the bullets, one by one, into the cleaned belts. The crews' crank-type ammo loaders would have made the work a lot easier, but they were broken.

I had my squad set up as three two-man teams, each team doing the final wipedown and loading rounds into the belts.

The rounds had to be loaded evenly, or they would jam the machine gun when it was fired. At that time, the men in my squad were Larry Gerkin, Hap Poloshian, Curly Woods, Stash Zega, Yogi Milana, and Jerry Smith. Jerry had been wounded at the Matanikau, but his wounds weren't serious and he was now back on duty. My squad was one man short at the time. John Case, also wounded at the Matanikau, had been hit in both legs and evacuated from the island.

A second case of inept leadership occurred at precisely the same time as the machine-gun near disaster—this one with tragic results. I don't know who the leader was in this case, but I saw the results of his incompetence with my own eyes. We were working at our berm-line beach defense position, about 150 yards from the Kukum boat landing area. That gave us a panoramic view of Ironbottom Sound.

Our navy had converted several destroyers for transport duty, and one of those four-stackers had come in with supplies. It was now anchored off Kukum Beach while we were cleaning the machine-gun ammo. I knew those ships firsthand, at one time or another having made practice landings from the USS *Little*, *Gregory*, and *Colhoun*. They looked identical from a distance, and it was only later that we learned that this ship was the *Colhoun*.

It was a clear, hot, sunny day, and as usual, while we worked on the beach, the air-raid siren went off at the airfield. There had been a Japanese air raid earlier that day, but it had been overcast at the time, and I don't believe much damage was done. Now the sky had cleared and the Jap bombers were coming back. That was a little unusual, their returning so soon, but it wasn't unprecedented. The siren was loud enough to be heard anywhere along the coast and well out to sea. There was no question that enemy bombers were approaching and would be overhead within about ten minutes. I glanced out toward the destroyer, expecting to see it preparing to get under way, with all men at their battle stations.

The destroyer USS *Colhoun* in early 1942. Months later, in August 1942, the marines of L-3-5 watched helplessly from the beach as a well-placed Japanese bomb sent the *Colhoun* to the bottom.

U.S. NAVAL HISTORICAL CENTER

Larry Gerkin was looking out at the destroyer, too. "That guy will start taking off like a wounded pony in a minute or two," he remarked.

"Yeah," somebody else said.

They were both wrong. All was quiet on the ship, with no sign of movement and no men on deck. It was almost as though no one were aboard.

Hap Poloshian was the squad's philosopher. "Maybe they'll make smoke in a minute or so and stick around to fight."

"Whatever they do," Yogi said, "they'd better do it real soon. I can hear the planes' engines. A lot of company will be here in a few minutes."

The ship remained sitting out on the sound, like a car in a stateside parking lot. Pretty soon the planes came into sight, right on time for one more of their daily frolics with the U.S. Navy and Marine Corps. The *Colhoun* remained as motionless as a stoned goose, while about fifteen two-engine Bettys approached. We watched the bombers as they seemed to be making one of their standard approaches toward the airfield. Then they saw the same thing we did: the perfectly motionless *Colhoun*. The bombers veered, and suddenly they were coming directly over our position, heading straight for the *Colhoun*. We could only sit dumbfounded and watch the planes' bomb-bay doors open and the bombs come down, all of them headed for the *Colhoun*.

None of our own planes were up at that time. In late August '42, we had too few fighters, and when these Japanese planes came over, I don't believe any of our fighters were operational. Our antiaircraft guns began firing as soon as the enemy bombers came into range, but I don't recall that they scored any hits.

The first couple of Japanese bombs did score hits, however, directly on the *Colhoun*'s fantail. Even though the ship had been converted for transport duty, it continued to carry a stern full of depth charges—and the Jap bombs exploded directly on top of them. The series of blasts that followed was huge, with smoke billowing and steel parts flying sky-high. As the smoke

The Second Half of August 1942

began to clear, the only section of the ship still in one piece was the bow, which now stood out of the water, pointed skyward. Within seconds, even the ship's bow disappeared, making one more addition to Ironbottom Sound.

The enemy planes had done their damage and were gone. Almost immediately a Higgins boat took off from Kukum Landing, headed toward the spot where the *Colhoun* had gone down, searching for survivors. Before long, the boat returned to the landing, and from our position, it didn't appear to be overloaded. Official naval records state that the *Colhoun* had brought much-needed food to Guadalcanal that day but had been sunk shortly after unloading its supplies.

Thank you, Admiral Ghormley, for that piece of information. The fact is that everybody in the 1st Marine Division knew more about what happened to the *Colhoun* than Ghormley ever did. He never appeared on Guadalcanal. Fortunately he was soon replaced by a better man: Adm. William Halsey.

In fairness, it's difficult to blame the *Colhoun*'s fate on Admiral Ghormley. What many of us wanted to know was, Who was responsible for the ship just sitting out there? It's unlikely that the *Colhoun* was inoperable, but if by chance it was, then why didn't the captain order the men to abandon ship before the planes arrived? They would have had plenty of time to get away.

In the very good book *Guadalcanal: The Definitive Account of the Landmark Battle,* author Richard B. Frank apparently had to rely on a doctored account from the Navy Department, because his story of the *Colhoun* differs in several details from the event that L Company and other marines witnessed firsthand. Frank reports the incident as taking place on August 30, which is probably correct. To the best of my recollection, it was at the very end of August. He also states that no marine fighter planes were in the air because at the time of the attack, the available fighters were being refueled by ground crews. That could very well be correct. It is in his account of the bombing that his details differ from what we saw.

CHAPTER 4

September 1942

OUT ON PATROL

Before Pearl Harbor and before we'd ever heard of Guadalcanal, I received the standard 1st Marine Division rifleman's training. In our day, an important part of every rifleman's instruction was reconnaissance, or how to go on scouting patrol. To the best of my knowledge, it still is. We were drilled over and over in the details of what we had to know and do as scouts, until we could perform our duty in our sleep. Every squad in every rifle company had to take its turn at scouting patrol, so by the time we landed on Guadalcanal, we were experts at it. When the sergeant signaled or said, "Scouts out," the scouting detail moved out immediately. We'd been well trained by the Old Breed, and what they taught us eventually helped to save many of our lives.

On the Canal in 1942, my training and my rank as corporal and squad leader, then later as sergeant, put me in charge of many regular scouting details. As often as not, my being in charge just happened. We'd be ordered out on patrol, and nobody would tell us who was in command. I'd look around to see who was in charge. There was no officer and no sergeant. There was another corporal in our platoon—a hell of a nice guy, but you couldn't count on him for much. "So okay, let's go," I'd say. As corporal, I was in charge.

One day in early September, it was my turn to lead a five-man mission. By now the days had become a blur. We didn't know what day it was, or care. If the chaplain said he was going to hold a service, you figured it might be Sunday, or maybe not. The only important things were food, medicine, and staying alive. So we moved out from the western edge of the MLR, staying close to the beach, moving through coconut groves in the direction of the Matanikau River. This was L Company's assigned area to scout out and keep under steady observation. Squads were taking regular turns at scouting, so every man was likely to go out two or three times a week, a little more or a little less, depending on how many men were incapacitated on a given day by malaria or dysentery.

On this particular day, I led my scouting patrol off the MLR at about 0800 hours. We had worked and trained together so often that it was no longer necessary for us to speak, once I'd given the initial order to designate the first point man. After that, it was all automatic. We moved out, then changed point at regular intervals, our progress always dictated by the terrain, the foliage, and our immediate surroundings. We traveled light—no loose clothing, nothing that might snag on any type of branch or bush, no equipment that might rattle. We each carried a rifle, cartridge belt, ammo, water, and a first-aid kit. Nothing else, not even dog tags.

By this September day, we'd been on the Canal and in combat conditions for about a month, and our uniforms were starting to fall apart. That was all the more reason for us to be careful and avoid snagging our clothes on anything. Practice had taught us how to walk without snapping twigs under our feet. We passed information among ourselves with a nod of the head or a slight pointing gesture with our rifle. We moved our eyes constantly, looking in every direction, on the alert for anything out of the ordinary. By this time, we'd come to know every other man's move and gesture, and we instinctively understood its meaning. We used our ears like bird dogs, and we listened to every jungle sound, every tropical bird screech, every rustle in the brush, alert to any unusual noise. We knew very well that our lives depended on every move made by each man in the patrol. We'd also learned how to use our noses, smelling and sniffing as we moved along. We knew well enough that each one of us stank; we were seldom able to bathe and never able to change clothes. We also knew that the Japanese suffered from the same conditions, and that the odor they gave off was different from our own. To our noses, the Japs had a sweet-sour smell.

We had moved forward a considerable distance without incident, and by now we were nearly to the Matanikau River. Then we heard it. Seeming to come from out of nowhere, we heard a clear, strange little voice that cut through the ordinary, more subdued jungle sounds.

"Hello! Hello!"

We froze on the spot and then sank very slowly, very quietly to the ground.

"Hello! Hello!"

That odd little voice had to be carrying a good hundred yards through the jungle. My hair stood on end, every muscle and nerve in my body strung as tight as banjo wire. Who in hell was dumb enough to wander into my patrol area? Which dumb SOB was so stupid that he called out to us and gave our position away? Even the Japs had more brains than to call out like that. But there it was again.

"Hello! Hello!"

Instant fright gripped each man in the patrol. All I could do was hold my breath and pray.

"Hello! Hello!"

Suddenly it struck me that the weird greeting was coming from overhead—from somewhere in a tree. Nobody had ever taught me what to do in a situation like this, but by now I was sure the voice was coming down to us from the treetops. Who the hell was up there, and why was he hollering down at us? Could it be the enemy? A trick of some kind? Plenty of Japanese spoke English. I still couldn't decide what to do. When on a scouting patrol, we'd been instructed over and over again not to fire a shot or engage the enemy in any way, except as a last resort.

As I raised my head, I saw our point man rise slowly up to his knees. Our eyes met and he nodded, looking upward. Then he began moving his elbows, making motions like a chicken flapping its wings. His message registered loud and clear: It's not a man, it's a bird. The voice came at us again.

"Hello! Hello!"

We started to get the picture. The island was full of macaws and parrots, and one of them had spotted us from up in the trees. One of them that had been taught to talk by somebody who spoke English. I was in charge of the patrol, which meant that I had to decide what we'd do next. I made the only decision that seemed sensible. We had to abort this mission and get the hell out of there fast. There were bound to be Japs somewhere nearby, and they must have heard those crazy little "hellos." By now the Japs would be trying to figure out the location of the marines that the bird was saying hello to.

I rapped the stock of my '03 rifle twice with my knuckles. That was our signal to fall back. I motioned, and we all started moving back in disciplined scout formation, but quietly and rapidly to remain undetected. As we began what we called our retrograde movement—or in plain English, getting the hell out of there—we startled a flock of fifty or a hundred wild macaws or parrots. They immediately took flight, making an awful racket, just the way a flock of pigeons does when they all take off at once. It was hard to tell who was more startled, the birds or us. Worse, those beautiful birds did what they usually did when they flew off in fright. They crapped. All over *us*. Meanwhile, the talking bird called out a couple more "hellos," but now from a greater distance. Before long, we were a hundred yards or more from where it had all started.

We returned to our lines and I made our report, feeling a little foolish. At first I wasn't sure our story would be believed. The NCOs and officers accepted our tale with grins on their faces, but they knew they'd better pass the word throughout the entire sector, figuring that sooner or later future patrols would run into that feathered bigmouth. A few days after our "hello" incident, we learned that an English missionary who had fled from approaching Japanese had turned his pet parrot loose.

Many other patrols ran across that talking bird as the Guadalcanal campaign wore on, and on a number of occasions, I heard that parrot saying, "Hello, hello!" to some other squad, somewhere far off in the jungle's distance. Those "hellos" told us that the bird had caught sight of a Japanese patrol, decided to greet them, and was now giving *them* fits.

THE JAPANESE LANDING CRAFT AND THE CARIBOU WITH SIX LEGS

One day our entire 1st Platoon was patrolling along the beach, approaching the location where the Matanikau River empties into the ocean. A shot-up and abandoned Japanese landing craft had been on the beach long enough that it was starting to serve as a landmark. When you stood on the beach, you could see it from quite a distance away. When you approached and looked inside the craft, you could see a little hutlike structure that housed its engine. The craft had a front ramp for troops to disembark, and the ramp was down (our own navy had not yet approved the convenience of a ramp for us marines), with its front dug into the beach sand. On several earlier patrols, some of our guys had seen a solitary Jap running either onto that craft or off it—disappearing somewhere inside or leaving the wreck and disappearing into the bush beyond the beach. At times when patrols had spotted the Jap, none of our men had ever been close enough to do anything about him.

But on this day, our platoon was headed all the way to the riverbank, and soon enough we were very close to the beached hulk. We made no unnecessary sounds, so we must have remained undetected until we were nearly on top of it. Then our man who was nearest to the beached hulk stopped suddenly. He motioned silently to Flash Flaherty, who was in charge of that day's patrol. As Flash moved forward to see what was wrong, the lone Jap appeared suddenly from around the opposite side of the hulk. He was a small man—they were all small—and wore trousers, a white naval blouse, and a cap. Before any of us could react, he dashed up the ramp and disappeared into the craft.

Immediately our whole platoon spread out around the hulk. At that point in the campaign, none of us knew any

Japanese, and the Jap probably didn't understand a word of English. Even so, we started shouting at him: "Come out of there, you son of a bitch!" and other such profanities. He stayed put and we couldn't see him or hear him. The only place he could have been hiding was in the little hut that served as the engine housing.

"Maybe we can get somebody to drop a grenade in there," Flash said. The top of the engine compartment was visible from where we were situated, and it was open.

"Yeah, but how?" I asked. Any one of us going up the ramp to drop a grenade into the compartment would make a good target for whatever weapon the Jap had with him.

"The best way is for one man to climb over the craft's gunwale," Flash said.

Hap Poloshian was delegated. Flash and I crouched a few steps behind the spot where the hulk's ramp dug into the sand. We had our weapons ready. Poloshian, off to one side, grabbed the craft's gunwale and pulled himself aboard. The rest of the platoon remained surrounding the craft on three sides, ready to protect us if the Jap came out at us with a weapon.

Poloshian dropped the hand grenade into the compartment, then hustled back over the gunwale and dropped to the ground. The grenade went off a moment later, and the Jap appeared suddenly. He ran out from his makeshift shelter, coming straight at us, swinging a large, deadly looking knife. As he hurled himself toward us, he was screaming something in Japanese at the top of his lungs.

It was all over in seconds. From a distance of not more than ten yards, Flash shot him with his .45 and I fired at him with my rifle. As he fell, I saw that my bullet had hit him in the face. That was the end of that poor Jap.

He'd been wearing one of those Japanese soft military hats. Flash took the hat. Later, somebody back at our MLR told him that the insignia on it belonged to a naval commander, so he kept it as a souvenir. But exactly who the Jap was and what he was supposed to be doing at that beached hulk was something we never learned.

You developed a sixth sense on this island. Once out on a patrol, we needed to keep our senses alert and trust our instincts. If something didn't look right or feel right—even when I couldn't say exactly why it *wasn't* right—I knew we'd better not move into that suspicious area. Sometimes I couldn't say *why* it was suspicious, but my instincts told me something was wrong. That sixth sense was telling me that a couple of Japanese were hiding in the underbrush just ahead, and they were watching our every move.

Once it worked the other way around—and we found ourselves watching one of *them*. On this particular day, I was out with just my squad, and we approached the Matanikau by following a route a little farther inland and away from the beach. As we neared the riverbank, there was an open grassy area of maybe a hundred yards or more that went straight to the river. The grass wasn't tall at this point, and we had a clear view to the river. Among the island's native animal life were caribou, which, before the war, I believe the native Melanesians tended as cattle. By the time we were on the Canal, the caribou were all running wild. On this day, we stopped as we approached the grassy stretch to the river, and in the distance we saw three of those caribou. Our presence must have startled them, because they began to move away. The odd thing about it was that two of the caribou moved off in one direction, and the third moved off in another, toward the safety of jungle underbrush.

My point man motioned to me, and I joined him. "Look at that caribou," he said.

"Yeah," I said. "Something's wrong with him." I couldn't tell exactly what it was, though. We watched the animal more closely, watched the way it was moving, and finally I saw what was wrong.

"Goddamn it," I said. "That caribou's got six legs."

"Well, I'll be damned," somebody else said.

Those two extra legs belonged to a lone Jap who was hanging on to the animal, running with it and keeping himself behind it, where he hoped we couldn't see him. We just watched that six-legged caribou run off to safety. We were too far away from our MLR, and we didn't want to start a firefight any more than he did. So this time, we just let the Japanese soldier and his caribou cover run off to safety. He probably thought he had been pretty clever.

YOGI MILANA, CHAMPION SWIMMER

Everybody was concerned about the food problem, from command all the way down to the lowliest private on the line. Those two tablespoons of Japanese rice, seasoned with plump maggots and served twice a day, just weren't enough to sustain the men. Looking back on the situation now, I marvel at how, despite the adversity and deprivation, our morale never hit rock bottom. It was only our supplies that sank that low.

I was in the defense line that extended along the beach, west of Lunga Point, and then swung inland at a forty-five-degree angle through a coconut grove and up to the top of a ridge. The beach was our platoon's secondary defense position, our primary position being the MLR's western perimeter as it swung inland across the Copra Cart Road and through a coconut grove. L Company's other platoons extended the MLR farther inland and up on the ridge. On this particular morning, we were at our secondary position, guarding the beach. The night had been quiet, but lo and behold, as we looked out to sea at first light, one of our own destroyers sat anchored and motionless not more than seven hundred yards offshore. It must have arrived quietly during the night, then dropped anchor, unobserved by all on shore. Nobody on the ship was topside. The destroyer sat outlined against the sky and looked as peaceful as a car parked in a driveway back home. It was the first U.S. ship we'd seen in a couple weeks, and it was a welcome sight.

Yogi Milana and I were sitting in the sand and talking about it with another squad leader from our platoon, Cpl. Hank Klemicki. Before Pearl Harbor, Yogi—better known to his parents and to our company clerk as Pfc. Richard E. Milana—had been a student at Brooklyn College, where he was on the swimming team. Rumor around L Company had it that he also did yoga meditations and exercises, which was how he got his nickname. Yogi has a different explanation for his name and insists to this day that it's only the guys in L-3-5 who call him Yogi. Everyone else calls him Dick or Richard—but to us, he was and is Yogi.

"Somebody's got to be aboard," Yogi remarked. "I can smell breakfast."

Damn! So could I.

More guys in my squad heard the magic word and came over to join the discussion. "Breakfast," Hank said. "Yeah! Just smell that delicious aroma!"

We could all smell it, and it was wonderful. The aroma of cooking breakfast drifted ashore on a light breeze—coffee and bacon and all those other kitchen fragrances that smelled like home. It almost drove us nuts.

There were about a half dozen of us by now, up on our feet and gazing with longing at the destroyer. We talked about all that wonderful food we were smelling, telling each other we wished we were aboard, sitting at a table and eating just one decent meal. Living on starvation rations, and most of us sick with tropical illnesses, we were all losing weight. By the time we finally left the Canal, we'd each lost between twenty and thirty pounds. But on that particular morning, I don't think any of us truly realized how hungry we always were—not until we smelled that good old stateside chow being cooked.

Yogi came up with a bright idea. "What if I swim out there and get us some chow?"

"Oh, yeah! Keep on dreaming. Why don't you flap your arms and *fly* out there," some of the men started taunting.

"Wait a minute!" I said. I was a squad leader, so maybe my opinion carried a little extra weight. Or maybe I just yelled louder than the others. "Wait a minute! Yogi's a good swimmer. He was on a college swimming team, for Chrissake!"

"Yeah?" Suddenly, the guys shut up and looked admiringly at Yogi. "Is that the truth, Yogi?"

"Sure, it's the truth. You think Marion makes up stories?"

"Yeah," somebody said. "I *know* he does."

"Shut up," I said. "I'm not making this one up."

Hope began lighting up their faces. We all agreed that Yogi had just come up with one great idea. One of the guys started flapping his arms and waving at the ship. Some of the sailors must have been watching us from the bridge, because before long, one of them appeared outside on the wing bridge. He began waving back. In those days, every man in the navy and marines had to learn semaphore, and on this occasion the knowledge came in handy. Our guy who had been waving began signaling in semaphore.

"Will you give us some chow?"

The sailor on the wing bridge signaled back: "Yes, but how?"

"Someone will swim out to the ship."

While the semaphore messages were going back and forth, Yogi had sat down in the sand and assumed what looked to me like a yoga meditation position. Maybe he was only trying to muster up enough strength to make the long swim, but to the rest of us, it looked like a yoga position.

"Hey, look at Yogi," one of our guys remarked, amazed. "He's doing yoga!"

"What the hell's yoga?" another guy asked. Back in those days, most Americans didn't know much about yoga.

"Never mind," I said. "Just let him do it!"

Meanwhile, we started making plans. Yogi would swim out to the ship while two of us on the beach covered him for sharks with our '03 rifles. When we spotted Yogi coming back, Hank would swim out, meet him halfway, and assist in getting that precious chow ashore. Somebody mentioned that we were breaking a few rules.

"To hell with rules, regulations, and everything else!" one of the guys said.

"Damn right! All's fair in love and war," somebody else said.

That made sense to me. We were definitely at war, we were in love with the idea of getting some decent food for a change, and we were hungry as hell. And the sailors out on the destroyer were willing to give us some chow!

Yogi had peeled down to his skin. He was up on his feet, then into the water. Within seconds, only his head and shoulders were visible. Soon we could see just his head and thrashing arms. Yogi was making good progress, and we were getting excited. We watched until he was so far out that we weren't always able to spot his head on the water's surface. Fifteen minutes passed, maybe twenty. Then we saw sailors moving around on the ship's deck, reaching down. Next we saw Yogi. Sailors were pulling him aboard, and there was no mistaking him, his hair long and wet and gleaming pitch black in the early morning sunlight. In the battle zone, we didn't have the luxury of a barber's chair, and we all looked pretty scruffy. We watched the sailors help Yogi on deck. Then they all disappeared into a passageway. He was out of sight but safe. We cheered and yelled.

Then we sat back down on the sand and waited, which was the only thing left for us to do.

"Jesus, he's probably eating bacon and eggs," Hank said.

"Or maybe ham," I said.

Somebody else moaned. He must have been picturing the food we were talking about and longing for some of it.

"I wonder what kind of food they'll give him to bring ashore," Hank said.

Nobody answered, but we each had ideas of our own. Anything but rice, I thought. We waited, and we waited some more. It was almost too much for us to bear.

Meanwhile, none of the other marines on the Canal had the faintest idea what our guys were doing or why we were doing it. And nobody above the rank of squad leader—and that included only Hank and me—gave a damn.

Another twenty minutes passed without any visible sign of activity on the destroyer. Then several figures appeared topside—a couple of sailors and Yogi. He wasted no time climbing down the ship's net, while the sailors began lowering an object into the water near him. From our distance, we couldn't make out what the object was, but we figured it had to contain food. Yogi was in the water now, the sailors looking down at him from the deck, watching him start to swim away. We were watching, too, but from our distance, all we could make out was that object floating in the water. Then it did more than just bob on the surface. It started coming toward us and was making good progress. That meant Yogi was pushing it ahead of him as he swam toward shore.

"Wish me luck," Hank shouted, then dashed into the water and began swimming toward Yogi. He was on his way to help bring in the cargo. They met about halfway out, and together now, they towed their cargo toward shore. By this time, the floating object was close enough for us to make it out. The sailors had rigged up a small wooden raft, about three feet square, and had lashed a supply of canned food on it. Yogi and Hank touched bottom and were splashing ashore, carrying their treasure between them. We ran down to meet them, yelling, and for a change having something worth cheering about.

It wasn't yet 0700 hours, but on this unusual morning, several marines from Company L-3-5 had themselves one hell of a good breakfast. My most vivid memory is of sitting in the sand and opening one of the cans, then taking beautiful, luscious yellow peach halves out of the sweet syrup. Damn, but they tasted good!

Yogi had already eaten breakfast back aboard the destroyer, but he never did tell us what he'd had. That's all right. Whatever it was, he'd earned it.

To this day, I doubt that our company commander, our platoon leader, our first sergeant, or our platoon sergeant ever found out about our special breakfast that day. If any of them read this, they'll know now. Meanwhile, I wonder about the crew on the destroyer, and if any of them have ever told the story or ever wrote about the crazy marine swimmer who boarded their ship to scrounge breakfast for some of the troops back on the beach. I'd like to hear their version of the story. Anyhow, after all these years, I do owe them one thing.

Thanks a lot, guys! You made our misery and hunger a little easier to bear.

SEPTEMBER 12–14 ON L COMPANY RIDGE

Late on the evening of September 12, 1942, the Japanese command on Guadalcanal started a well-coordinated land-sea-air attack on the marine-held perimeter. The ground attacks concentrated on three main points. The enemy went against our eastern perimeter, which was defended by the 3rd Battalion, 1st Marine Regiment. The Japs also thrust northward at our southern perimeter in what became their main assault. That was the now-famous battle of Bloody Ridge. The third point they attacked during the battle was our western perimeter, defended by my own L Company, 3rd Battalion, 5th Marines under the command of Lt. Col. Frederick C. Biebush.

The main thrust at Bloody Ridge lasted from September 12 through 14. It has been written about and studied many times over and is regarded by most historians as the critical turning point of the Guadalcanal campaign. If the Japanese had been able to take Bloody Ridge, Vandegrift's command post and Henderson Field itself would have fallen. And Guadalcanal probably would have been lost. As the official battle histories tell us, the marines under Col. Merritt A. Edson held Bloody Ridge and saved both the airfield and the command post. Meanwhile, a lesser-known chapter of that battle took place on the western perimeter, where we did our own share of fighting.

L-3-5 held a line west of the Lunga River, about five thousand to six thousand yards west of Bloody Ridge. Our own main line of resistance, or MLR, would look like a shallow bow shape on a map, beginning at the beach's berm line, extending across maybe thirty yards of sand beach to a dirt trail that we called the Copra Cart Road, then crossing the road and stretching through a little more than a hundred yards of grass and coconut grove. Beyond the coconut palms, our MLR went uphill for another hundred or so yards on hard coral to a V-shaped ridge that I'll be calling L Company Ridge. I believe some Japanese maps designated it Tora Ridge. The ridge itself was coral, and so hard that the men who held it couldn't dig in. In all, we were three platoons strong. My own 1st Platoon, led by Lt. John "Flash" Flaherty, commanded the coconut grove and the Copra Cart Road, which led westward, parallel with the beach, toward the Matanikau River. Somewhere down at the other end of that road was a large unit of Japanese combat troops. In fact, if you went down to the shoreline and looked toward Matanikau, you could see a beached Japanese landing craft in the distance. Inland, holding the opposite end of L Company's part of the MLR from where my platoon was positioned, 2nd Lt. Edward Farmer's 3rd Platoon held L Company Ridge, our defense line's all-important high ground.

My platoon's position started from the beach, straddled the road, and went into the grove. Dug in on the side of the road nearer the beach, we had a thirty-seven-millimeter gun that came from Regimental Company. We had the gun dug in so deep that only its barrel was above ground level. At the road's other side, we had a water-cooled .30-caliber heavy machine gun from M Company. Also along our line we had several light .30-caliber machine guns and at least five BARs, plus riflemen positioned between the automatic weapons. L Company's platoons were short-manned, but in the coconut grove we were well dug in, well spaced, and camouflaged with care. Lieutenant Farmer's platoon was less well protected. Their problem was the ridge's solid coral rock. It was so hard that it was impossible for the defenders to dig in with any of the equipment we had on hand. Being out in the open put them at a clear disadvantage, but that ridge had to be manned, and it had to be held. Far off on our left flank, the Japanese were already attacking Bloody Ridge. Our own sector remained quiet, but that wouldn't last long.

One of my old cobber friends, Art Boston, was up on the ridge with Farmer's 3rd Platoon. Here's how he recalls the night of September 13–14.

> Our job was to defend the ridge near the new fighter airfield and from there down to the beach. We had to stop any enemy coming through that line. One night, we'd just gotten through unloading barrels of gasoline

for our fighter planes, and we were tired. We went back and took the positions that we held every night, and we weren't expecting any kind of attack on our part of the line. But when we were up on our ridge, pretty tired, word was passed to us that we were having a 50 percent alert—in other words, with two men in a foxhole, one of us would have to be awake at all times.

Although L Company's section of the MLR had remained quiet to this point, we'd been hearing plenty of fireworks in the distance, as the Japanese were making their main thrust at Bloody Ridge. Our orders were to hold fast at the far western sector of the MLR and await a Japanese attack from the west. Art Boston's recollection of that night continues:

> On the first watch, I was sitting up with Smitty [Pvt. Milton H. Smith] because I couldn't sleep. And I put little pebbles in the ration cans, and we hung them on the barbed wire so that if anybody or anything hit the wire, it would give a little *tinkle-tinkle.*
> Well, the wire started tinkling. I said, "Smitty, I'm going to fire three rounds down there and see if I can get anything stirred up." So I fired three rounds, and I stirred something up all right—our lieutenant.
> Lieutenant Farmer came running up to the top of the ridge and said, "Did you fire those three shots, Boston?"
> I said, "Yes sir. There are Japs down there. I can smell 'em."
> "What do you mean, you can smell them?"
> I said, "It's not a body odor or anything like that. It's just—I don't know what it is, but I know it's them."
> "Look," he said, "don't do any more shooting. The guys are getting all upset."
> I said, "I *want* them to be upset. Because if there's Japs out there, they could come through here at any time."

Lieutenant Farmer went back down, and pretty soon I heard the tinkling again. I took another shot, and the lieutenant came back up. "Boston, I don't know what I'm going to do with you. You're directly disobeying an order in a combat zone."

I said, "Well, sir, I won't do that again."

He said okay and left us, and it wasn't much later when I heard quite a bit of rustling out there—down the ridge from our defense line. I looked at Smitty and I said, "Smitty, he didn't say anything about grenades, did he?"

Smitty said, "No, he didn't."

So I pulled the pin on one and gave it a good heave. It went off, and after that there was no more tinkling on the barbed wire. I think Lieutenant Farmer began to realize from reports somewhere else down our line that our boys were hearing movements out there. He didn't make an issue about the grenade. He just came around and told us, "Keep alert and knock off the firing. Next time you hear anything and you think it's Japanese, one of you come down and report it."

Well, I had the twelve o'clock–to–dawn watch that night. And I hate to admit it, but I did something that I could have gotten shot for. Sometime shortly before dawn, I just fell asleep, and when I woke up, my watch said five-thirty. I just said, "Oh, my goodness—!"

Smitty was sleeping because it was his time to sleep, but he woke up soon after that. I pulled out my cigarettes and offered him one. He said no and stuffed his Red Man tobacco into his cheek. He loved that chewing tobacco. So I lit my cigarette and I leaned back to take it easy—which is when I heard this wicked screeching:

"Ah, Malines—you die! Ah, Malines, you die!" It was like a singsong chant.

Now our whole line was wide awake. We were in position, and we all knew what was coming. Sure enough, the Japanese hit the barbed wire, and they were stopped right there. Firing opened up on both sides. Our Browning automatics and our machine guns started firing, not to mention our .30-03 rifles, all of us firing. My rifle got so hot that as soon as I got a round in the chamber, it would go off, before I could pull the trigger.

While Boston and his platoon were up on the ridge, we were down in the coconut grove. When the attack began in our section that early morning of September 14, it was still dark, less than an hour before sunrise. We heard the Japanese approaching when they were still 150 yards from our defense line. That gave us time to get ready. We had no way of knowing their strength, but I read years later that they were three of Colonel Oka's companies. The main body of that force came up the Old Copra Cart Road. My platoon was waiting for them in the palm grove, and now we were starting to see them. In that early morning darkness, pale moonlight peeking through the palm trees gave us a clear view of the approaching columns. The Japs were rattling equipment, bullshitting, joking, not making any effort to be cautious. Their equipment was reflecting glints of moonlight. We could see clearly that each column was led by an officer who wielded a saber, and their sabers shimmered and flashed in the moonlight too. Those carefree champions were coming in to attack us in a close-order route march, approaching our line in columns of three. Either they didn't realize how near we were to them, or they were too dumb and too arrogant to give a damn. Word was passed up and down our line: "Hold your fire until our thirty-seven-millimeter lets go."

In previous campaigns, those Japanese were used to seeing their opponents pick up and run away from them as soon as they came into sight. Their enemies had panicked on a number of occasions on the Asian mainland in China, Malay, Singapore, and Burma. This was the first time the Japanese had ever come up against an outfit that refused to pick up and run. I should add that this outfit—*my* outfit—had nowhere to get up and run *to*. So the only thing we *could* do was fight. Oka's troops were about to meet their match.

The Japanese main assault group, still in formation, approached to about twenty-five yards from our line when the thirty-seven-millimeter let fly with the first of a dozen or so canister, or grapeshot, rounds. *"BLAM!"* Our whole line followed suit, opening up with all weapons. Machine guns and BARs swept their lanes of fire. Riflemen took targets, picking off Japanese who were trying to get away. The Japs sent very little return fire in our direction. They never got the chance. For the Japanese on the road and in the coconut grove, it was all over in less than ten minutes. Our company's 1st Sgt. William McMullen was among our own wounded in the coconut grove. He was one hell of a nice guy, but he was evacuated and I never saw him again. Platoon Sgt. Ben B. Selvitelle, a good friend of mine, took McMullen's place as first sergeant, becoming the youngest first sergeant in the entire division.

The L-3-5 casualties in that sector of our defense line were extremely light, but the story was different at the top of L Company Ridge, the sector that Art Boston held. The marines holding that position were in serious trouble several times over the next twenty-four hours, and I experienced it firsthand because later that day, I became one of them.

Our battle in the coconut grove was all but over, but we were still hearing plenty of gunfire up on the ridge, where Farmer's men were maintaining their positions without the benefit of cover. Their only defense was primitive but effective—the couple strands of barbed wire and the ration cans with pebbles in them. Whenever an approaching enemy touched that wire, the stones would rattle like hell and give him away.

The third Jap column approached Farmer's ridge positions the same way that their other columns had come into our coconut grove, in a close-order route march, talking among themselves, their equipment rattling. Several BARs and the riflemen on the ridge opened fire on them before they could reorganize and attempt an attack. Even though our defense positions up there were mostly above ground because of the ridge's hard coral, the men in Farmer's platoon held their ground, and not one of them let up fighting until he was wounded to the point of being unable to continue without medical attention. The Japs reorganized and attacked our ridge again.

By now we were fighting in broad daylight. Every time they tried to sneak up through the jungle growth to the open crest of L Company Ridge, the cans rattled and our guys opened up with their BARs and .30-caliber Springfields. But the Japs gave back plenty of return fire, too. At the V point on the ridgeline, about a half dozen wounded L-3-5 marines were forced by a Japanese attack to withdraw about ten yards. They formed a new position a little way back down the ridge, at the military crest of the ridge. Holding their position at that point, they never—and I mean absolutely *never*—withdrew another step until the Japanese assault terminated in failure hours later. Art Boston puts it like this.

> When you're in combat, and you've got a certain area that you've got to look after, you're oblivious to everything else going on around you in other areas. That's how it was with us during that fight. At that same time, Colonel Edson and his Raider Battalion were taking an awful lot of fire down the line on Bloody Ridge. They could have lost the whole thing, but they kept their position, and it was just by sheer—I don't know what you'd call it—determination, maybe. They would *not* give in to the superior force of Japanese that was hitting them. They suffered pretty high casualties, and we suffered casualties on our own ridge. And it just shows how much a person can stand at a time like that. We were taking a good beating up on our ridge, and down on the beach there was shooting left and right, where the other L Company platoons were stopping a Japanese advance.

We had a brave bunch of kids that night, and there were a lot of cases where medals should have been given out but were never issued, because there was no officer to see what they did, our officers being few and far between.

Meanwhile, some of the attacking Japanese had made it to our ridge's top, and it was our job to get them off of there. This phase of the assault—Company L-3-5's defense of our ridge—is seldom mentioned in the official battle reports, and where historians have picked up on it, we get only brief mention. But had the marines of L-3-5 failed to hold their positions, the overall operation that history books call the battle of Bloody Ridge would have had a different outcome.

By late morning, the young warriors who had survived the initial phase of the Jap assault had moved their wounded back down from the ridge. Lieutenant Farmer was one of the wounded, having been badly hit in the arm and side. He was later given a medical discharge, went to law school, and eventually became a circuit court judge in Michigan. His BAR man, whose nickname was Limey because he'd been born in England, also was badly wounded. Jim Motsinger, Harold Pazofsky, and about a half dozen others were clobbered on top of their ridge—but man, did they ever account for themselves! They were as tough and as stubborn a band of fighting men as any that the United States military has ever been fortunate enough to produce. No communications, no artillery or mortar supporting fire, and they still stacked those attacking Japanese while protecting the ridge with only some old, rusty barbed wire and tin cans with pebbles.

Sometime before noon, Lieutenant Flaherty pulled my squad after Captain Spurlock told him to take some men up to the ridge and see what we could do to help reinforce it. Michael S. Smith, in his fine book *Bloody Ridge: The Battle That Saved Guadalcanal*, sums up what we did in a single sentence: "Second Lieutenant John 'Flash' Flaherty, Sgt. Ore Marion, and eight other men from the platoon in the grove helped

Farmer hold his ground." This is correct, but there's quite a bit more to the story.

Flaherty was one damn fine marine. Nothing to the contrary should be read into the fact that on a few occasions, he and I had some impolite verbal exchanges on points of disagreement, also known as yelling matches. I don't think blame should be put on either of us, but on the fact that we were two very young men stressed out by battle conditions and intensely aware that we were nearly always in immediate danger of being killed.

Flaherty took off from the coconut grove, moving from cover to cover, with me and my squad directly behind him. We were running, and I was bent way over forward. I was directly behind Flaherty, and Hap Poloshian was right behind me. A Japanese machine gun opened up when we were about halfway up the ridge. The bullets missed Flaherty by inches. This former Yale football player was well over six feet tall and made a huge target. He stopped on a dime, then tripped and fell backward, which was a good thing, because it probably prevented him from being hit by the enemy machine gun's second blast. I was a half pace behind Flaherty as he fell toward me, my rifle at the ready, with bayonet attached. He stumbled backward, lurching directly into my bayonet, which dug about a half inch into his calf. He let out a yell. You couldn't really blame him.

"I'm wounded! I'm wounded!"

"Where?" I asked.

"In the leg!"

"That ain't a wound. It's where my bayonet pig-stuck you."

"Why the hell did you do that?" he yelled.

"I didn't do it. You fell on it!" I yelled back.

Back and forth went our stupid dialogue, and for all I know, the Jap machine gunner was out there waiting for us to finish arguing before trying to take another shot at us. Finally we calmed down. "Give me your bandage and I'll wrap it up," I told him.

He was still grumbling while I was applying the bandage. "I'll have you court-martialed for this," he said.

"Good!" I said. "Have me court-martialed right away. I'm not happy here."

He didn't have me court-martialed and somehow we both managed to survive the ordeal. Years later, at a get-together in Boston, Hap Poloshian reminded me of that bayonet accident. "Holy shit, why did you remind me of *that?*" I laughed, and Hap laughed too. Now we were able to laugh about it. But that morning, my squad was halfway up on L Company Ridge as replacements for the wounded that Lieutenant Farmer's platoon had suffered. During most of that time, we exchanged sporadic small-arms fire with the Japs at the very top. They couldn't dislodge us, and we weren't having much luck dislodging them from the ridge.

After a while, Flash had to go back to get his leg taken care of, so there were no officers up on the ridge and no sergeants, the only NCOs being corporals Clarence Aldridge, Frank Haberle, Hank Klemicki, and me. We spent several hours up there with our men, doing what we could to hold our position, but we had practically nothing to hold it with. I think what saved our day, and finally made it possible for us to hold our own and drive the Japanese off the top of the ridge, was the fact that we'd mustered about a half dozen VB rifle grenades—that and the arrival of our mortar man, Carl Kelly from M Company, with maybe three or four rounds for his sixty-millimeter mortar. We answered the small-arms fire from the Japs at the top of the ridge by lobbing rifle grenades up at them. Then Kelly came up on the military crest with us. He sat with his mortar tube on the ground between his legs, and in order to hit the Japs above us, he had the tube positioned almost straight up and down. "Carl, that son of a bitch is gonna come straight down on top of us," I said. "I've gotta do it this way, Ore," he told me. "It's the only way I can get them."

To his credit, none of his mortar rounds came down on us. They dropped right on the ridgetop where the Japs had their small foothold. After each round, he would move the mortar tube over a little bit, then drop another round on them. I think that saved our day on the ridge. Either he got the enemy, or he forced them to keep their heads down. The few Japs who survived eventually got the hell out of there. Meanwhile, we'd been hollering down the ridge toward our rear all morning, calling for artillery support, but we didn't get any until after Kelly's mortar rounds and our own half dozen or so rifle grenades had cleared the enemy off the ridge. By afternoon, after L Company had beaten back the worst of the Jap attacks, somebody called up to us that our artillery was going to send out a few rounds. I think they were firing a 105-millimeter.

That help has been summarized very briefly on page 243 of battle historian Richard B. Frank's generally excellent book, *Guadalcanal: The Definitive Account of the Landmark Battle*. "After thrashing through the jungle all night, one [Japanese] rifle company attacked in daylight a Marine position on the west of the perimeter held by company L, 3rd Battalion, 5th Marines (Lieutenant Colonel Frederick C. Biebush). They were driven off with the help of a timely artillery barrage. . . ."

What Frank doesn't say—and probably didn't know—is that the friendly artillery barrage did nearly as much damage to us as we'd done to the Japs. I was one of four corporals positioned on the military crest with our squads. This was in the afternoon, and we'd received word that our artillery was finally going to give us a little support, after all the begging we'd done throughout the morning. The other squad leaders and I were talking about the fact that to maintain the defense perimeter in our sector, we had to have our men form a continuous line from the top of the ridge, then back down into the coconut grove. Because we corporals were the only rated men on the crest, it was up to us to decide how a defense line needed to be established, starting from our ridge and extending down to where the rest of the company was dug in. The other squad leaders with me were Aldridge, Haberle, and Klemicki.

I had five guys in my squad, and the other three squads each had about the same number of men. "I'll go down and find out where our flank is positioned, then I'll work my men into positions leading back up toward this ridge," I told them. "Then I'll pass the word, and you guys can tie your squads in with mine."

Just about the time they were saying, "Okay. That sounds all right—" we heard the artillery *boom* sounding from our rear.

"Goddamn!" I yelled. One of the other guys shouted, *"Short!"*

The way it sounded, we knew the shell would be coming in on top of us. Having been shelled a dozen times or more by both enemy battleships and field artillery, we'd come to know what was coming in, and where we had better not be. We recognized the friendly fire as coming from a pair of our 105s. I dove backward, in a down-the-hill direction. I think I was still in midair when that damned thing landed near where I'd been kneeling. It was a powerful blast that sent me flying backward, and I couldn't even draw a breath. In that instant, I sensed that the Man just turned the page that had my name written on it. My clothes were torn and twisted, my helmet went flying off somewhere, and there was dirt in my eyes and mouth and ears. I thought that was the end for me. It wasn't, but it was damn near the end for the other squad leaders.

For a few minutes, I was off in a world of my own. I couldn't feel or see a thing. I couldn't even hear anything. Next thing I knew, I was lying on the ground, spitting out dirt, and frightened. There had to be a wound somewhere on my body, and pain to go with it, but I wasn't feeling much of anything. Then I began to hear moans, crying, and all the bad noises that come as an aftermath to a disaster. When I was able to look around, I saw my fellow corporals—all three of them—badly wounded. At that moment, it dawned on me that Cpl. Ore J. Marion had made it alive through another day. Aldridge was lying in the dirt with a chunk of muscle hanging out of one of his arms. That bloody arm was filled with little pieces of metal. Klemicki was sprawled in the dirt, one of his legs at about a forty-five-degree angle away from normal. Haberle was out cold, lying in his own blood. He was full of shrapnel, his entire body riddled with pieces of steel, and I could tell he was hurt bad.

Aldridge later underwent three or four major operations and eventually was able to move his arm in a normal manner. He stayed in the corps, retired after twenty years, and died a few years after his retirement. Klemicki had to undergo several operations on his leg, and he spent several years in and out of hospitals before he returned to civilian life. We keep in touch. As of 2002, Hank was doing well, living in Florida, and playing golf as often as the weather permitted. We never heard what became of Haberle after he was evacuated. We could only hope for the best. To this day, I don't know how or why I escaped serious injury, but somehow I didn't have one piece of shrapnel in me.

The men in my squad had been all hunkered down when the shell exploded, and nobody was hurt. As far as I know, the men in the other squads weren't hurt either. Just their squad leaders. I had escaped with one more very close call. Other things like that incident had happened to me before—and would happen again—but that short artillery shell was the closest call during my four months on Guadalcanal. You never get used to those things. Never.

Klemicki, Aldridge, and Haberle were so badly wounded that we couldn't wait for help to come up to us from a corpsman. Several of the men carried the squad leaders down the hill where they could be taken care of. As for the rest of us—we had a job to do, so we stayed. We didn't have a choice in the matter.

We maneuvered the men in our squads the way we'd planned. I tied my squad in on the right, and Aldridge's squad—now minus Aldridge—tied in with me. Later that day, when we got up to the top of our ridge, we found about a half dozen dead Japanese, probably the victims of our few rifle grenades and Carl Kelly's mortar rounds. The rest of the attackers had vanished into the jungle, their assault thwarted. We stayed on the ridge the rest of that day, then all through the night and into the following morning, holding our position. The Japanese attack had failed, and nothing more happened in our sector during that night or the next day. Just sporadic small-arms fire here and there.

The following day, Major Barbey and Lieutenant Colonel Biebush, L Company's commander, came up on our ridge. Barbey formed a reconnaissance patrol that included my squad, and we took off, moving down off the ridge into the jungle foliage, roughly into an area where part of the Japanese attack had originally come at us. We couldn't have been much more than 100 or 150 yards out from our MLR when we discovered what had happened to the Japanese dead. At first we encountered no enemy at all, alive *or* dead, but we knew were moving in the right direction because we were following a trail of bloody bandages. Then, before we could see where the Japs had dumped their dead, we heard it. We heard the droning buzz of millions of flies, swarming in a dark cloud over a large area of stinking ground. That's where their bodies were—there must have been a hundred of them at that location. The retreating Japanese had tried to cover their dead, spreading shovelfuls of dirt over the corpses, but the arms, legs, faces, and torsos were barely covered, and the flies were thick and buzzing all over them. Flies were everywhere, and the stench of dead flesh was everywhere.

It was clear to Major Barbey and to the rest of us that the Japs who had survived the battle were nowhere nearby, so we returned to our positions on the MLR. The battle of Bloody Ridge—and of our own L Company Ridge—was over. The scattered Japanese who retreated from the Bloody Ridge attack, which was to our east, gradually drifted back in a westward direction. We were able to spot many of them off in the distance, making their way in the direction that took them toward the Matanikau River. They were completely disorganized and in bad physical shape. Some of them no longer had weapons.

If the Japanese had been able to exploit the situation when a few of them succeeded in making it to the crest of our ridge, they would have been down to the new fighter strip in no time at all. But they had taken casualties—a lot more casualties than we took—and it seems that there weren't enough Japanese left to sustain their attack.

Marines on the Canal. If the clean uniforms and healthy appearance of the men are any indication, this photo was probably taken very early in the campaign. NATIONAL ARCHIVES

The Japanese who attacked our sector of the perimeter had clearly intended to stay and take over. On top of L Company Ridge after the battle was over, we found a dead Japanese officer still clutching two leather briefcases chock-full of new Japanese currency. My guess is that they either planned to hold pay call or were going to try to buy the airfield from us. Or maybe that champion was a card shark or dice-rolling hustler, ready to open up shop as soon as the firefight was over. In fact, the firefight *was* over. The Japanese assault on Bloody Ridge—and the simultaneous attack on our own L Company Ridge—had ended with their defeat.

The thwarted Japanese attack that later became known to the world as the battle of Bloody Ridge was genuine good news, and as such, it made it into the American newspapers right away. Here are the headlines over the story that my family read in the *Buffalo Evening News* on September 16.

**ALL OUT ATTACK ON SOLOMONS
FAILS TO BREAK MARINES' GRIP**

**JAPANESE SEEK
TO REGAIN BASE
ON GUADALCANAL**

**Heavy Fighting on Land and
Sea and in Air in Progress
Since Saturday Night, Navy
Announces**

(copyright 1942, the *Buffalo Evening News*)

LEAD 'EM BY THREE LENGTHS—OR, IT WORKED IN WORLD WAR I

I believe it was late September when one of L Company's officers gathered our platoon together for a short discussion. That was usually reason to worry. I don't remember any meeting during that period when a good scoop was passed our way. The officer, a lieutenant, told us a little about our air support situation—or lack of it—which was getting more serious by the day. The reason for this discussion, he said, was to tell us how we, the raggedy-assed troops, were going to give the flyboys some help. We all agreed that if we could give them help of any kind, they sure deserved it. Our group of fighter pilots, which had become known as the Cactus Air Force, was doing a terrific job with too few planes, not one of which was any longer in good shape. That made their already dangerous job doubly dangerous. Ernie Snowden recalls watching our flyboys taxiing their Grumman Wildcats on the runway, the planes' glass canopies pulled back. The sight reminded him of guys back home driving off in convertibles, which seems to lend the pilots' job an air of glamour. In fact, their job was a lot more dangerous than it was glamorous.

The lieutenant went on: "We have only two or three airplanes that can fly at any given time. Our pilots have been going up two or three times a day to tangle with those Jap Zeros and bombers, and they don't come back down until they run out of ammo or gas, or are shot down. One of the pilots has an idea: When he runs out of ammo or starts getting low on fuel, he'll try to get a Zero on his tail. He'll try to take the Zero down low, so that we can open up on the Jap from here on the ground. Maybe we'll get lucky."

Damned if that didn't sound like a neat idea. Back in training, we had practiced something we called "snapping in" on aircraft, which roughly translates into taking small-arms potshots from the ground at a low-flying plane. That was practice. Now we were going to get a chance to try the real thing. "No problem," we'd been told by the sergeant who'd instructed us at practice. "Just lead the plane by three lengths. It never failed in World War I."

So the lieutenant's idea sounded good to us. "Hell, this'll be like a turkey shoot," one of our guys told him. "We'll do it like we were instructed. We lead 'em by three plane lengths and we can't miss 'em." The rest of us agreed. Maybe the lieutenant's news wasn't so bad after all. We were getting a chance to help the flyboys, and a little diversion while we were at it.

Midmorning the next day, and we were in our regular defensive positions in our coconut grove, which faced toward the Matanikau River, when some two-engine Japanese bombers came overhead. We watched two or three of our Grumman Wildcat fighters go after them and start giving them hell. A couple of Japanese Zeros now joined the fight, trying to protect their bombers. We watched the show as we lay on the ground next to our spider holes. That was the only thing we *could* do from our position: watch.

Suddenly a guy a few yards away from me shouted, "Look! He's bringing that sucker in!" Coming toward us from the Matanikau's direction, a Grumman Wildcat fighter had a Zero on its tail. The Grumman that our guy was yelling about was dancing around in the sky like a one-legged goose, and the Zero was staying right behind it, following its every move. Both planes were coming toward our coconut grove—which is to say, they were coming straight at us. The Wildcat flipped on its side, its lower wing cutting the air between two rows of tall coconut palms. The Zero stayed on its tail.

By now we were all in firing position, exactly the way we'd been taught—right knee on the ground, left foot planted firmly in the dirt, left arm extended all the way forward with left hand on the upper rifle stock, right elbow up, right index finger on the trigger. The planes were coming in fast, but we were ready. Now they were precisely overhead. We led, we aimed, we fired.

The Springfield '03 rifles and the pistols got off maybe one round apiece. The BARs and Tommy guns did a little better. Two rounds. That was all. The planes were gone. It was as though nothing had happened. Just like that, it was over.

It wasn't until later that day that the lieutenant brought us together again for a little critique of our glorious experimental turkey shoot. Before he could get started on his report, we interrupted, telling him what a magnificent try we'd given it. "Maybe we didn't shoot him down, sir, but we sure worried the hell out of him...."

"That Zero must look like a sieve!"

"That Jap pilot must be having a nervous breakdown by now. Hell, our guy'll probably bring those Zeros in for us every day from now on."

The lieutenant kept cool and calm. He listened for a minute, and then it was his turn to talk. "Men, that pilot is a good flier and a good friend of mine. He told me he'll do that maneuver again when we're served steak and eggs three times a day on this island. He doesn't think any of your shots hit the Zero, but you sure did succeed in putting three rounds into the tail of his Wildcat. He has absolutely no faith in your marksmanship. Absolutely none. You were supposed to lead those planes by three lengths. Not four lengths. Not five lengths. Three goddamn lengths."

With that, the lieutenant walked away.

He left us talking amongst ourselves. "What the hell do they want from us?" one guy muttered.

"Yeah," another of our guys said. "Next thing you know, they'll want us to *fly* those planes for them."

The first guy said, "We led 'em by three lengths, didn't we? So we hit the wrong damn plane. What do they expect from us? Miracles?"

Somebody else piped in. "It wasn't our idea, anyway. The planes go by with a whoosh, and they expect us to hold an exact three-length lead. Hell. We got crazy people leading us in a crazy war."

"Yeah," the first guy said. "If we had food in our stomachs, we'd have heartburn by now."

But that flyboy wasn't kidding. That was the first—and the last—fly-by of that kind that had anything to do with us. So much for the good idea we'd inherited from World War I. Like so much else, it wasn't worth a damn in World War II.

PROMOTION TIME

By late September, jungle warfare had taken its toll on us. Chronic lack of food and medical supplies, malaria-carrying mosquitoes, and other tropical diseases were taking more marine casualties than we were losing in combat. Nearly every one of us was suffering. My platoon had moved out to our isolated ridge and established our position, but practically before I knew it, both Lieutenant Flaherty and our platoon sergeant were gone to the field hospital, both down with malaria attacks. By the last couple days of September, and without anybody to tell me, I'd become the senior man in Company L-3-5's 1st Platoon. That put me in charge whether I liked it or not.

Our other two platoons were in the same fix. The 2nd Platoon had lost Lt. George Mead, killed in action at Matanikau back in August, then they'd lost Lieutenant Farmer when he was badly wounded in the September 13–14 Japanese attack on L Company Ridge. That left Cpl. Raleigh Bright in charge. The 3rd Platoon was only a little better off. It had lost its lieutenant to malaria, which left Platoon Sgt. Walt Sincek in charge, with Cpl. Paul Morris his second in charge.

I had the 1st Platoon dug in on the military crest of our area of responsibility. By that time, the entire platoon's strength was down to a dozen or fifteen men. Every one of us was sick, with malaria, diarrhea, or both, and we were all physically weak from lack of food and sleep. Back in those days, the marines didn't have "talking doctors" or psychiatrists, and we didn't know the meaning of depression. Everybody in every one of our platoons was in the same physical and mental condition. We lived on several tablespoons of captured Jap rice per day—that is, if anyone brought it out to us. Our water situation was about as bad. Not enough of it, and sometimes it wasn't available at all.

Somebody "in the rear with the gear"—which is to say a Mighty Plan Maker at Company Command—decided that we should cut our field of fire at the foot of our ridge. That's Marine Manual terminology for cutting down the area's tall grass and foliage to provide visibility in case we ever had to fire on the approaching enemy with our automatic weapons. According to the manual, cutting a field of fire is what is supposed to be done as soon as your position is established. But what we discovered the hard way was that the Japanese didn't cut their own fields of fire, and on more than one occasion, our guys walked right into the path of fire of their Nambu light machine guns. In other words, the Japs' attitude was "screw the manuals," which is what they did. We suffered for it. What's more, on too many occasions, cutting our fields turned out to be a dead giveaway, revealing our own positions to the Japs.

I'd been acting platoon leader for a day or so when somebody from our company showed up with a grub hook and a rusty old machete left over from one of our banana wars. They were our tools for cutting a field of fire. For the following day or two, I sent three men at a time down to the bottom of the ridge and into a ravinelike area to do some bushwhacking below the field of fire for our BARs and our one light machine gun. What should have taken half a day under better circumstances seemed to go on forever. We couldn't make much progress, because the men were too sick and too weak for that kind of work in jungle heat and humidity. The routine called for two men to whack away at the foliage while the third man kept them covered with his weapon. For extra defensive protection, we'd strung a strand of barbed wire below the area where the men were cutting. It was the same idea as Lieutenant Farmer's trick during his platoon's defense of L Company Ridge. We hung a rusty ration can on the wire and put a couple of pebbles into the can. If someone or something touched the wire, the can rattled and gave us warning.

On the second or third day of this brilliant military exercise, and with all my men too sick to do much work, I decided to get the damned job over with fast. I picked out two men who weren't as sick as the others. Then I led them down the ridge. I decided that I'd cover them with my rifle while they used the cutting tools and finished up this useless, futile exercise. After about an hour, one of my men up topside on the ridge called down to us: "Patrol coming in."

"Good," I called back. "Do they have any chow?"

We continued our work for about another five minutes, when I got another call from the ridge. "You're wanted up here."

The problem was that if I climbed back up to the crest, my two grass cutters would have to come up with me. They couldn't work down there without anybody to cover for them. "You'd better tell him to come down here," I called back. "Because once we come up there, our work's over for the day."

The next voice that came down to me from the ridge belonged to my assistant and BAR man, Larry Gerkin. "Goddamn it! Get your ass up here!" Gerkin never talked like that to anyone unless it was something serious. The nearest he usually came to cussing was to say, "Jeez—" This, I guessed, was something serious.

We struggled up the steep embankment. The ground was so rough and we were so damned weak that it must have taken us ten minutes to pull ourselves, drag ourselves, and sometimes just crawl back up to the ridge. At last I got to the top, and I was sucking wind through all my orifices. I found myself standing face-to-face with a gentleman (he must have been a gentleman) dressed in clean khakis, with clean-shaven face and neatly trimmed hair. His attitude was what I call "Naval Academy impatient."

"Are you in charge here?" he asked.

I figured that this champion must be a bird colonel at least, and a true stalwart warrior, so I stood at strict attention. His detail consisted of about eight men guarding him. There I stood, all five-feet-six-inches and one hundred pounds of me, my hair long and hanging, no shave or bath for maybe two weeks. I replied to our young hero, "Yes, sir. I'm in charge."

"What were you doing down there?" he asked.

"We're finishing up cutting our fields of fire, which I am not in favor of doing."

"If you're in charge, why are you down there working?" he demanded.

"Sir," I said, "these men are sick. I felt that under these conditions, I could show them my concern."

"What is your rank?" he demanded.

"Sir," I said, "I am a corporal."

"Corporal," said this brave warrior. "As long as you have one man under you who can stand and work, you will supervise and oversee the job. If you can't understand that, we can always revert you to the rank of private."

I was standing at attention and listening, but I was looking at this well-fed, well-groomed officer, and I was thinking, "Up yours." What I did say was, "Sir, if you're going back to the MLR from here, can we have your water?"

Every man in his detail had two water canteens hanging from their belts, and we hadn't had water for a couple days. I didn't give our hero a chance to answer my question. "Water, men!" I shouted. "Come and get it!"

From out of their dug-out holes in the ground and from out of the underbrush came a dozen or so men from my dirty, unshaven, raggedy-ass platoon. They were really just a bunch of kids who needed a lot of things but were willing to settle for something as simple as water. They looked like kids because that's exactly what they were. But later on, somebody describing the Guadalcanal campaign called them the "Magnificent Bastards," and that's what they were to me. A bunch of raggedy-ass magnificent bastards—and to this day, I love every last one of them, above and below the sod.

This visiting detachment didn't want to exchange canteens with us, because anybody could see that we were a bunch of unclean, diseased slobs. Instead, they let us pour the water from their canteens into ours, losing several precious gulps of water that splashed on the ground in each exchange. To this day, old veterans who were on the Canal but weren't out on the MLR are unable to understand the desperate situation we were in. The one good thing that happened that day is that once that chicken-shit officer in his pressed khakis turned around and led his detail off our ridge, I never saw him again. Through the rest of my twenty years in the corps, I never laid eyes on that jerk a second time.

We didn't have much when we were out on that ridge, but by this time, we did have a field telephone. Next morning, my telephone man was lying on the ground maybe ten feet from me, with the field phone up to his ear. He turned to me and said, "Looks like they're going to make some promotions in the ranks. The battalion switchboard man was just telling me they're going to promote about a half dozen guys to sergeant."

"That's real neighborly," I said. "Let me know what comes of it all."

For a while I just continued lying there with a blank mind and not giving much of a damn about anything. Then I started thinking about those promotions, which I knew were now being discussed back at headquarters. What about me? Why the hell can't they promote me? All right, I'm one of the regiment's junior corporals, but so what? Who the hell's got the responsibility of leading this platoon out here on the front line? *I* have! *I'm* doing the job. I started thinking about that asshole in the clean uniform, threatening to demote me, his only reason being that I was helping my men. So he threatened to demote me—the hell with him. Why shouldn't I be promoted instead?

"Edwards," I said, "give me that phone."

I cranked up the phone, and the company clerk, Ralph Rivera, came on. I told him I wanted to speak to the first sergeant. "The first sergeant isn't around," Rivera said.

"How about the new company commander?" I asked. "Captain Smith."

Rivera told me that the acting first sergeant, who happened to be my old buddy Ben Selvitelle, and Captain Smith were at a meeting at battalion command. I asked him who was there who had some authority, and Rivera told me that the exec officer, First Lieutenant Guffin, was there. I told Rivera that I had some kind words I wanted to exchange with Guffin. Mister Guffin, who was a nice guy and a competent officer, came on the field phone.

"Lieutenant," I said, "I've been told some promotions are going to be made. The reason I'm taking up your time is to ask if my name will be on the promotion list."

"To be honest with you, your name wasn't mentioned in any of our conversations," Guffin said.

"Mister Guffin," I said, "in all the special details and all the extra details I've been assigned, no one has complained or found fault with my performance. I know that I'm a junior corporal in the regiment. If you guys don't think I'm ready for promotion or you don't think I'm competent to be promoted, then you'd best send someone out here to take over the platoon. Because right now, I'm the only man who's leading it. And that somebody had better be here by the crack of dawn, because I'm pissed, and I'm going to come in early tomorrow morning and report for brig time for leaving my post."

Lieutenant Guffin was a good warrior. I liked him personally and I didn't intend to give him a hard time, but at the same time, I was telling myself that what's fair is fair. So now I told the lieutenant, "I'm out here and I'm responsible for what's left of this platoon. We're all hungry and we're all sick, dirty, stinking, and unwashed. I'm holding these poor meatheads together on this goddamned hot ridge, and if command doesn't think I'm acting responsibly and capably, then the only thing that makes sense for them to do is to relieve me.

"Mister Guffin," I went on, "if by sunset I'm not informed that my name will be on that promotion list, you'll see me shortly after 0800 hours tomorrow morning."

Guffin sympathized, but he went on and on with a song and dance, the conclusion being that he'd see what he could do, but that he couldn't promise me anything. That's how our phone conversation ended.

Just as the sky was getting dark, we got a tap on our field phone. It was Sgt. Ben Selvitelle, and he wanted to speak to me. I got on the phone.

"Ore," he said, "I don't know what your conversation with Guffin was all about, but I've been told to inform you that your promotion to sergeant will be effective on October 1, 1942.

Congratulations, old buddy. And by the way, I've just been promoted to gunny sergeant."

"Thanks for the info, Ben," I said. "Congratulations to you, too."

Ben deserved his promotion, too. He was a damned fine marine who stayed in the corps for thirty-five years, getting a commission and rising to the rank of lieutenant colonel by the time he retired. He held several important jobs and was always a credit to the corps and to his country. Because of the age factor, he couldn't be promoted higher than lieutenant colonel. But as of the following day, October 1, 1942, Ben was the youngest gunnery sergeant in the entire 1st Marine Division. As it turned out, the awful month of September 1942 ended on a good note for some of us.

CHAPTER 5

October 1942

THREE FLYING FORTRESSES
There was something unusual happening on Mount Austen, the thirteen-hundred-foot rise that formed the normally unchanging green backdrop for our island ordeal. Back in August, when we first arrived on the island and looked up at the side of Mount Austen, the only thing we saw was heavy green foliage that covered it in an unbroken climb to its mounded top. When we stood facing out to the beach and the deep blue bay beyond, Mount Austen was back over our left shoulder, its heavy, dark green foliage punctuated only by the zigzag rises of barren coral ridges that accented the surrounding jungle lowlands. But one day there was a line on its surface, plain for all of us to see, as if somebody had started moving the foliage.

The line kept getting bigger and bigger. You had to be blind not to see it, but no one said anything officially. After a time, you learned not to report everything you saw. Report something funny going on, and before you knew it, you'd be on a two-day hike, trying to find out what the Japs were up to. So we never said anything about that bare-looking line cutting through the foliage. At about the same time, from the ridge we were on, we could see Japanese ships landing troops at Point Cruz.

I believe it was the beginning of October when General Vandegrift came up on our ridge, and we called out to him, "Hey! How're y'doin, A. A.?" We were in battle, everything was informal, and Vandegrift didn't mind when he showed up somewhere and the men called him A. A. The A. A. stood for

Alexander Archer. Somebody in our company called out, "What the hell are you doing up *here*, general?"

"I just got a message from General MacArthur," he told us. "He's sending some planes to help us out. They should be coming by very shortly!"

That was something worth looking for. So we waited and waited, but it wasn't shortly—and after a while, we sensed that the general was getting impatient. Finally we spotted planes in the sky, three of them, and they were very high. I'd never seen an airplane flying that high. They were big four-engine bombers, B-17 Flying Fortresses, which at that time were the largest planes in the U.S. Army Air Corps, the forerunner of today's Air Force. The planes were coming toward us from the general direction of Florida Island, and for all I know, they might have come all the way from New Guinea. Now, high over the bay, they were as plainly visible to us as to the Japanese transport ship that was unloading troops off Point Cruz. It seemed clear to every one of us on the ridge that the enemy transport was our bombers' logical target.

Then, when the B-17s were roughly halfway between Savo Island and the Guadalcanal shoreline, they opened their bomb-bay doors and down came the bombs. They weren't anywhere near the Japanese ship. Probably not within a mile of it. All the bombs came down in the middle of the bay, exploding as they hit the water, which was the middle of nowhere. Then the three planes veered off and disappeared. The Japanese transport ship continued unloading its troops, and there were no additional bombers, no more bombs. As the B-17s flew away, Vandegrift jumped up and yelled, *"Jesus Christ!"*

He took off his helmet and threw it on the ground. He cussed some more, then picked up his helmet, slapped it on his head, and went stomping down and away from our position.

"Stop up and see us again sometime!" a couple of the marines called, but he probably didn't hear them. He was too furious about what he'd just seen the flyboys do. There weren't even any Zeros up in the sky to try to stop them. Every time one of our planes flew a mission, its crew got credit in their records, whether they accomplished anything or not. That day, I guess they were more interested in completing their mission than in whether or not they found and hit an enemy target.

THE HOWITZER: WITH A FRIEND LIKE THAT, WE DIDN'T NEED ENEMIES

This early October incident started shortly after dinnertime—that was a stretch, calling a skimpy ration of wormy rice dinner. Our platoon was ordered to get our gear, move out of our coconut grove position on the western edge of the MLR, and dig in down on the beach. The scoop had it that a Japanese fleet with troop transports was headed our way and would probably appear around midnight. Within about ten minutes, we were digging new spider holes on the beach, making them a little deeper than usual, pampering our weapons, and establishing watches that would continue between nightfall and 2300 hours. After that, it would be all troops on alert.

Just before sunset, two jeeps pulled up to our beach position, one of them towing a seventy-five-millimeter howitzer, the other pulling a large searchlight and a generator. The battalion's exec officer arrived shortly behind them, and he was soon in deep discussion with the artillery officer and his crew. We saw them pointing out along the beach in the direction of Matanikau and Point Cruz. Our own platoon leader, Lt. Flash Flaherty, was not invited to this high-level and very-big-deal meeting, which had him feeling as left out as the rest of us. "The hell with 'em," I heard somebody mutter. "Who gives a damn about what they're doing with that gun and searchlight."

By the time sunset neared, the big searchlight was positioned to face in the same direction the artillery masterminds had been pointing: toward Matanikau and Point Cruz. The light wasn't turned on yet, but we saw plainly where it was pointing. We also saw the crew break out a half dozen or so rounds of howitzer ammo. At that stage of the campaign, we all knew that the Japanese were strutting around on the Matanikau–Point Cruz area like they owned the damned place and planned on setting up permanent housekeeping there. For our own part, we were harassing hell out of them whenever we had the chance. And when our air guys had a plane that could fly, they were anxious to help us by dropping an extra bomb or two into that area.

Night in the jungle always comes suddenly, and as usual, darkness came that evening like gangbusters. Immediately the generator started up and the big searchlight came on. It illuminated the beach line, then swung all the way out to Matanikau, lighting up the area so that it looked like high noon on California's Long Beach Turnpike.

We raggedy-ass marine infantrymen had been blasé about this mysterious artillery operation, but our attitude changed the moment that damned searchlight came to life. Now we were coming to life, too, because we knew the light was bound to draw enemy fire. Back then, and to the present day, if there is anything that a gravel-crunching marine infantryman hates, it is something or somebody who might draw unfriendly fire into his area. Drawing enemy fire at night is worse than doing it during the daytime, and we were well aware that a bright searchlight coming from our area was detrimental to our health and well-being.

The artillery crew received fire orders, and the night was suddenly shattered with a *Blam!* They fired on a flat trajectory along the beach and into Matanikau. There was a pause for correction, followed by another six or eight deafening rounds of *"take that, you lousy Jap bastards!"* In a way, we were lucky. There was no return fire. Within minutes, the searchlight was out, the jeeps started up, and both the howitzer and the light were gone. That left us with another long night to stay alert and wait for daybreak.

Around midnight, a couple of Jap warships eased our way, looking to find out where that gunfire had come from. And then, for the following twenty minutes, guess who got plastered with enemy shellfire: the 1st Platoon of L-3-5. There we were, crouched at the bottom of our spider holes, hugging the walls for dear life, and cussing at both the enemy and our own artillery champions.

It could have been worse, since all they did was scare the hell out of us. We didn't take any casualties, and the feared Japanese assault on our beach never took place.

THE BEST BUNKER
As the Guadalcanal campaign wore on and weeks turned into months, our spider holes were starting to break down. Japanese ships would pay their offshore social calls most evenings and send us a few rounds just so we wouldn't start thinking we owned the damned place. Then, later at night, Washing Machine Charlie would drop a few bombs to let us know it was time to change the watch. During daylight hours—usually late morning or early afternoon—Major Smith and one or two others from the Cactus Air Force would get our few operational Grumman fighters off the ground, and that usually gave them a chance to tear up a couple of Jap bombers, though it didn't stop the Japanese from dumping a flock of bombs all over the place. In quieter moments, Pistol Pete was likely to drop a few indiscriminate rounds into our sector, just to keep us honest.

Let me describe our spider holes, and why, when we got some time on our hands, we started thinking about building something a little more luxurious. A foxhole typically was a narrow trench with two or three or more guys in it. We found out real quick that a better way to protect ourselves, especially from the air attacks and falling shrapnel, was to build something we called spider holes. You'd dig in the wet, sandy earth with your helmet, say six feet down, in a column just big enough for you to stand up in. Everyone made his own, so you fashioned it the way you wanted it. Most of us built a little sand stool at the bottom on one side and widened the spider hole out a little so you could stretch your legs. You might cut out a little shelf for a canteen or a jug of water. You'd lie on the ground next to your spider hole, and when the shelling or bombing started, you'd jump into it and pull two sandbags together overhead to close it off. We were so close to the ocean at high tide that we'd get a little brackish water splashing around at our feet. Spider holes offered pretty good protection, but they weren't very comfortable.

With all that shelling and bombing and other commotion beating hell out of our spider holes, we were understandably nervous. That's when we decided that we'd build a bunker, a first-class bomb shelter to surpass all others on Guadalcanal. We managed to get in a little planning between the routine of daily patrols and incoming enemy fire, and then we started digging our shelter, using our few entrenching tools along with a couple of shovels the Japs had left behind. We also found an old Japanese saw that we could use for felling trees. Our plan called for a dugout, seven feet square and seven feet deep. Its entrance would be a slide so we could get in there fast when the shit hit the fan. Its covering top would be made of coconut logs, topped with a layer of Japanese sandbags, and with more sand piled on top of the bags. It would be the island's most magnificent bunker, bar none!

Our bunker's site was in the coconut grove beyond the west-facing end of the new fighter strip. Some of our guys dug while others sawed fallen trees. The Japanese saw was the type that cuts only on the pull stroke, but it was all we had, so we made do. Larry Hardrock Gerkin was honcho on the tree-cutting detail.

Work being intermittent, it took us about a week to complete our masterpiece. With the final sandbag in place one hot, muggy morning, we stood around our bunker and told each other what an excellent engineering feat we'd accomplished. From now on, we assured ourselves, we'd have no more worries during Japanese shellings and bombings. A visitor from the next platoon came over to help us admire our accomplishment, so Gerkin invited him below to inspect our bombproof marvel.

Just about then, the air-raid siren sounded. Minutes later, we heard, then saw, five or six Japanese bombers coming in our direction, the red meatballs shining on their wings in the full sunlight. Gerkin and the others stayed down in the bunker, and the rest of us remained in the open, waiting to see where the planes were going to release their bombs. By now we were pros at this game, able to estimate where the bombs would land from the moment we saw them drop out of the planes. And now that we had this magnificent bunker, all we had to do was slide into it for protection, just in case a couple of the bombs appeared to be coming too close.

As we watched, a couple of our Grummans went up into the sky to give the bombers hell. That could have been reason enough for the bombers to start releasing their loads a little early. Instead of falling toward Henderson Field, those bombs would be hitting the earth in our vicinity. We started diving into our new bunker headfirst, because the bombs were coming straight at us. We listened to the approaching explosions. The first hit was short, but in line. The second walked in a little closer. The third hit our bunker smack on top and right in the middle. And there we were, about eight of us, hunched down in that sucker!

The noise was deafening. The logs serving as our bunker's roof came partway down on top of us, followed by sand. For several minutes after that, none of us could hear a thing. We couldn't see a thing, either, because our eyes were full of sand. We were sputtering, spitting sand out of our mouths, and digging like hell to get out of that damned hole. Finally I managed to pull myself out of the rubble and up to solid ground, then reached down and helped a couple buddies out behind me. We were all out by now except Hardrock Gerkin. He was still down there, but we knew he was alive and conscious because we could hear him caterwauling like a scalded mule. He must have been holding hundreds of pounds of dirt and logs on his back. Now we all knew that Gerk was the strongest man in L Company, and maybe the strongest man in the entire 1st Marine Division, but there's a limit to what one man can hold on his back. What's more, we all knew that if anything bad was going to happen to anybody, it was going to happen to Hardrock first. We dug with our hands, pushed and pulled logs out of the way, and finally pulled Gerk out of the structure that, for barely an hour, had been our finished magnificent bombproof shelter.

It took a little while to get the sand and dirt out of our eyes and mouths and the fright out of our systems. We cursed the sons of the Rising Sun. We cursed their bombers, and we cursed Tokyo Rose for good measure. By some miracle, nobody was hurt, and as we realized that and started recovering from the shock of our close call, we found ourselves laughing. We filled up the "best bomb shelter on Guadalcanal" and went back to our less comfortable but safer individual spider holes.

Speaking of Japanese bombs, here is one of the funnier examples of bad information that made it back to the homefront at a time when Japanese Betty bombers were appearing overhead every day between August and December 1942 to plaster us with bombs, and when Washing Machine Charlie was drifting in every night to shake us up a little with a bomb or two of his own. This headline appeared in the *Buffalo Evening News* on September 14. I wonder which war this story was talking about.

**Jap Planes Get Little Chance
To Drop Bombs on Solomons
Only 10 Missiles Fell While U.S. Fliers, Antiaircraft
Guns Blasted 30 Enemy Ships Out of Air**
(copyright 1942, the *Buffalo Evening News*)

THE OCTOBER 7–9 BATTLE OF THE MATANIKAU

It was the crack of dawn on October 7, and all hands in L Company, 3rd Battalion, 5th Marine Regiment were awake. We were busy filling our canteens with water and getting extra rounds of ammunition. Both the 2nd and 3rd Battalions of the 5th Marine Regiment had been ordered to move west from our MLR and advance to the Matanikau River, and that included us. We were getting ready for what would later be officially listed as the Matanikau River Engagement, October 7–9, 1942.

As we moved out, word came to L Company: "This time, you're going to be in reserve."

"Jesus, it's about time," one of my guys muttered. "We're finally getting a break."

"They must've made a mistake," somebody else remarked.

Nobody in my unit seemed to be thinking the situation out, and none of us realized what would be in store for us before the day was over. Being "in reserve" is not always an enviable position. In fact, it's often downright hazardous.

Our mission was to hold our position on the river's east bank and be prepared to cross it if and when we received orders to do so. The 1st Battalion, 5th Marines, moved through our position and were soon well out ahead of us, heading toward the Matanikau River. Following them were I and K Companies of our own battalion. Other units that participated were the 3rd Battalion, 2nd Marines, which had come from Tulagi, and Col. Merritt Edson's Raiders, who, back in September, had played a large part in the defense of Bloody Ridge. At the same time, Col. Lewis "Chesty" Puller's battalion, which was part of the 7th Marine Regiment, was somewhere out on the opposite side of the Matanikau, on a flanking mission.

Our company moved down the Copra Cart Road, using the same route Colonel Oka's Japanese troops had taken in mid-September, before we'd stopped their advance on L Company Ridge. The difference was that back then, they'd been coming at us from west to east. Now we were going after them, from east to west. When we were about halfway to the river, we got orders to fall out on each side of the road. I heard somebody in my platoon say, "I could fight a war like this all my life." Famous last words. Up ahead, we started hearing small-arms fire—first our own, then the higher-pitched sound of Nambu light machine-gun fire. The Japs were shooting back.

It wasn't long before a jeep came bumping along the road, returning from the firefight. It carried three or four wounded marines. We were about to find out that I and K Companies had run into trouble at a spot located just before the Matanikau crossing. That was the first piece of bad news: the Japanese were supposed to be on the *other* side of the river, but they were on *our* side of it. L Company's runner appeared and approached our platoon to relay an order: "Move forward to the Old Man." By that, he meant that we were ordered to go to our company commander, Capt. Lyman Spurlock. We moved forward and found our CO conferring with an officer from battalion headquarters. By now I had my sergeant's stripes, which put me in charge of my platoon, since Lieutenant Flaherty, the official platoon leader, was still temporarily out of action with malaria.

Our CO and the battalion officer turned to L Company's platoon leaders, which on this day, included me: "Move up to the line, and hold it until I and K Companies join you on your left and right flanks. Then gradually pull back and let them fill the gap until their flanks join."

He didn't tell us the exact nature of the situation, only what we were expected to accomplish. There had to be a reason why that gap existed in the first place, but nobody was about to give *us* reasons. Common sense dictated one of two probable choices: one, the terrain was so bad that it was nearly impossible to move through it; two, the enemy had some very bad things in place on that spot. Whatever the situation, we would now have to face it.

Another runner appeared to guide us toward that gap in the line, and we started moving out. The runner led my platoon up to a spot where the vegetation was so thick that if I'd stuck my hand forward and into it, I couldn't have seen my fingers. It was the edge of what today they call a rain forest. On the Canal, we just called it jungle.

Our guide pointed off to one side and told me, "K Company is over there." Then he indicated the opposite direction: "I Company is over there. Good luck." With that, he left us.

Directly through the thick vegetation ahead of us was the east bank of the Matanikau River. Rifle fire crackled around us. Now and then, we heard what was becoming the too-familiar cry from a wounded marine: "Corpsman!"

Our platoon's three squads—none at full strength—started to deploy. We left one squad in reserve while the other two began penetrating the thick jungle. Immediately all hell broke loose. Enemy machine guns accompanied by an unknown number of riflemen opened up and started having a field day at our expense. They just weren't supposed to be on our side of the river, but nobody had the nerve to tell them as much. Anyhow, we now knew why the gap existed in our line: both reason number one and reason number two.

A couple of our guys got wounded right away. Pfc. Joe Parker was one of them. Before the Guadalcanal campaign was over, Joe would be wounded three times and was finally evacuated from the island, but he somehow survived it all. On this occasion, he was down and couldn't move, and it was a long time before a corpsman was able to get to him. For what seemed like forever, he was in clear view of the Japs, who just let him lie there as bait. We knew that if any one of us tried to get near him, we'd be clobbered by the machine guns they had in place, waiting for us to come out into the open. I don't know how our guys finally got Joe out of there—only that they eventually managed to save him.

I learned later that before our arrival, another marine platoon had tried to fill the gap at the spot where my platoon was now positioned, and their dead and wounded were now scattered among us in the jungle growth. In short order, several of my own men joined their ranks. We remained pinned down in that position for twelve hours.

You lie there or crouch behind the cover of a tree, wondering what to do next. You know the enemy is only fifty feet away. You can hear them. You call back and forth to your buddies, and the Japs can hear you. We didn't know a word of Japanese at that time, and they probably couldn't understand anything we were shouting. So you just sit tight. You learned patience, because if you didn't have patience, you were going to die.

When I tried to fill in the gap between K and I Companies with L Company's 1st Platoon, I made several mad dashes from one temporary shelter to another with Hap Poloshian. The underbrush around us and in front of us was very thick. We finally made it to a spot behind a banyan tree, its trunk maybe four feet in diameter. The Japs were dug in at about the thickest part of the underbrush with several machine guns and a number of riflemen. They kept tattooing our tree with everything they had. On our side, where we were protected from their line of fire, it sounded like tom-toms. Their rifles and machine guns had our whole unit pinned down and stuck where we were. Our only way of communicating was hollering back and forth among ourselves, which we did. Through bursts of gunfire, we also could hear the Japanese shouting back and forth.

By late afternoon, we heard a lot of thrashing behind us, and Maj. Lou Walt of the Raider Battalion appeared from out of the brush. He was in a kneeling position, making himself a good target for the enemy. I started to holler, "Get down—"

Whatever else I had to say was lost in the noise of hell breaking loose, all of it directed at Walt. He went down damn fast and miraculously escaped without a scratch. I could see the shrubs, vines, and everything that grew around him being cut down by bullets. After a while, the gunfire quieted down, and Major Walt crawled in a little closer to our position.

"I wanted to see what was holding you people up," he said. "I found out pretty fast, didn't I?"

With that, he crawled out backward, heading in the direction he'd come from, and it wasn't until the next morning, after the fiasco was over, that I saw anybody else from the Raider unit. Major Walt was a good officer, and when Lt. Col. Merritt Edson was promoted to full colonel after Bloody Ridge and later given command of our 5th Regiment, Walt came with him. Walt was always looking things over, making sure the details were carried out. Having the judgment to select men like Walt and other top-flight officers to assist him was a major reason for Colonel Edson's success in the corps.

Two or three years after the war, I had an opportunity to read what was considered an official account of the October

7–9 Matanikau battle in a book titled *The Old Breed: A History of the First Marine Division in World War II*, by George McMillan. This account is inaccurate in several details. McMillan states correctly that L-3-5—my unit—joined the firefight in the morning at about 1000 hours, or approximately three hours after we'd started moving down the Old Copra Cart Road from our MLR. I assume he's also correct when he goes on to say that our regiment's 2nd Battalion turned slightly left—which would be inland—as they approached the east bank of the river. But he's mistaken when he claims that they marched to the river without opposition. I could hear the opposition clearly enough, as could everybody else in the 3rd Battalion. McMillan does qualify his statement a little, saying "the only fly in the ointment were some Japs that 3-5 had bottled up on our side of the river." Again, he's inaccurate. We didn't bottle them up. They were very well dug in, and it's more nearly correct to say that they had *us* bottled up. The situation didn't change in any important way through the course of that day. On the following day Merritt Edson's Raider Company came in from reserve to join the fight.

McMillan goes on to say that during the first night, a comparatively small company of bottled-up Japs did nothing, while several of our amphibious vehicles ground around in the darkness to confuse them. I don't recall any of our vehicles being there at the time. What did happen was that through much of that very dark night, the Japs made very little sound—maybe firing an occasional shot or two from their Nambus to keep us alert and make us nervous.

Then, in the middle of that night—or what was more likely the very early hours of the following morning—McMillan says that those "bottled-up" Japs rushed out of their position, screaming and hollering, and running toward the beach, which was very close to where they'd been dug in. So far, so good. He goes on to say that their charge inflicted heavy casualties on our Raiders, who were positioned nearest to them. This is a mistake, because the Raiders didn't show up until after daybreak, and by that time, the battle was over. At that time, I saw Raiders crossing the Matanikau River at the sand spit where it flows out to sea. I knew several of the Raiders' NCOs either personally or by sight because that outfit had been formed back at New River when they took men from the 5th Marines' 1st Battalion. I point out McMillan's mistake here because I believe it has been picked up in good faith and perpetuated by many other military historians who reported on this battle.

But McMillan and others are correct about the Japanese charge. Attacking in pitch darkness, they burst out from where they'd been dug in. The unit they ran into wasn't the Raiders—it was us. They moved along the beach, yelling and shooting, running into our battalion's I and K Companies and through our own L Company. It was mayhem first-class, with bayoneting, screaming, shouting, and the constant crackle of small-arms fire in that black night. My outfit was right in the middle of it all, bullets flying in every direction, men running every which way, all of us scared, confused, and firing blindly half the time. Long after it was over, I talked about that awful night with Curtis "Speedy" Spach, one of my old cobber friends who was in L Company's 3rd Platoon. He told me, "I was sticking everybody who came running near me with my bayonet and just hoping for the best."

After the Japs' nighttime breakout, they moved along the riverbank toward the beach and the sand spit at the mouth of the Matanikau. Art Boston recalls that one enemy soldier stumbled and fell across his feet. The combat was that close. Both the Japanese and our guys fired in the dark whenever they thought they saw movement. We couldn't see anything, but we could hear plenty, and we could practically smell and feel the movement all around us. I remained hunkered down until first light, when I could see what I was doing and know why I should do it.

To sum the battle up, we stayed in our position, toughed it out, and held that position through the night and into the morning. The Raiders appeared shortly after daybreak, moved through our lines, crossed the Matanikau River at the sand spit, and disappeared.

As first light of day crept over the jungle floor, the after-battle scene looked like an artist's rendition of Dante's *Inferno*. There were bodies all over, ours and the Japanese, some on top of others, many of them dead, others wounded. Somehow I had survived it and remained standing. In the space of maybe twenty-five square yards around me, all was quiet except for an occasional moan or a weak cry.

"Water—"

"Help me—"

A Japanese officer lay on the ground, a bullet wound in his neck, gasping, and asking in English, "Water, please—"

One of our two doctors showed up and started working fast on a lad from either I or K Company. The kid had been slashed across the stomach with a cutlass or sword, and for most of the night, his intestines had been laying beside him in the mucky black sand. From somewhere, the doc had managed to get hold of a dirty white undershirt, which he put over the kid's chest. The doc had two corpsmen running back and forth, to and from the river, filling helmets with water, which he used to rinse the coils of the kid's guts, before placing them on top of the skivvy shirt that was on the kid's chest, and protecting them from the sand. The kid lay there in shock, chewing on a piece of wood to keep himself from screaming, as the doctor had no anesthetic. The kid just bit down hard, gnashing his teeth on the wood. I don't know whether he survived, but if he did, he didn't have his own teeth any longer.

Several weeks later, during our battle at Point Cruz, the same doctor who was now trying to save the life of the disemboweled kid was himself killed in action while working to save the life of another badly wounded warrior.

But now I looked over the battlefield and waited for word—any word—from a superior officer to tell us what to do next. You knew there were bodies piled up in the brush. Where you could, you dragged them out carefully. They weren't just bodies—they were the guys you lived with. You shared booze with these guys, shared women—and bingo! They were gone. You tried to forget it. Wipe it out. I don't know if you ever can. You subconsciously expected it to happen, expected buddies to get killed, but you couldn't go berserk over it.

Sometimes you counted noses. Or you went around and looked for someone, hoping he was wounded but still alive. "Where the hell is so and so?" you asked a buddy.

That's what my platoon assistant, Larry Hardrock Gerkin, must have been feeling when he eased up to where I was standing and told me he wanted to go over to the area where L Company's 2nd Platoon was situated. He told me he wanted to check on "the kid."

The kid in this case was Pfc. Luther L. Rhodes, a very young lad who had joined L Company directly from boot camp, just before we'd left New River, North Carolina. Back then, just about everybody in the corps got a nickname, whether they asked for one or not—and this kid, having the name Rhodes, naturally got the nickname "Dusty." When the war started, he'd probably lied about his age and claimed to be eighteen to get the marines to accept him. In those days, and with a war going on, the recruiting offices were less fussy about birth certificates than they are today. To look at Dusty Rhodes, you'd probably guess his age to be anywhere between fourteen and seventeen, though most likely not more than sixteen. He had a big shock of very light blond hair and a boyish face to go with it, and I don't think he was old enough to shave. In other words, he really *was* what Gerkin called him: a kid.

There were a few older wise guys in Rhodes's platoon who picked on him, mainly because he was so young—what they called a "chicken." But he was a spunky kid and would flare up at his antagonizers, often going at them with fists flying. We older guys (I was all of twenty-one) didn't take the situation seriously at first, but after a while the bullying started to bother us. That's when my good buddy Larry Gerkin decided enough was enough.

October 1942

One day several young blowhards had ganged up and were giving Dusty a hard time. I noticed that the kid was sobbing, but his fists were flying. Larry noticed it, too, and decided on the spot that we'd all seen and heard enough. Larry Gerkin was about five-foot-ten, not unusually tall, but he was husky, tough, and very strong. I'd once seen him pick up a six-footer and throw him through the air. Larry had small hands that made small fists, but they were hard fists that could knock you cold. Under all but the most extreme circumstances, he was a very gentle man, but rile him and you'd be facing a bulldog. When the occasion called for it, he was also as quick as a ferret. Now he jumped into the center of the brawl, and within a second or two, several of the bullies suddenly went flying without wings. Rhodes was on the ground, but Larry had one foot on his chest to hold him down and keep him out of further trouble. Gerk wasn't even breathing hard.

"I've watched you one-balled bastards pick on this kid since he came aboard," Gerk said to the guys he'd just picked up and thrown. His foot was still on the kid's chest. "You've made him into a good fighter, but I'm telling you here and now that the next son of a bitch who gives this kid a hard time is going to irritate me. And if you irritate me, I promise to bust your fucking head wide open so everybody can see the shit that's in your skull instead of brains." They knew that from then on, anybody who fucked with that kid was fucking with Gerkin. "Pass the word," he told his battered antagonists. They knew that when he said, "Don't fuck with this kid anymore," they had damn well better listen to him.

From then on, Dusty Rhodes would go to Gerkin the way a kid will usually go to his father or a big brother. Maybe he'd have a problem, and Gerk would hear him out, give him some advice, and say, "Okay, son." He always called the kid son. "You'll be all right." Gerk thought very highly of that kid.

But on this day on Guadalcanal, Gerkin and I stood in the middle of a battlefield, the battle now ended, but the blood, death, moans, dismembered bodies, and general ugliness were all around us. No sooner had Gerkin told me that he wanted to go and check on the kid, when I saw Dusty Rhodes's corporal and squad leader coming toward us. He spoke to Gerk.

"Larry, I've been looking for you."

"Oh?" Gerk said. "How's the kid?"

"That's why I came over here, Gerk," the corporal said. "I wanted you to know the kid got hit last night."

"How bad?" Gerkin asked. "Will he be okay?"

"Look, Larry," the corporal said. "It was dark, all hell was busting loose, and I don't know *what* the hell happened." He stopped talking for a second, then said, "He's dead, Larry—and I just wanted to tell you personally."

Gerkin didn't say anything. He lowered his head and kicked at the dirt a couple times. He didn't say anything at all, and I didn't say anything either. There was nothing I could tell him. The only decent thing I could do was to keep quiet and leave Gerk alone.

Finally Gerk looked up again and asked the corporal, "Where is he? Where's the kid?"

"He's over here a little way," the corporal said.

Gerkin looked at me. "I'm gonna go take a look at him, Ore."

"Okay, Larry," I said. "Go ahead.—No, wait. I'll go with you."

So we followed the corporal over to where his squad was situated, and as we got there, we saw the kid's body.

Gerkin choked up and let out a sob. There in front of us, in the midst of all the dead and wounded, two men from the 2nd Platoon were rolling Dusty onto a poncho. My thought then, and my vivid memory today, sixty years later, was how white Dusty's light blond hair looked as they wrapped him in the poncho.

Gerkin pulled himself together and went directly to the two men who were getting ready to take the kid's body away. He said to them, "Don't drop that kid while you're moving him in that poncho. Don't bump him on the ground, or I'll kick the shit out of both of you."

"Okay, Gerk," one of them said quietly. "Don't worry. We'll take good care of him."

Larry wandered off somewhere, and it was about thirty minutes before he showed up again. I never heard him mention the kid again or say anything about him. Not ever. I understood his silence perfectly. It was the only way you could keep on going and keep yourself from cracking up altogether. Death was everywhere, but to keep going, we had to push the dead out of our thoughts. And from that day on, I never heard anyone mention Dusty Rhodes's name in Larry Gerkin's presence. Today I allow myself to think of that kid, and I think also of several others I knew who didn't make it off the Canal, or off several other Pacific islands. It still hurts, thinking about them. By now they should be old men like me. Old men who have lived long, eventful lives. But they didn't make it past their boyhood. Soon after Gerkin came back from wherever he had wandered, I'd gotten word to prepare for moving the platoon out of the area.

A little earlier, before I received that order to move out, a jeep appeared, coming toward us on the Copra Cart Road from the direction of our MLR. It turned out to be General Vandegrift. It so happened that the general's driver was an old friend of mine from before the war, dating back to the time when we were stationed together at Guantánamo. I caught sight of him at the wheel, and I went over to talk with him and exchange scuttlebutt. That's how I happened to get a ringside seat for what occurred next.

It turned out that Vandegrift was trying to make contact with Col. Lewis "Chesty" Puller, whose battalion of the 7th Marine Regiment was situated well across the Matanikau. The general had a radio and radioman with him in his jeep. At the same time, one of our Higgins boats was located out on the bay, a few hundred yards from the mouth of the Matanikau and just beyond rifle range from shore. The Higgins boat also had a radio, which now served General Vandegrift as his relay. At that time, radios were few and far between on the island, and the radios we did possess didn't have much range. Using the Higgins boat's radio as relay, the general managed to make contact with Puller's unit. The message coming our way from somewhere across the river and from out of the jungle highlands between Point Cruz and Kokumbona was from Puller, who insisted that he had the Japanese on the run. I don't know; maybe he *did* have them running, but Vandegrift now wanted Puller to move back. The general had just received word that a very large Japanese task force had left Rabaul, and that it was loaded with troops and headed our way. Vandegrift wanted every marine hunkered down inside our MLR to man our beach defenses in preparation for a direct seaborne invasion. It turned out that such an attack was not part of the Japanese plan, but at that time, and from where we were situated, it remained a very likely possibility. Vandegrift was making the sensible decision to defend against such an invasion.

But from where I happened to be standing as a witness, it was clear that the general was having trouble getting his message through to Puller. Vandegrift's radioman kept repeating the general's message: "Break off from battle and head back to the MLR immediately." That order didn't get a reply, and the general had his radioman continue to repeat it: "Break off from battle and head back to the MLR immediately." Still no answer, and I could see that the general was getting pissed off. We knew well enough that Puller was getting the message, but it wasn't a message he wanted to hear. He was pretending it wasn't coming through, and the general was getting more and more impatient. After a couple more tries, Vandegrift said to his radioman, "Tell him that's a direct order."

That message *did* get a response. We all heard Puller get on the radio from his end, and I recognized Puller's voice myself: "Who's giving me this order?"

That's when the general really got pissed. There went his helmet, bouncing on the ground, the same way we'd seen him throw it on the day the B-17s dropped their bombs into the ocean instead of on the Japanese transport ship.

"Goddamn it!" Vandegrift shouted into the radio. "Lewis, this is Archer! Get back here now! *I'm* giving the goddamned order! I want to see your men down on the beach and running in this direction. Have them coming this way, and do it fast!"

Within less than fifteen minutes, we could see Puller's battalion down on the beach and moving our way, exactly as the general had ordered them to move: fast. I believe that incident cooked Puller's goose with Vandegrift and other senior officers on the Canal for the rest of the campaign. Puller redeemed himself later, but after that day, it appeared that he was not one of Vandegrift's favorite officers.

THE OCTOBER 13 ENGAGEMENT AT THE MATANIKAU

Less than a week later, on October 13, our 3rd Battalion was back in the vicinity of the Matanikau River. The Japanese transports had arrived from Rabaul, as Vandegrift had been warned, but the enemy had made their several landings well away from our MLR, at staging areas where they were preparing for new land-based assaults. With the threat of a direct Japanese assault on our beach now greatly reduced, L Company moved westward from our MLR one more time. We crossed the Matanikau, but on this occasion nearly a mile upriver, on a crude makeshift bridge known as One-Log Bridge. We'd been in the thick of a pitched battle the night before, and by this time, my platoon consisted of no more than about ten physically beaten warriors. As the unit's only currently active sergeant, and with no officer with us, once again I was effectively the platoon leader. We were tired, and most of us were sick from one or another of the things that were common on the Canal: malaria, jungle rot, bad food, practically no food—you name it.

After we'd crossed the Matanikau, we made a left turn, an inland turn, and moved up a hillside to relieve a company that was partially dug in on a ridge. From this position, we could see Point Cruz sticking out into the sea directly below us. It was late afternoon by the time we made it to the top of the hill. I don't know why, but it always seemed to happen that way. Our timing was such that relieving another unit always seemed to occur in late afternoon, which never gave us time to check our surroundings adequately or dig in better before dark set in. We dug in at our ridge positions just before dark, and that night, my platoon had an encounter with—of all things—dogs.

We'd relieved a platoon from the 7th Regiment. They were damned eager to get off that ridge. As they were pulling out, one of their riflemen told us, "Those dirty bastards had a couple of dogs sniffing around and yapping in front of our line last night. You'd better keep an ear open for them after it gets dark."

That was odd. We'd never heard anything about dogs before. We went about our business, occupying positions, tying in with the platoons on our flanks, and getting ready for one more tropical nightfall, which we knew very well would come early and fast. We settled down without delay, each of us in two-man positions, and everything fell quiet until a little after midnight.

At about that time, we heard movement coming from the bottom of the hill. It had to be the Japs. They probably were trying to be quiet, but in that undergrowth, each step sounded like an elephant doing push-ups. We heard them coming closer. Occasionally we could make out a word or two, softly spoken in Japanese. Then, for the first time, we heard a couple of soft yips and yaps and whines.

Throughout the entire Guadalcanal campaign, we never had the luxury of being able to spray the countryside with ammunition every time we heard a suspicious noise or movement. Our supplies were always critically short. Every round of ammo was valuable. Beyond the supply problem, fire discipline had been pounded into our heads through all our training. Whenever you fire a weapon at night, you immediately give away your position, which dramatically increases the odds of your next of kin getting an unwelcome telegram.

We were all dumbfounded by the yips and whines. There was no doubt it was dogs. We hadn't heard the sound of barking dogs since New Zealand. It was a familiar and friendly sound, but in the middle of a jungle combat area, it became something else—a weird experience that raised our hackles. Maybe half an hour passed, and gradually the sounds and movements came closer: footsteps in the jungle undergrowth, whispers, the whine of a dog. A quarter moon came out, which gave us just a sliver of light. It wasn't much light, but it was enough for us to make out shadowy figures moving in on us.

Now was our moment to act. We threw two hand grenades from our position, then a third. We followed up those three explosions with a brief crackle of gunfire. We each fired three or four rounds, but no more than that. Yells came from the Japanese, a few more yips and yaps from the dogs, and that was it. We signaled among ourselves, and everyone in the platoon checked in okay. No casualties. There was nothing more for us to do except wait. There were no more sounds of movement, no more whispers in Japanese, and no more sniffing or whining. Deathly quiet descended upon us for the rest of the night.

With the first faint light of daybreak, we began to make out the terrain and see each other in our positions. With daylight, we received orders to reconnoiter a short distance down the hill and try to find out what the Japs had been up to—if anything. We didn't have to go far. Immediately in front of our position, we found the bodies of about a half dozen Japanese and two small dogs that looked like a pair of beagles. They weren't more than puppies.

As soon as we got back to our positions, orders came for us to saddle up, move out, and cross back over the river. Coast watchers had reported another Japanese convoy headed toward Guadalcanal.

That was my only experience with Japanese war dogs. Maybe they weren't war dogs after all, but just some Japanese soldier's pets, brought to the Canal from another island. There were also rumors, which proved to be true, that their food situation was even worse than our own. Maybe they were serving dogs at chow time. But as I looked at those dead puppies on that ridge, now hot with the morning sun and filled with the stench of decaying bodies, the sight of those dead puppies left me feeling sad. Enemy armies were fighting and killing each other, but these were only innocent puppies.

Three marines display a captured Japanese sword. The man at far right is Ore Marion's good buddy and fellow squad leader Cpl. Raleigh Bright. ESTATE OF ORE J. MARION

With morning light and a lessening of immediate danger, my platoon's overriding need was for water. By now we didn't have a drop of water in any of our canteens, so I decided to take a few men, go down to the Matanikau, and fill our expeditionary cans with river water. We continued our practice of adding a few drops of iodine to each can. It didn't help the water's taste any, but it killed the dangerous bacteria. That's what we were told, anyway.

Quite a bit later that day, we got orders to recross the Matanikau and start moving back toward our MLR. With the rest of L Company, we retraced the route we'd come by, recrossing on One-Log Bridge. Back across the river, we moved up to the summit of another small ridge, where our company was met by the battalion's exec officer, Maj. Robert O. Bowen. I was within earshot of the conversation he started having with our new CO, Capt. John Smith, and I overheard a little of what they were talking about. I didn't like what I heard. It had something to do with barbed wire. Bowen was explaining to Smith that he wanted to set a trap for the Japanese on this side of the Matanikau. He planned to send back to the MLR for one or two rolls of barbed wire, which some of the men from our company would be detailed to string along this ridge as a tactic to waylay the advancing enemy.

At best, I was only half listening, but the little that I gathered was not good news. Which lucky platoon was going to get stuck with this harebrained detail?

"Hey, Marion, come on over here," the CO called.

Oh shit, I thought, as I went over to join them.

"Did you hear what the major was saying?"

"No, sir."

That wasn't what he wanted to hear, and he let me know it. Finally Major Bowen explained his idea a second time for my benefit. I listened, but as he went on talking, I was thinking: He believes the Japanese are going to be stupid. He thinks they'll fall for a dumb trap that won't slow them down for five seconds. I didn't say anything right away. I listened as the major continued to make his point.

"The Japs will get to the wire, and it'll slow them down. That's when your platoon holds them off. You'll fire on them and slow down their movement."

Oh sure, I thought. It was starting to get late in the day, which meant that my men would be doing this lousy job in the pitch dark. Worse yet was the fact that they'd be working in a totally unfamiliar area. But I listened and didn't argue. Instead, I waited until the major was finished, then I asked a few simple questions.

"How much longer will it be before the barbed wire arrives?"

"Well—." He hesitated. "I'm sure we'll get it up here soon."

Wonderful.

"Sir," I said, "pretty soon it's going to be dark. We'll have to work in the dark. It's impossible to string barbed wire effectively when you can't see where you're going or what you're doing." He didn't have an answer for that. "What's more, we can't string wire without stakes. Are we getting stakes with the wire?"

"Well, no. You'll have to chop some wood if you need stakes."

"Just a minute, sir. What do we use to chop wood? How do we make these stakes? We haven't got any tools." He didn't have an answer for that, either. "Here's something else," I said. "It's hard enough stringing barbed wire in broad daylight with our bare hands. Do we get gloves so we can handle the wire?"

"No, we don't have gloves. We're lucky to have the barbed wire."

Maybe *he* was lucky to have the wire. I didn't feel very lucky. I was asking questions he couldn't answer, and he was getting exasperated with me. I didn't give a damn. My questions were making sense, and his answers weren't. It was just about then that a runner came into sight and approached us. As usual, radios weren't available to us, and runners were our only way to communicate.

"Major, hold everything," the runner called as he reached us. "I've got a message for you."

The major took the message, and I watched silently while he opened it and read it. Finally he looked at me. "Okay. Disregard everything I said. Let's move. We're all going back to the perimeter right now."

I was saved. My platoon was saved. They'd have hung us out to dry, and we'd never have made it back. Instead, we now did what the major said, which was to move out right away. It grew dark while we were still moving back to our line. By the time we reached our MLR, we were moving in the dark. If it hadn't been for that runner and his message, my platoon would have been trying to string barbed wire in that same pitch blackness. We'd have been in a hopeless fix.

I'd been on the Canal for a little more than two months, and by now I'd gradually come to understand that my platoon and I were on our own. Lieutenant Flaherty, our platoon leader, and several of our NCOs were back in the field hospital. They were down with malaria, and all that remained of the platoon were me and what was left of my men. By mid-October 1942, I'd seen enough combat to know that the first thing I had to do was look after myself and my men. A few of my superior officers didn't always seem to share my attitude.

THE JAPANESE NAVY ZEROS IN ON GERKIN

Everyone who was on the Canal during the big combined Japanese air raid, land artillery, and naval bombardment in mid-October will always remember it. For two straight days, there was always a shell or a bomb falling into our narrow-boundary perimeter. It was a situation that prompted the frustrating kind of anger that comes to men who are taking punishment but can't retaliate.

The Japanese were getting ready for another big attack on the marine perimeter, but the news story that my folks back home read in the *Buffalo Evening News* on October 10 "accentuated the positive," as one popular song from the 1940s put it. You had to read past the headlines to realize that the going was tough for us guys in the foxholes.

JAP WARSHIP SUNK, 2 HIT IN SOLOMONS
U.S. WARPLANES
BLAST CRUISER,
TWO DESTROYERS

. . . The enemy succeeded in reinforcing his troops on Guadalcanal, site of the American airbase in the Solomons, despite the resistance from Navy and Marine Corps Air Forces.
(copyright 1942, the *Buffalo Evening News*)

After the Guadalcanal campaign was over, each of us would tell his own story of weird things that had happened to him or his buddies during those seemingly endless hours of bombardment. The yarns range from bouts of dysentery between shell and bomb bursts to fighting the gray rats that didn't like what was happening above ground any more than we did and insisted on trying to share our spider holes with us. We hated those gray critters nearly as much as we hated the Japs who were trying to kill us.

If anything strange was going to occur in L-3-5's 1st Platoon, it was probably going to happen to Larry Hardrock Gerkin, BAR man extraordinary. Gerkin was not a "foul-up" or a "cork-off." On the contrary, he was one marine who was on the ball, conscientious, always ready to help a buddy, and honest as the day is long. And even though he had the strength to throw a six-foot man six feet across the ground, his nature was gentle, kind, and caring. Hardrock didn't have an enemy in the world that I ever heard of, but that didn't prevent crazy things from happening to him on a regular basis. Such occurrences would leave him shaking his head and saying the nearest thing to a curse word that was part of his regular vocabulary: "Jeeezz!"

On the first night of that huge Japanese naval bombardment, our 1st Platoon was one of two platoons of L Company that was pulled away from positions outside the perimeter and moved to beach defense along the berm line. The new Fighter Strip Number Two was located behind us.

We'd been bombed from the air and shelled by field artillery throughout the day, and as it began to grow dark, we looked out to sea and saw the Japanese fleet moving in. Now it was their turn to try to finish us off. Their destroyers moved close in, formed a line, and started a barrage that has been written about many times and by many marines who survived that awful night. It might seem odd to anybody who has never been in combat, but shelling, bombing, and high-angle fire in general don't shake up experienced riflemen too badly—*if* they've had time to dig in properly. And we were well dug in. We were shaken, rattled, and rolled, and it's possible that a marine hasn't really lived until he experiences those big shells coming through, zipping close overhead or skidding along the ground and sounding like runaway boxcars. For all the fireworks that took place on that long night, L Company suffered no serious casualties.

With the morning's first light, I climbed out of my spider hole and took a look around, just to make sure the world was still there, still round, and still in orbit. The area was a complete mess. Very few guys were up and around yet. One or two cobbers poked their heads up out of their holes like ground squirrels. I could see the glazed look in their eyes—punch-drunk and sleepy. Dud shells littered the area. The Japanese Navy had been shooting at us with high-explosive and armor-piercing rounds that hadn't hit anything solid enough to set them off. So there they lay among our spider holes, as though daring us to bang one of them on its nose and fly directly off to hell in the explosion that would follow. Being out of my spider hole, I was one of the first to notice two unfamiliar marines walking through our area and looking at the duds. The visitors turned out to be our ordnance people.

I decided that I'd better check heads and count butts, just to make sure that all my men were still among the living. "Poke your heads up and let me see your beautiful, eager pusses!" I shouted.

One by one, heads began popping up. Everyone was accounted for—except for one man: Pfc. Larry Hardrock

Gerkin. I looked around, trying to recall the exact location of Gerk's spider hole, and as my eyes found the spot where I expected him to be, the truth hit me. *"Holy Kee-rist!"* I yelled.

A huge Japanese naval shell was plugging the top of Larry Gerkin's hole! I ran straight to the spider hole, and a couple of the guys came with me.

"Gerk! Are you okay? Can you hear me down there?"

His voice came back, muffled but clear enough: "Stop asking questions and get this goddamn thing off me!" This had to be really serious—Gerk was actually cursing. And for good reason. The damned shell had plowed a twenty-foot-long furrow along the ground and stopped directly above Hardrock's head.

The two ordnance men were close by. I gave out a yell, and they came running toward us. It turned out to be a simple matter for them to lash a line around the shell. Carefully we helped them pull, and pretty soon the top of Gerkin's spider hole came into view. Next came Gerkin's head. Almost casually, he emerged from his hole.

"Jeez," he said. "I was starting to get a little nervous down there. What took you guys so long?"

I noticed one of his hands. "Gerk, what happened to your hand?"

It turned out that during the night, when the earth shook extra hard and the dark sky over Gerkin's spider hole deepened to pitch blackness, he had reached up with his left hand to try to feel what had happened up there. What was worse, his hole suddenly grew hot as hell. He put the palm of his left hand on that heat-radiating projectile, burned himself, then sat down at the bottom of his hole, where he waited out the night and hoped nothing would hit that monster that had just become his roof.

If what happened to Hardrock Gerkin back then happened to a military man of today, our modern warrior would receive at least one Purple Heart medal, a couple weeks of R&R, a promotion of at least two stripes, and maybe even a court-martial for impersonating an officer. But on the Canal back in 1942, a corpsman spread a little greasy salve on Gerk's burn and covered it with a skimpy piece of gauze. An hour later, our platoon headed back out to the jungle side of our perimeter, and the only thing that Hardrock got was his butt chewed out because his BAR was full of sand.

THE MYSTERY PLANE
By mid-October, the Guadalcanal campaign was finally being recognized by the press reporting to the homefront as a major engagement. Battle reports from the Canal were making the papers on a daily basis.

> **JAPS ARE EXPECTED
> BY LAND AND SEA**
> **Washington, Oct. 12 (UP)**—Japan appeared
> to be preparing a pincers offensive today
> in an attempt to isolate and then crush the U.S.
> Marine garrison defending their strategic
> base on Guadalcanal Island . . .
> (copyright 1942, the *Buffalo Evening News*)

That story was accurate. The Japanese were preparing for what turned out to be their final major assault on Henderson Field.

One miserable October day in the middle of the Guadalcanal campaign, I saw a mystery airplane. Before anybody starts thinking I was hallucinating after too many run-ins with the enemy, I'd better add that plenty of others saw that mystery plane, too. One thing about it was not at all mysterious: It had a shiny red meatball on each wing, which made it not only a mystery plane, but an unfriendly mystery.

At that point in the campaign, Company L-3-5 was taking a lot of shit from every direction on the compass. I was a buck sergeant in one of two platoons that had been moved up to ridge positions, just off the main perimeter. By this time, even the dumbest marine on the island had figured out that Henderson Field was what the entire Guadalcanal campaign was all about. I don't guess we knew yet what we were supposed to be doing there, except that we couldn't get off the damned island. While the Japanese Army continued giving us a rough time on the ground, Japanese airplanes and ships at sea were attacking the airfield—and us—regularly, and in large numbers. Luckily, marine fighter pilots manning Grumman Wildcats were downing Japanese planes in large numbers, with much-needed help from our land-based antiaircraft gunners.

The night before the mystery-plane incident was a typical bad night for us. Before the moon came up, we were shelled from the sea. Then Washing Machine Charlie, the two-engine Jap bomber with engines that sounded like an old washing machine motor, came over and paid his nightly visit. He'd rumble overhead and drop a couple bombs into our area, hoping for a lucky hit. Sometimes the bastard got one, though that night, all he did was make us duck into our spider holes and pray, while a couple of thuds shook the ground. After Charlie went away, Pistol Pete or his Japanese kid brother sent in a few rounds, just to keep us troops honest and on our toes. Pistol Pete was our nickname for a Japanese land artillery piece that shelled us with regularity.

At the crack of dawn, we looked out to sea from our high point on the ridge. Off to the west toward Point Cruz, we could make out a couple of good-size Japanese ships that were feverishly unloading troops. There wasn't a damn thing we could do about it, so we ignored it—as though nothing were happening out there. By that time on the Canal, you had to be good at ignoring the unpleasant things you couldn't do anything about. If you didn't ignore them, you'd soon be looking around the bend for the streetcar that was going to come and take you home. For us snuffies, staying alive had become the point of every battle, more so because we knew we had been abandoned.

For the time being, all was quiet on our ridge, which gave us a few minutes to tell each other that we wished we were back stateside. If that was asking too much, then we wished we could at least get a cup of good hot coffee. That was asking for too much, too. Our talk was interrupted when six Zeros appeared from out of nowhere. They were coming in our direction. Like most high points on the Canal's terrain, the covering growth on our ridge was too sparse to give us hiding places. That left us visible and in constant danger from the air. The Zeros were going to take advantage of that situation right now. They'd spotted us and were zooming in directly at us.

We moved fast to save our lives, scrambling to the opposite side of the ridge from where the Zeros were approaching. They strafed, but by the time their bullets came whistling in, we'd taken cover on the ridge's safe side. They roared overhead in a flash and kept going into the distance behind us. We turned our heads and watched them, hoping they'd disappear forever. Not a chance. Our position on the ridge was too tempting. They wheeled around and came at us again, which forced us to hurry back over to the ridge's opposite side, then hug the dirt while more of their machine-gun bullets peppered the ridge.

They put us through that ordeal three more times. We didn't take any casualties, but all the time we were running from one side of the ridge to the other, we were scared and were bitching, cursing, shouting at each other, and yelling at the sky: "Why the hell are you picking on *us*? Go down to Kukum and strafe some shore party guys! Go strafe the airport, like you sons of bitches usually do! For Christ's sake, give us a break!"

Not that they heard us, or gave a damn, but the Zeros finally gave up and disappeared. Safe for the moment, we looked down at the fighter airstrip and saw one of our own planes taking off. The first thing I thought was, "You're a little late, goddamn it!"

One of the other guys said out loud what I was thinking. "Where the hell were you when the goddamn Zeros were coming at us?" he yelled.

But even if our pilot could have heard us, he had something different in mind. We watched him scooting no higher than treetop level, and then heading out to sea, toward those Jap ships that were still being unloaded. Our pilot flew his plane straight over one of the ships, and then dropped a single bomb directly down and into its hold. *Boom!* That, anyhow, made a few less enemy troops that we'd have to deal with.

While we watched, he turned his plane around on a dime and headed back toward the airfield. He'd made it about halfway home when those six Zeros decided to come back, but this time they were leaving us alone. They had spotted our plane and were heading straight for it. It began to look as though every one of those Zeros was fighting each other, trying to get the first crack at our plane. Our pilot was flying low, in a vulnerable position, and badly outnumbered. He did the only thing he *could* do: He began taking evasive action, and we lost sight of him as he maneuvered still lower, flying and banking among Guadalcanal's tall palm trees. All he could hope to do was get back to the airstrip and put the plane on the ground without getting himself killed.

We learned later that he made it. I heard that he was out of the plane even before it came to a complete stop, and that he ran like hell while the Zeros dove in on him, strafing the ground around him and pockmarking his plane with holes. But by the time he was on the field, we had something entirely different to grab our attention: the mystery plane.

One of our guys let out a yell. I looked his way and saw him pointing toward an approaching, low-flying airplane of a type we hadn't seen before. It was coming toward us from over the Matanikau–Point Cruz area, which meant that it had to be a Jap, probably flying in from Rabaul. As it got closer, I made out its details: It was a slow-flying, twin-engine, noncombat plane with a big, shiny red meatball on each wing—and its winner of a pilot was now bringing it in at treetop level with its wheels down, showing every sign that he was coming in for a landing. *Landing on our airfield!*

"What's that crazy bastard doing?" one of our guys yelled.
"Holy shit! He's coming in for a *landing!*"

By now we were all heads-up, wide-eyed, and watching. Not one of us could believe what our eyes were showing us. Weeks in combat had made a few of the guys so blasé that they hadn't even bothered watching when our pilot damn near wrapped himself around jungle coconut palms to evade the Zeros. But now even those nonchalant warriors were watching the mysterious Japanese plane, their mouths wide open like the rest of us. It was one more example of an old combat soldier's saying: "If something weird hasn't happened yet, just wait a minute and it will."

Soon the mystery plane was broadside to us, and we could see four windows on our side of its fuselage, with faces looking out through those windows—at *us*. Those faces belonged to Japanese officers wearing white uniforms, and the fact that we could make out that much detail tells you how close the plane was to our ridge. It couldn't have been much more than seventy-five feet from our position, floating in at about the same elevation as our ridgetop.

No one gave a signal or said a word, but nobody had to. The meatballs decorating that plane said it all for us. Every one of us started firing, using every weapon we had—Springfield '03s, BARs, tommy guns, machine guns, even .45 automatics. For maybe ten or fifteen seconds, we fired and kept on firing with everything we had. I got off only about three shots, and I don't know if any of mine hit the plane, but it was so close that they might have. From positions below the ridge and from several different directions, other marines were also firing on that misguided champion of a pilot. The plane was flying so low and so slow that we couldn't have missed it with a rock. At least a hundred tracers along with rounds from all kinds of weapons went through that fuselage.

The plane took a sudden, sharp dip below ridge level and sank into the treetops, out of sight and into jungle growth. The next thing we saw was the explosion, and some of the thousand flying pieces that recently had been the mystery plane. My guess is that somebody back at their headquarters had given these Japanese a bum scoop, leading them to believe that the airfield was captured and they could land safely. It had to be something like that, because this clearly wasn't a combat plane, and it wasn't a reconnaissance plane, either. We could plainly see that it was a slow, two-engine passenger plane filled with officers in their white uniforms.

Before an hour had passed, all excitement and talk about the mysterious Japanese airplane was ended. We had more immediate things to worry about, which included staying alive. We spent several more days patrolling from that ridge, or gathering and reporting information when our position from that high vantage point enabled us to spot enemy activity. Then we were sent down to a new position in the coconut groves, where we prepared for a new offensive operation that would send us back to the Matanikau River.

The airplane incident was just something odd that had happened. Then we went back to coping with more basic things: staying alive, getting enough food and water to keep going, getting ammunition so we could keep fighting. But to my knowledge, mystery has always surrounded that incident, and sixty years later, I still wonder about it.

I've compared notes with a few other marines, but we never came up with anything more than speculation. Marines from companies other than L-3-5 helped shoot the plane down, and some of them might have examined the wreckage, or maybe they saw something that day that we didn't see. Whatever the real story turns out to be, two platoons from Company L-3-5 once helped shoot down an enemy plane. That isn't a claim many infantrymen can make.

It had been way back in early August when the U.S. Navy's defeat at the battle of Savo Island sent Admiral Ghormley scurrying for safety, pulling our fleet out of the area and leaving us marines stranded. But it wasn't until the middle of October, when the tide of battle was clearly turning in our favor, that the

Savo Island engagement and its losses were made known to the folks back home.

> **Marines Enlarge Hold on Guadalcanal;
> 2 Jap Cruisers Hit, 15 Planes Downed
> OCT. 9–11 BATTLE
> COSTS U.S. ONLY
> PAIR OF AIRCRAFT**
>
> **Announcement of New Victory
> Follows Disclosure That We
> Lost Three Heavy Cruisers
> in Clash Aug. 8, 9**
>
> (copyright 1942, the *Buffalo Evening News*)

It should go without saying that the good news in these headlines was vastly exaggerated and American losses minimized. Anyway, the U.S. Navy had finally gotten around to admitting a defeat.

TANKS AT THE MATANIKAU

I don't know anybody in our unit who was keeping track of dates, but the history books say it was at about dusk on October 23 when the Japanese sent ten light tanks across the narrow mouth of the Matanikau River. We couldn't know it at the time, but it turned out to be a part of the last effective Japanese thrust toward Henderson Field. The first tank was knocked out as it tried to cross the sand spit at the shore, and then the tanks behind it were destroyed one by one. My platoon was a short way upriver during that shoot-out. Ernie Snowden saw them.

> We weren't far up from the river's mouth when the Jap tanks tried to cross. I remember our half-track dug in on our side of the river, dug in like it was on a ramp, with just the barrel of its seventy-five-millimeter gun sticking out above ground. That was the time when Lt.

> Thomas O'Neal and I were pinned down by Jap machine-gun fire. It was cutting the weeds right over our heads. I told the lieutenant that when the Jap fire let up, I was getting out of there. He said no, but I waited for my chance and got out of there anyway. I made it behind a big tree, where it was safer, and that's where I found the rest of the men in my squad.

Curtis Speedy Spach was in L Company's 3rd Platoon and even closer to the tank action during that battle.

> I didn't know the Japs had any tanks with them, because up to then I hadn't seen one. But the damn tanks were there that evening. I heard something roaring, and I thought it was low-flying Jap planes. Then here came those Jap tanks, right at us. Our half-track was dug in, and its gun knocked the tanks out. When the Japanese opened the tanks' hatches to crawl out, we cleaned them up.
>
> Sergeant Anderson and his crew from our 5th Regiment's thirty-seven-millimeter guns had one of his guns dug in on the Matanikau line. That gun plus the half-track, which had a seventy-five-millimeter gun, combined to knock out most of the tanks before they could start to cross the river and reach our positions. I believe only one Japanese tank made it as far as the sandbar, which was partway across the river. At that time, it came under heavy small-arms fire from several of our units. Then a marine from a neighboring unit disabled that lead tank by jamming a tree limb into one of its tracks. The tanks behind it were stranded, and their crews were all killed.
>
> A week or two later, we returned for what turned out to be one final time to that sand spit at the mouth of the Matanikau. We were on our way to what would become the Point Cruz battle. The disabled tanks were still there at the sand spit. My thoughts, as I saw those tanks for a second time, were: "Why didn't one of our units blow the damned things up and get

them the hell out of there?" Each one of those tanks would have been an ideal hiding place for a sniper, had the Japs thought to take advantage of them. It was the same kind of question I'd asked myself about that big copra hut we'd encountered on Beach Red when we'd first landed on the Canal three months earlier. That had been another ideal place for snipers. Why hadn't our naval artillery knocked that hut flat before we landed on the beach? We'd been lucky on D-Day, and we would be lucky a second time in early November, when we crossed the Matanikau on our way to Point Cruz. But you'd like to hope that somebody in command might be thinking of the ordinary gravel cruncher's welfare, rather than just relying on luck.

CHAPTER 6

November and Early December 1942

POINT CRUZ

The last time I saw the little village of Matanikau would be just about the last time anyone in the world would ever see it, because it isn't there anymore. Point Cruz, a neighboring piece of rocky land, still juts into the ocean, but the spot where a tiny cluster of native huts was once the village of Matanikau is now part of Honiara, a city with a population of somewhere around forty-four thousand. Today Honiara serves as the Solomon Islands' government capital.

The entire region around the Matanikau River had been the scene of several battles, and it had become known as one of the bloodiest combat zones of the Guadalcanal campaign. Because L Company was the farthest west unit positioned on the marines' defense line, our squads had to take regular turns patrolling the abandoned cluster of huts where the village once stood. We called it a village, but Matanikau wasn't more than eight or a dozen native huts, each with a thatched roof and walls of palm fronds and palm branches woven together. The sides of each hut were open to the air, and the huts were clustered together no more than an easy stone's throw apart. This cluster of huts sat on the landward side of a little dirt road no wider than a good-size kitchen table. Beyond the huts was nothing: just thick jungle growth covering rising terrain.

By the time we first entered the village, the natives had abandoned it and were living up in the hills, away from the combat zone. We'd seen a few of the natives' bodies that first time, but historians who wrote about piles of bodies at Matanikau got it wrong. The village is right down at sea level where the natives could fish for subsistence. It's hot and damp. A body lying on the ground there first bloats up, and then bursts out of its clothes within twenty-four hours. Give it another forty-eight hours, and there's very little left. Bodies usually don't pile up in a tropical environment.

It wasn't long before we torched those huts so we'd never have to concern ourselves with the enemy hiding in them and waiting for us in ambush. So by November, between the trucks, the tanks, and the artillery fire that had crunched over the area, there was no longer a village of Matanikau, and there never would be again. It had been pulverized.

Today, from the very spot we were standing that November, you can book an excursion cruise, including some scuba diving, out to what Honiara's website describes as some "important WWII sites." Honiara brags about its nice cafés, restaurants, and bars, and even sports the three-star Iron Bottom Sound Hotel, where you can get a room for under seventy-five bucks a night. Old ex-marines like me think back to that desolate spot of nothing that soaked up our buddies' blood, and we can only say, *"Can you believe that one??"*

Some guys went back later as tourists. But I never wanted to go back. I didn't leave anything on that island worth going back for except my youth—and one helluva lot of my good friends. And I can't recover either of them.

Well, nobody was thinking about tourism during the first week of November '42. As a marine in L Company's 3rd Battalion, 5th Regiment, I played a small part in what the official history books now call the Matanikau–Point Cruz engagement. I recall crossing the makeshift pontoon bridge that had just been rigged across the Matanikau River by the 1st Engineers Battalion. That crossing was at the sand spit, where the river empties into the bay, the same spot where several Japanese light tanks had been put out of action and destroyed on our previous visit. We crossed the river within yards of those burnt-out, abandoned tanks. We were lucky one more time: there weren't any snipers hiding in those tanks. Across the river, we passed the wreckage of Matanikau village. My depleted platoon moved forward along the beach against a background crackle of steady small-arms fire and the thuds of explosions coming from several different directions.

By now I was an ancient warrior, a buck sergeant in L Company, and because at the moment I was the 1st Platoon's senior man present, I was also platoon leader by default. Following me were eleven seasoned marines; I'd estimate their average age to be an elderly nineteen. Even readers who don't know much about how combat units are organized might be puzzled by the fact that our platoon had only eleven men, but the simple fact is that we had lost most of our regulars. Casualties from illness, wounds, and KIAs had whittled us down. I was one of the few NCOs in my unit who hadn't been knocked down by malaria. My luck ran out a few weeks after we were taken off the Canal and were supposedly safe. I caught malaria in Camp Cable, informally known as Camp Swampy, outside the handsome city of Brisbane, on Australia's east coast. As several of my old cobbers often remark to this day, there were more and bigger mosquitoes at Camp Cable than the ones we had to fight on the Canal.

But now we were moving toward Point Cruz, with gunfire and explosions all around us. The worst of it came from a short distance straight ahead, where the Japanese were retreating, but not without putting up a fierce struggle. At the start of the Point Cruz operation, L Company had been placed in a reserve position, right behind the attacking units, which in our sector were the 3rd Battalion's I and K Companies, plus the machine guns of M Company. These and other units had already engaged the Japs in the flattened remains of Matanikau village, driving them out of there. Until late October, the Matanikau–Point Cruz area had been a major point for the Japanese to unload men, supplies, and equipment as they prepared for their unsuccessful try at taking Henderson Field back from us. But at this stage in the campaign, the Japs' only movement was backward.

The fighting moved forward along the coast on this early November day, my platoon advancing directly behind the worst of it. My band of eleven men would plug the line in one area, reinforce it in another, and then join with other units to take part in an assault at still another point. At one spot, the Japs had two antiaircraft guns that they had lowered until their barrels were horizontal. This enabled them to fire on a flat trajectory, the shells coming straight at us at a height of about four feet off the ground. It was diabolical—and lethal. I saw what was left of one of our guys who'd caught a round in the chest from one of those guns.

As we moved in on Point Cruz, I saw one of our battalion corpsmen, accompanied by our doctor who had tried to save the life of the disemboweled marine on the morning following our early October battle at the Matanikau River. They were hurrying past us in the direction of Point Cruz to attend another seriously wounded man. Just a few minutes later, the corpsman met us again on his way back. This time he was alone. Not stopping, he breathlessly told us that the doctor had been killed before he could reach the wounded marine. It couldn't have been more than a few minutes later when a very young warrior, really just a kid, came staggering and running past us from the same direction, holding his bloody left eyeball in his hand.

We'd gone another few dozen yards forward when the battalion exec officer approached me. "Have your men fix bayonets and prepare to charge. I want your platoon to swing to the right and help I Company run those Japs into the bay." A swing to the right would put us directly on Point Cruz. "Fix bayonets" is just about the most blood-chilling order that a combat infantryman ever gets. It took us kids forever to engage the bayonet-retaining lugs on the muzzles of our rifles. Our hands were shaky and jerking, because we were trying to hold our nerves together. Then the order *"Do it!"* came down, and our world became total mayhem: shouts, screams, and small-arms fire.

At this point in movies and novels, you get detailed accounts of heroics, but my guess is that the guys writing the stories and directing the films have never been anywhere near

November and Early December 1942

hand-to-hand battle. I'm talking about combat filled with screams, blood, bullets, violence, and death. I'm talking about the sounds, the taste, and the stink of death. I was there, and like most others who have undergone that experience on hundreds of different battlefields, I didn't remember a hell of a lot when it was over. For the most part, I still don't recall very much. And I give thanks to the "Man up topside" for blanking out my memory of events that are too horrible for any sane man to *want* to remember.

What I do recall is that after a while—don't ask me how long—the worst was over, and I was still among the living. My platoon, or what was left of it, had joined I Company. By that time, we were at the tip of Point Cruz, which was nothing more than jungle scrub brush and rocks that jutted into the bay.

At Point Cruz, Sergeant Diedrick from Company I-3-5 and some of his men were at the shoreline, firing their rifles at random into the water. All I could see was small, dark-looking objects bobbing on the ocean's surface. Diedrick stopped firing and looked my way when I approached.

"What the hell are you shooting at?" I asked him.

"The bastards are trying to swim back to Japan," he said.

Those dark, bobbing objects were the heads of Japanese soldiers, swimming away from Point Cruz to save their lives. I assume their intention was to swim back to shore somewhere to our west, where they might be able to find relative safety. The guys from my unit joined in, firing at the Japanese in the water. I don't know if any of them made it back to shore, but it's safe to say that none of them made it back to Tokyo. Anyway, we did what the exec officer had told us to do. We ran the Japanese into the bay.

That wasn't the end of the day for my platoon. Nobody below regiment level had radios, so on this occasion, official communication came from a runner. He told me that orders were to take my platoon to the rear, moving back across the Matanikau. We were being relieved. I got my men together, and we moved back. A fresh unit—from the 2nd Regiment, I think—became our replacement as the assault's main thrust now moved west and beyond Point Cruz, pushing the Japanese back in the direction of Kokumbona.

On our way to the rear, we had to cross a small creek with muddy banks that dropped two to four feet down to the water's edge. I was first to step down into the water, and I signaled my platoon to follow. The man directly behind me had been assigned to my platoon from another unit, which is why I can't recall his full name today. He was a kid from New Jersey with a genuine "Joisey" accent, and we'd nicknamed him "Greek." He was carrying our light machine gun. He took a step off the steep bank and planted one foot down into the mud. Then he slipped, lost his balance, and fell on his ass with a *splat*. As he fell, the machine gun flew out of his hands, also into the mud. He sat in several inches of thick mud, looking completely helpless. It could have happened to anybody—me included—but I had to keep the platoon moving, so I let him have it.

"Get up!" I shouted. "And get that machine gun out of that mud or I'll wrap my rifle around your thick skull!"

He looked up at me and groaned, then said something I didn't catch. Maybe I wasn't intended to catch it. I yelled some more, and he still didn't get up out of the mud, but this time he yelled back. We were busy exchanging pleasantries, and none of us noticed that just beyond the creek, off to our left and nearly hidden from us behind tropical growth, a jeep had parked just off the side of the Copra Cart Road. Somebody near the jeep moved, which caught my attention. I looked up. Standing beside the jeep and watching us was a man every marine on the Canal recognized: Gen. Alexander A. Vandegrift. Another tall, thin, high-ranking officer stood next to the general, but I didn't recognize him. A third man wearing U.S. Navy insignia sat in the jeep. They were all looking down at the creek bank, their interest caught by our accident.

I was naturally astonished, and my reaction was automatic: "Hi-ya, A. A.!" I called. "Hi-ya, General Vandegrift!"

But I still had to deal with Greek and his machine gun in the mud, so I turned back to him. He sat unmoving in the slime, and he looked sad. My motor-mouth started operating in top form, and by now Greek had reached the limit of his endurance. He started yelling back. We yelled at each other for about a minute, spicing our conversation with church-service language. The rest of the platoon started joining in, then we all shut up when the tall officer standing next to General Vandegrift stepped forward, made his way down to the creek bank, took hold of our fallen warrior's arms, and lifted him out of the muck. Then he reached into the wet mud, picked up the light machine gun, and gave it to poor Greek. By now I saw the officer's insignia. This man, too, was a general.

He took one long, mournful look at our mud-caked warrior, then looked back at General Vandegrift. "Good Lord. This man is so exhausted, he can hardly stand."

General Vandegrift nodded. "My men have been through hell, General Patch."

Holy Christ! General Vandegrift and General Patch! Maj. Gen. Alexander Patch—as every World War II history book will tell you—was commander of the army's Americal Division, the unit that relieved us marines and mopped up all remaining Japanese resistance on Guadalcanal after we evacuated. But at that moment, I simply said the first thing that came into my dumb head.

"Say thank you to the gentleman," I instructed my mud-laden warrior.

"That's it! Just what I need to hear!" Greek yelled back at me. "A guy with clean clothes lifts me out of the goddamn mud and tells me I look tired. Then a no-good sergeant tells me to say *thank you*!" He looked straight at me as he yelled, and I felt sorry for him, but I couldn't show it. "This no-good sergeant's done his best to get me killed the past few days. And now I gotta say thank you to a guy in *clean clothes*! Look at *my* goddamn clothes!"

Greek had a wonderful Jersey accent. He was yelling louder than the sounds of the occasional small-arms rounds that were still zinging and crackling not all that far away. I let him yell. Get it out of his system. The top brass let him yell, too. Somebody told me later that the navy man in the jeep was Admiral Halsey.

Finally we made it back to an assembly area, and a runner pointed out a location where I could have my men fall out and catch our breath. Our rest area put us on safer ground than we'd occupied for many hours past, but small-arms fire continued to crackle around us. The safest place for any of us to be was close to the ground. "Your company's other platoons will be here shortly," the runner told me. He was right about that detail. Moments later, I caught sight of my old buddy Sgt. Walter Sincek leading his platoon back toward our area. Walter was a well-built six-footer, a guy you didn't want to cross, a fighting fool. He had been in the marines for four years before World War II, had come back after Pearl Harbor as a corporal, and by the time we were on the Canal, he was a sergeant.

Nearly all of us had nicknames, many of them chosen to use during a firefight. Many of them included sounds that the Japanese had trouble imitating. Walter's happened to be "Chum." Don't ask why. Somehow the name Chum had been given to him, and it had stuck. Walter had a big, deep, resonant voice and a slow way of talking that always broke me up—even on a terrifying day like the one we were having now. As his platoon moved into the rest area, Walter turned and faced his men.

"All right, fall in, men," he commanded in his deep voice. He almost sang his words in a monotone with a throatiness you hear in western Pennsylvania, around Pittsburgh. He was expecting his men to assemble in ranks before giving them permission to fall out and rest. Nobody moved. "My command was fall in, men," Walter intoned. "Doesn't anybody here understand English?"

Bullets continued to fly in our vicinity. Corporal Morris, one of his squad leaders, piped in.

"Sergeant? You know, it's pretty dangerous falling in here."

"Corporal Morris, you heard my command." So there they stood in platoon formation until Walter got his "present-or-accounted-for" report.

"Okay. Fall out, men," Walter said in his bass voice. "But remain in the immediate vicinity."

"Okay, Chum," somebody in his platoon replied.

"Do not call me Chum," Walter intoned. "We cannot be chums now. We're no longer on the line, and my name is Platoon Sergeant Sincek."

"Yes, sergeant!"

I was lying on the ground watching the charade, and by now I was breaking up with laughter. At one moment we'd be scared shitless, and the next moment we'd be laughing. I knew Walter too well to take him seriously. His men fell out, and he came over and sat down next to me. "Goddamn. I don't know how much more of this I can take, Ore," he rumbled in his deep voice.

"Walter," I said, "I've had it up to here myself."

We'd all had more than we needed or wanted. But we were still alive, and though we didn't realize it, the worst was nearly over for us.

THE USS *ATLANTA*

Back in late October, our operation planners had decided to set up a delay defense position at the south end of the MLR. L Company was elected. We were moved to a ridge about a hundred yards forward of our MLR in the direction of Mount Austen. This wasn't an extension of the MLR; it was a forward outpost leaving roughly a seventy-five-yard gap in the MLR, and placing three undermanned platoons alone on this new ridge. The purpose seems to have been to surprise, disrupt, or delay any assault that the enemy might attempt from the Matanikau direction. In other words, in the event of an attack, L Company was supposed to give them hell, and then be hung out to dry. Before going out there, we'd been told that we were to dig in and hold our position to the last man. The question nobody ever answered for us was, Then what? Who the hell does the last man report to?

This was a hush-hush move, and we found that out the hard way. As we had dug in at our new positions, one of our own planes flew overhead, took a good look, moved away, decided we must be Japs, then came back and dropped a bomb on us. Luckily it missed. The Japanese found out about us anyhow. It didn't take them more than a day to discover what we were doing, because their daily flight of Zeros would zoom in and strafe us. We dug in and fortified our positions, took turns making patrols in every direction, and settled down to a monotonous routine, the high point of which consisted of our two tablespoons of Japanese rice seasoned with maggots, served twice a day, day after day. If we wanted water, we went back behind our lines and got it for ourselves.

No American ships or airplanes came in, and we were positioned on high ground that gave us a good view of sea, sky, and any airplane soon before it landed or just after it took off from our airfield. The only friendly planes we ever saw were two or maybe three patched-together F4F Wildcats that at any one time were able to take off and have a go against the Jap bombers and fighters that visited the Canal regularly. This routine went on for quite a while.

We were back on our outpost one night in mid-November. I was temporarily top man in L Company's 1st Platoon, with both the platoon sergeant and Lieutenant Flaherty still in the field hospital with malaria. Checking back into the pages of official battle histories, it turns out that the night I'm talking about was Friday, November 13. But I'm sure none of us knew the date at the time, or even that it was a Friday. Nor did we know we had purchased ringside seats—the best seats in the house—for one of the Guadalcanal campaign's biggest and deadliest sea battles.

There were two platoons—maybe thirty of us holding our positions—sitting out in the open in total darkness on the coral ridge within easy daytime view of the bay that spread out before us. Our line of sight took us over the top of a grove of tall coconut trees that separated us from the beach roughly two hundred yards away. But it was night, and all we saw was black. We knew the Japanese came right in with their ships at night. You could smell them, smell the different food aromas from the ships. And you could feel the heat and smell the fuel up on the ridge. The Japs would come in after dark, but they wouldn't fight. There usually wasn't anything out there to fight. But it was different on this night.

By now we knew the Japs were out there again, and we were just sitting around on the ground out in the open. We had no reason to be afraid. It was good and dark. Then, maybe about ten o'clock, all of a sudden, the Jap spotlights burst on and *biff, bam, bam,* in quick succession, they started blasting away at some target at sea. An echo from a blast of a big cannon rolled up the ridge. "Damn. Catch a load of that one," someone said. And then our navy started in. We didn't know any of our navy's ships were out there, or even that they were anywhere near the Canal. What we did know was that the Japs weren't shooting at nothing. We knew they weren't shooting at us. And we knew somebody—it had to be our guys—was giving it right back to them.

In a typical night battle, our navy would wait for the enemy to "cross the T," whatever the hell that means, but the Japanese would throw on these big spotlights. And then they'd both start blasting away. Between the flashes and the booms lighting up the pitch blackness of the night sky, it was like an old-fashioned knock-down-drag-out street fight. What a show, with a flash breaking the darkness and just briefly lighting up shadows in the bay. Then a quick blaze of fire and another flash from the other side. And another boom. Then a flash over there to the left. Then the echo of a bang, like the end of the fireworks display on the Fourth of July. As we watched the flashes and ricochets light up the night, and heard the artillery booms and bangs between the flashes of light, someone said, "Goddamn, we're kicking the crap out of those Shambos." Shambo was one of the less polite names our guys called the Japanese. From our vantage point, we didn't know who was doing what. The marine who made that comment was being optimistic. "Yeah," someone else said, "I *hope* we are."

On that night, we had a field phone hookup with our company command post, located back at the MLR. Somebody from

CP got on the line and gave us the scoop that our cruiser task force was kicking hell out of the Japanese Navy. But the truth is that everybody on shore was guessing—and hoping.

In fact, both the American and Japanese Navies suffered heavy losses during that night's battle. Though tactically it was a stalemate, strategically it was an American victory, because it prevented the landing of a large Japanese ground force on the island.

All the time, the flashes and booms continued to crack the darkness. But as hard as you strained your senses, you couldn't see what was taking place right before your eyes. You might see the reflection of water, or the shadows of steel forms in the dark right after a sharp blast, but you couldn't put details on the shadows. I'd estimate the battle raged for thirty to forty-five minutes that night, first close in to the beach and then farther out. Even when the spotlights came on, you couldn't see much. The firing would start. Everything was flash-bang over here and boom over there. Off and on; back and forth. All you knew was that a lot of hitting was going on.

We were probably a quarter mile from the action at one point. You could smell the powder from there. We just sat there tense on the ridge, not really understanding that one of the war's major naval battles was spread out before our eyes. There were no cheers, no shouts. Now and then someone said, "Goddamn!" after a bright flash followed by the sound rolling up over the ridge.

What happens when you're fighting in those circumstances is that all your senses are heightened, a natural reaction in order to stay alive. Your smell, your hearing, your sight, your peripheral vision. You hear a little sound. Oh, that's a land crab, you say to yourself, and you ignore it. You even recognize each other by smell. We didn't bathe; we all stank. You got to know the guy in the darkness by his particular odor.

So we watched as the action seemed to move away from the beach and then subside. And then we smelled the battle in the darkness.

Our platoon's only form of communication with the outside world that night was a field phone operated by a young kid named Billy Edwards. At about the time the tropical dawn began lighting the sky, Edwards woke me up with the report that last night's sea battle hadn't gone too well for our side. I looked out to the bay, and close to shore I made out what appeared to be a heavy cruiser that had been hit pretty badly. Edwards told me he'd received word that it was the USS *Atlanta*. That rang a familiar bell. One of my childhood buddies, a kid I grew up with back in Buffalo by the name of Roger Pigeon, was a gun turret man on the *Atlanta*.

What I could see of the ship didn't look good. The forward deck no longer appeared to have any gun turrets. I asked Edwards what else he'd been able to find out, and he told me the *Atlanta* was being scuttled because she was dead in the water. He repeated to me what he'd gotten on the field phone: "Her crew has abandoned ship and most of them are now on the beach. Others from the *Atlanta* made it to Tulagi. Survivors from some of our other sunken ships are on the beach, too."

What we all learned later is that during the Guadalcanal campaign, the Japanese Navy had introduced a new gimmick to night sea battles, while our navy champions were still fighting sea battles the old way, which the textbooks called "crossing the T." The new Japanese way worked better. Taking advantage of the night's darkness, they would steam in close, pick out one or two of our ships, turn their big, bright spotlights on them, and open up with everything they had. They were giving us you-know-what-from-where, while our master tacticians were still looking for some way to "cross that T" in the middle of those pitch-dark tropical nights. The U.S. Navy was learning the hard way.

That morning, looking out through the mist, we made out another wounded cruiser that appeared to be under tow by a destroyer. A couple more of our destroyers were limping, smoke coming out of them from below decks. I saw still another cruiser smoking—I'm guessing it was the *Chicago*—with

The cruiser USS *Atlanta* just a few weeks before being badly damaged off Guadalcanal on November 13. It was scuttled the following day. NATIONAL ARCHIVES

a good part of her fantail missing. Looking down at Ironbottom Sound from our ridge was like looking down at a battlefield after the battle was over, except that our badly wounded weren't only men, but also the ships they manned.

I wondered what had become of my old neighbor and childhood buddy, Roger Pigeon. I told Edwards to get Company on the phone, and then I took the phone and spoke to my good friend Ben Selvitelle, the first sergeant. He turned me over to the company exec officer, Lt. Tom Guffin. I asked for permission to leave the ridge for a couple hours. I wanted to check out the beach and look for Roger Pigeon. Since I was temporarily the senior man in L Company's 1st Platoon, Guffin was understandably hesitant about letting me leave the platoon. Finally he gave permission, provided that I get my scroungy body back up on our ridge no later than noon. That was fair enough.

In no time at all, I was ready to go down to the beach—my utility uniform torn and filthy, my face showing a couple weeks' growth of beard, my last haircut dating back from a short time after Christ made corporal. I told Cpl. Larry Gerkin that I'd be gone until around noon, and that he was to take over until I got back. I had my usual breakfast, which was three or four gulps of fresh air, and headed off toward the beach.

The trek down to the shore took me about ten minutes, where I found myself in the midst of mayhem. Sailors were sprawled on the sand in groups, probably divisions or sections. I didn't see any wounded, though there had to be quite a few casualties after that ferocious nighttime battle. By now the wounded probably had been moved to the island's field hospital.

Looking out over the water, I took in the miserable sight of our ships, many of them close to shore and limping around aimlessly like wounded marines. The nearest ship, battered and with water almost up to her gunwales, but still standing tall, was what remained of the USS *Atlanta*. On the beach, in the middle of all the chaos, a pair of naval officers stood side by side, one of them looking at the *Atlanta* through field glasses. I took the opportunity to walk to the surf's edge, sit down on the beach, and do the nearest thing I could manage to bathing, which was to splash water on my face and hands, then submerge my helmet and collect some water to pour over my head.

Starved and filthy, I was in poor shape. I stood up again to my full five-foot-six, my weight down to about ninety-five pounds, and I shook the water off my body. I walked directly over to those two immaculately dressed naval officers. Clean-shaven, wearing starched khaki uniforms and cordovan polished shoes, they looked as though someone had carried them ashore. That didn't stop me. I approached them.

"Hey, guys, is that the *Atlanta*?"

As I was asking my question, I noticed that one of these winners had a small eagle insignia on his left collar, which gave him the rank of U.S. Navy captain. Captain or not, he was standing on my beach, where I'd stood many a watch. Under those circumstances, as far as I was concerned, that insignia of his meant navy beans.

The two officers looked back at me, taking in all my scrounginess, the expressions on their faces giving me the feeling that they were glancing at some mysterious new form of lowlife. To his credit, the officer with the eagle on his collar decided to be civil.

"Yes, that's the *Atlanta*," he said. "If you want to take a good last look, you can use these glasses."

He started to remove the strap from behind his neck, which I admit was a neighborly gesture, especially coming from a navy captain.

"No thanks," I said. "I can see her fine, as close to shore as she is. I came down to the beach to try to find an old buddy and neighbor of mine. His name is Roger Pigeon. Either of you guys know the name?"

No, they didn't recognize the name, but one of them volunteered, "You might ask some of the men on the beach. Somebody might know him or know his whereabouts."

I thanked them and walked away.

I didn't have to go more than about ten paces before I was with a group of sailors sitting on the sand. Every one of them was covered with oil and grease, and they'd clearly had a rough night of it. I asked around, but none of them knew Roger.

Just about then, I remembered a simple fact of life on Guadalcanal that the pair of beautifully dressed officers should have known but apparently didn't. The captain had been civil to me, so maybe I owed him something in return. Also, those poor beaten-up, grease-and-oil-smeared sailors had already taken more than their share of punishment, so maybe it was time to do *them* a good turn. I walked back toward the officers and got their attention.

"In case you haven't heard about it, every day, just like clockwork between eleven A.M. and noon, we get an air raid. It might be a good idea to get these guys off the beach, 'cause if those airplanes come in on time today, you're going to have some nervous sailors on your hands."

They didn't say thank you, but I have a feeling that they appreciated my advice.

I left them and walked along the beach as far as Kukum, asking each group of stranded sailors if anybody knew Roger Pigeon from the *Atlanta*. All the answers came back negative. By noon, I was back where I belonged, on the ridge and with my warriors. The *Atlanta* went down and out at about that time. It wasn't until after the war was over that I learned about Roger. He survived. With other shipmates, he'd been picked up earlier that day and taken to Tulagi.

We did have the usual air raid that morning. The Jap planes came over before noon, as I'd predicted. I hope those two navy champions took my advice and got their sailors off the beach.

I guess you can't blame the Navy Department for putting the best face on the story of a ferocious naval engagement in which both the Americans and Japanese suffered terrific losses of both lives and ships. The story that my folks back home read in the November 17 *Buffalo Evening News* says little about our own losses at sea, but plenty about sunken Japanese ships. As it turned out, the November 13 sea battle was a strategic victory for our navy, but it sure didn't look like victory for those of us who saw its aftermath, looking out to sea from our Guadalcanal beaches.

**2 U.S. Admirals Give Lives
As Navy Wins Great Battle**

**20,000 TO 40,000 JAPS
ARE LOST IN SOLOMONS
AS U.S. SINKS 23 SHIPS**

**Brilliant American Action Causes Enemy
Vessels to Fire at Each Other; Our
Losses Are Comparatively Light**
(copyright 1942, the *Buffalo Evening News*)

That bottom headline got the facts precisely backward. It turned out that in the darkness and general confusion, it was our own ships that fired at each other, but what the hell. Our navy's victory was messy, and the margin of victory was narrow, but it *was* a victory. The Japanese fared much worse.

HARDROCK GERKIN TAKES A BATH

For several weeks during November, my platoon was dug in on that outpost on the high ridge about 100 yards out in front of our MLR. During our first days out there, a small patrol brought our food ration out to us once a day. After a week or so, an entire day might pass without that food patrol, which meant nothing to eat. Drinking water was also scarce, and water for sanitation was no more than a distant dream. It was hot, miserable, and isolated up on that ridge. As the weeks passed, we started to reach that stage where warriors stop caring about very much of anything. We were growing lethargic, which is one of the worst things that can happen to any man in combat. Normally, once a warrior reaches the "I don't care" stage, he is just one small step away from having his dog tags separated and a telegram sent home to his next of kin.

One morning on that ridge, we were paid an unexpected visit by a platoon-size patrol led by a full bird colonel. I happened to be lying in the shade when that colonel strode into our area. He was beautifully attired in pressed riding britches and shined boots, his hair was trimmed in a neat brush cut, and he looked ready to go out on a parade ground.

"Who's in charge here?" he asked.

"I am, sir," I said. The Man strutted around among our reclining figures, sniffing the bad aromas our bodies were giving off, and looking at us with disgust. As I saw it, the colonel had made one mistake by coming out here. Now he made his second mistake by asking me a direct question.

"When was the last time you men washed yourselves?"

Before I could answer, our little seventeen-year-old runner, who did double duty as our telephone man, burst out, "Why don't you ask us *another* stupid question? Why don't you ask us when was the last time we had water to *drink*?" I think his anger surprised everybody on the scene, including the colonel, but his outburst was justified by our situation.

The colonel didn't answer. Instead, he took his own canteen off his belt and handed it to me. Then he turned to the men in his patrol. "Break out your canteens, men," he told them.

"*Water!*" our young runner yelled. It was a magic word. Every man in our platoon came up and out from where he was dug in, and as each of them approached us, I looked at them and realized how sorry a sight we must have appeared to these outsiders. My men were wide-eyed, with haunted, zombielike expressions on their faces. Our uniforms were dirty and tattered, our faces were long overdue for shaves, and our hair was in need of cutting. Some of us were feverish with malaria, most of us suffered from dysentery, and all of us were gaunt and thin from lack of food. Most of all, *we were thirsty as hell.* In every sense of the word, we were raggedy-ass marines.

That colonel didn't have much more to say to us, but at least we had water that morning. And to his credit, he took word back to command that we were in serious need of relief.

Early the next morning, this buck sergeant received a long overdue and much welcome order to take half of the 1st Platoon down off the ridge and to the Lunga River to bathe. The idea was for us to wash ourselves and the utilities on our backs, which were the only clothes we ever had during our stay on the Canal. We were to shave our faces, and mainly to get the fly-attracting stink off our frames.

About eight of us were able to trek to the river that morning. We arrived at the shore of the Lunga River at a spot where a tall tree had fallen and extended halfway across to the opposite bank. That tree trunk was bleached white by sun and sand. Since we lacked soap, we would have to use some of that river sand to wash our bodies and our clothes. We grounded our weapons at the riverbank, undressed, and walked into that sweet, clean water to a point where we were about waist deep. Meanwhile, on the opposite side of the fallen tree, a short, older, thin-haired man was also bathing. He was alone. We were on one side of the fallen tree, and he was on the other, so none of us paid particular attention to him until Hardrock Gerkin glanced toward him and piped up, "Jeez, that guy's got a bar of soap."

The rest of us didn't say anything, but that didn't stop Gerk. He called out, "Hey, Mac. Where the hell did you ever get that soap?" Before the man had a chance to answer, Gerkin waded closer to him. "You mind letting me use a little of that soap?"

The older guy appeared affable enough. He turned halfway around toward us, extended his arm with soap in hand, and said, "Here, help yourself."

Gerkin took the soap without as much as a word of thanks and started lathering himself. From my short distance away from them, I recognized one small detail that had somehow eluded Pfc. Lawrence E. Gerkin. The man who had turned toward us and decided to be generous with his bar of soap was none other than Gen. A. A. Vandegrift.

Now, while we scrubbed our clothes with river sand and washed our stinking bodies clean, I stopped what I was doing and made an effort to get Hardrock's attention. It was clear that Gerk had no idea that the man he was talking to, the man whose soap he'd just taken, was our commanding general. Gerk remained blissfully unaware that I was trying to catch his attention.

"Boy, what a hell of a way to fight a war," he remarked to the general. "No chow, almost no drinkable water, and not enough ammo to start a decent firefight."

"Yes," the general replied. "It certainly isn't the best way to fight a war."

Gerkin nodded, then said, "What outfit are you in, buddy?"

"Headquarters," the general said, as though maybe he was one of the less important aides back at the CP.

"Hey, Gerk!" I called. "Come over here!"

Gerkin paid no attention to me. He scrutinized the general. "Jeez. You headquarters guys must be getting all the chow and the best supplies. Us guys out on the line get what's left over."

"It's not exactly like that," the general replied mildly.

I eased my way toward them, bent on rescuing Hardrock before he *really* stuck his foot in his mouth.

"Well," Gerkin persisted, "you guys *must* be getting pretty good chow. You still have a little gut going for you, Mac."

By now I was beside Hardrock, and glaring at him. The general observed us, quietly amused, from his side of the fallen tree, which gave me an opportunity to look at him and say in my most cheerful voice, "Good morning, general! How are you today?"

"I'm fine," A. A. replied. "And how are you men today?"

With that, Hardrock made a sudden splash and disappeared beneath the water's surface. The general was grinning. We exchanged a little more small talk until Gerk suddenly bobbed to the surface, extended his hand, and gave the general what remained of his bar of soap. There wasn't much of it left.

"Jeez, I'm sorry, general," he said. "But if I'm going to beat my gums and complain to *somebody* about this war, I might as well start at the top."

The general was laughing now. "You make a very good point, young man," he said.

And so it went—just another average day in the life of Pfc. Lawrence E. Gerkin, the 1st Platoon's peerless BAR man.

THE RAGGEDY-ASS MARINES TEACH THE U.S. ARMY
Maybe the single most important reason why we marines stayed on that godforsaken island and not only survived but defeated the Japanese can be summed up by that old cliché: self-reliance. After the campaign ended and the Japanese had been kicked off the Canal, specific descriptions of Marine Corps' self-reliance were printed in a little blue-covered booklet titled *Fighting on Guadalcanal,* published by the U.S. Army. I'm one among many guys who know something about how that booklet was put together.

Late in November, the 5th Regiment was pulled out of combat and moved back to a relatively safe area between Division Headquarters and the beach. By now we knew that the navy would soon take us off the island, and the main thing we had to do was wait for the ship that would pick us up. Our wait lasted about a week, at which time the transport ship USS *President Jackson* appeared offshore. The *Jackson* was our ticket out of there.

While we were waiting, we were bivouacked in grass country, not far from the Lunga River. One morning, for a change, the regiment managed to give us a little decent food, and after breakfast the first sergeant approached me, read off the names of several men from L Company, and told me to round them up. Chink McAllan and Red Byrne were on his list, along with one or two others, including me. Our order was to report to 1st Division Headquarters, where several army officers wanted to talk with us. We were told in advance that we'd be asked about the different techniques and tricks we'd developed, and which we'd found to be effective during our engagements with the Japanese. We made our way toward headquarters, and on the way, I recognized a number of men joining us from various units throughout the 5th Regiment. A captain assembled us and introduced five army colonels, all of them young hotshots, and all of them full bird colonels.

One colonel got the meeting started, and what follows is a close approximation of the talk he gave us.

"Men," he said, "General Marshall sent us out here from Washington on a fact-finding mission. We've just been to New Guinea, and now we're here on Guadalcanal to learn more details about staying alive and defeating the enemy in jungle combat. On New Guinea, our main job was to try to learn what the army's problem has been. Up to the present, we've supplied General MacArthur with just about everything he's asked for on that island, and his troops haven't accomplished a damned thing. Meanwhile, we haven't given you marines here on Guadalcanal much of anything, and you guys have done wonders. We want to know how you did it, and how you managed to succeed with so little help. We want to know about any little thing you believe you learned while you were in combat. Our intention is to put this information together and use it as part of a training program that the army is about to start at a base in Louisiana. What we're going to do this morning is talk to each of you individually. We'll ask questions, and all we ask of you is to recall as many details as you can. Tell us how you succeeded in the different situations that we'll be discussing."

With those words, the five colonels each took a spot on the ground. They sat down in the grass and called on us individually. We told them what we knew, what we did, and how we managed to do it. I sat down with one of the colonels, had a pleasant conversation with him, and responded to his questions. One unintentionally humorous question was, Which weapons and equipment could you have used?

When you consider that we won our battle mainly with the Springfield '03, a relic from World War I, while MacArthur's troops had spanking new M-1, .30-caliber, semi-automatic rifles, you have to start wondering what we could have accomplished if we'd received just a small fraction of the arms and supplies we'd been begging for—and never received. This isn't a complaint against the Springfield '03, which is a good rifle. It's just one instance among hundreds where the army got the new equipment and the marines got what was left over. Most of those leftovers weren't of the same high quality as the '03. Anyhow, we, the raggedy-ass 5th Marines, answered the U.S. Army's questions to the best of our ability, and as honestly as we knew how. When we were finished, we went back to our units.

I'd nearly forgotten about that morning until 1945, when I was in the 5th Division and training for what turned out to be the marines' landing on Iwo Jima. We had an army captain with us, and when I was introduced to him, he said, "Your name is familiar. Do I know you from somewhere?"

"It could be," I said. "I don't recall."

He seemed to think about it for a moment. "I know your name from somewhere," he said.

I saw him again the next day. "I knew I'd run across your name somewhere," he told me. "Here it is." He held out a small book, *The Blue Manual*, also known as *Fighting on Guadalcanal*, and two copies of *The Infantryman's Journal*. The *Journal* quoted a few things I'd said back on the Canal, and *The Blue Manual* quoted every word that I recall speaking to the army colonel. It also quoted replies from the many other marines who had been interviewed on the Canal that morning in early December 1942, along with frequent remarks about our replies from Col. Merritt Edson. Edson's remarks weren't critical of the things we had to say. In every case, he simply corroborated the information we'd given to the army. The army captain told me that these were the books he'd used back in Louisiana, when he'd trained troops in methods of jungle combat and survival. I hadn't seen those books or known of their existence until the day he showed them to me. He wanted me to keep them, which I did for several years, until I finally donated them to the Marine Corps Museum. Much later, a few excerpts from *The Blue Manual* also appeared in our veterans' newspaper, *Guadalcanal Echoes.*

What I had to say was no more and probably no less important than information the army colonels gathered from many other marines. One thing I noticed when I read the manual was that often, each marine had his own way of dealing with any number of different combat situations. Many answers varied from one marine to another, but all our answers shared the qualities of common sense and hard-earned experience. The excerpts that follow are just a few of the replies we gave, as they appeared in *The Blue Manual.*

> 2nd Lt. H. M. Davis, 5th Marines:
>
> Travel light. For example, to hell with the mess equipment! We used our mess cup and spoon for the first 15 days here, and enjoyed our chow. But you don't have to live like a gentleman in jungle warfare. Our mess equipment is too bulky for this type of warfare, and it makes noise.
>
> Not every man can lead a battalion. Find out who can lead your battalions before you go into the combat areas. (Col. Edson's remark: I would like to concur in that statement.)
>
> Plt. Sgt. C. M. Feagin, I Company, 5th Marines:
>
> We are learning the hard way to move quietly in this jungle. I have been fired at many times by snipers and haven't seen one yet.
>
> The sabers which the Japanese officers carry have proved to be worthless. I killed two Japs who came at me with sabers, and I got them first by shooting them. But I wished I had in reserve a good jungle knife. I don't mean a bolo, which we should have for cutting trails, but a knife with a 12-inch blade of good steel. We could use it against these Japs . . . [and also use it for]

cutting vines that catch on us [when we move through jungle terrain] at night.

Motor Section Sgt. T. E. Rumbley, I Company, 5th Marines:

Our 60 mm. mortars are fine weapons if you have observers who know their stuff. The mortar was not stressed enough in our training. . . . If the numbers on the mortar sight were luminous, with a luminous strip on the stick, we would not have to use the flashlight. This flashlight business is dangerous.

Cpl. Fred Carter, I Company, 5th Marines:

On the Matanikau River, we got to firing at each other because of careless leadership by the junior leaders. We are curing ourselves of promiscuous firing, but I should think new units would get training to make the men more careful. We learned not to fire unless we had something to shoot at. Doing otherwise discloses your position and wastes ammunition. . . .

I have been charged twice by the Japs in a bayonet charge. Our Marines can out-bayonet-fight them, and I know our Army men will do the same. (Note by Col. Edson: Incidentally, in our last push, we executed three bayonet charges.)

A Japanese trick to draw our fire was for the hidden Jap to work his bolt back and forth. Men who got sucked in on this and fired without seeing what they were firing at generally drew enemy automatic fire from another direction.

Every scout should be taught to look in the trees. I was a scout and was shot in the shoulder by a Jap in a tree. I look in the trees now. We take turns being scouts; so all should be trained as scouts.

Sgt. O. J. Marion, L Company, 5th Marines, a Platoon Guide:

You crawl when making an advance—unless you are to charge and make it. The reason is that all men who are hit are hit from the knees up, except for ricochets. We've been able to crawl up to within 25 yards of a machinegun that's firing over our backs. The Japs don't depress their machineguns. (Note by Col. Edson: I saw men of Company L doing this.)

Men get killed rushing to help a wounded man. If the wounded man would crawl about 10 yards to his flank, he can generally be aided in safety, as the Japs seem to fire down lanes in jungle combat. (Remark by Col. Edson: We have taught our men that the best way to aid a wounded man is to push ahead so that the wounded man can be cared for by the Corpsmen following behind.)

Men have to be trained to act individually, for when the firefight starts, the corporal can't see all his men, and further, when the order for an attack is given, any number of men are unable to see the man on his right or left. So you see, sir, it takes guts for men to get up and move forward when the signal is given. The men have to learn to depend on one another, and have confidence in each other.

I was caught in one advance when the Japs let us come through, and then rose up out of covered foxholes and shot at our backs. The best cure for that is a rear guard looking towards the rear.

A few years ago, a fellow veteran of the Canal wrote to *Guadalcanal Echoes*, inquiring about what he believed was a rare booklet. It turned out that he was referring to *Fighting on Guadalcanal*. Until then, it hadn't occurred to me that the booklet had become rare. I had my copy of it stashed in a footlocker, the same copy that the army officer had given me back in 1945. I searched around the house a little, found that old footlocker, opened it up, and sure enough, there it was. The booklet wasn't doing me any good anymore, so I mailed it off to the Guadalcanal Veteran's Museum. I'm glad I gave it to them, but I've thought about that booklet many times since then. Those of us who contributed to it, each in our own small way, would like to think it helped save a few American lives.

THE JAPANESE

When highly decorated and victorious Japanese commanders like General Kawaguchi, Colonel Ichiki, and Colonel Oka, all three of them in command of battle-tested troops, told their superiors that they would attack Guadalcanal, force the Americans to capitulate, and retake the island's airfield, they were as deadly serious as they could be. Up to that point, they had never known defeat. After years of rolling over and through all their enemies, they felt invincible. That was especially true as they prepared to face a motley crew of mostly young, untested, and abandoned American marines on Guadalcanal.

In the 1930s, the Japanese decided that the best and cheapest way to get minerals, lumber, and other resources was to invade Manchuria and just take it for themselves. With a few bombings, some well-placed artillery fire, and the advantage of facing an ill-equipped and poorly trained Chinese Army that was best at running the wrong way, the Japanese Imperial Army started its steam-roller exercises.

After conquering the Chinese Manchurian Army and invading that country, the Japanese Army intimidated the population by employing brute terror that included indiscriminate killing of men, women, and children, a scorched-earth policy, rape, beheading the educated, forced prostitution, forced labor, and imprisoning and starving still others for no obvious reason. At that time, a romantic Japanese composer wrote a famous song, "Manchurian Nights," which later got a new set of words from American fighting men and became known as "She Ain't Got No Yo-Yo." But if you happened to be a Manchurian, those nights weren't very romantic.

Well before the Japanese started their march south from Manchuria into mainland China, their reputation for brutality preceded them. When they went on the attack, word was quickly passed along that the Japs were coming, and Chinese troops faded into the mist. As a result, there were few documented battles, as the Japanese easily occupied most important sections of the country that had the largest land mass in Asia. The "rape of Nanking," the bombing of the USS *Panay*, and the bombing of downtown Shanghai continued to terrorize both the Chinese population at large and Chinese military forces.

As the Japanese moved south through Hong Kong, the Dutch East Indies, and Singapore, and even though they were greatly outnumbered in many of the battles, they rolled through Dutch and British defenses, partly because the reputation of their brutality preceded them, and partly because their enemies' will to stand and defend had largely disappeared. They conquered everything and everyone they met. The Imperial Japanese Army was invincible, and its leaders were arrogant. In 1942 on Guadalcanal, the Japanese Army saw its chance to teach the Americans the same lesson they'd been teaching everybody else.

Col. Kiyoano Ichiki, with a detachment of nine hundred of Japan's best soldiers attacked the marines' eastern perimeter, trying to cross Alligator Creek at the battle of the Tenaru River on August 20–21. Ichiki's force made a semi–route march that culminated with a banzai formation. The presumably battle-seasoned Ichiki seemed to think that as soon as those untested Americans saw his troops approaching, the U.S. Marines would do what everyone else had done: grab ass and run. But the good colonel soon found out that those young soldiers of the 1st Marine Regiment weren't grabbing anything. Instead, they stayed, fought back, and generally kicked butt. When it was over, Japanese dead littered the banks of the Teneru, and Ichiki's body was among them.

Maj. Gen. Kayotaki Kawaguchi and his combined force almost made it at Edson's Ridge on September 12–14, and again the marines didn't run. Short of ammo and short of chow, but having nowhere to go, the marines stayed, slugged it out against the numerically superior Japanese, and stacked them high. At the same time, Colonel Oka attacked marine lines at several places on the Matanikau end—L Company's combat area—while his troops advanced in a route march formation. Apparently he, too, was under the impression that we stupid Americans would see him, drop our weapons, and bug out. The stupidity was all his. My own unit played an important part in routing Oka. Today Japanese representatives search old battle areas on Guadalcanal, still trying to find the remains of Oka's troops so that they can return the bones to the homeland and enshrine them with the remains of their ancestors.

Throughout the Guadalcanal campaign, Japanese attacks went on and on, probing one place or another along the American line, until finally the Imperial Headquarters Staff in Tokyo began to understand that Guadalcanal had become a turning point in their Pacific land, sea, and air battle. The war was turning against them.

At Guadalcanal, the Imperial staff bit off more than it could chew. Its fighting forces ran into the U.S. Marines, then later found themselves up against the army's well-equipped Americal Division, which finally secured the island. Facing the marines, the Japanese were facing American fighting men who had been abandoned, who never had enough ammo or chow, but who had nowhere to go. The Japanese military ran into American sailors who'd gotten tired of getting kicked around and having to swim for their lives. They also ran into American airmen, flying in patched-up airplanes, but still capable of leaving deep, long-lasting impressions on those self-deluded leaders who had thought they were invincible. The battles of the Coral Sea, Midway, and Guadalcanal were a one-two punch, the first decisive blows that spelled defeat to the previously unbeaten Japanese Army and Navy.

In 1945, when Japan surrendered, I was with the occupation forces on the Japanese mainland. I was among the Americans who came face-to-face with Japanese troops being returned home from conquered lands and demobilized. As they turned over their weapons to us, hatred showed in their eyes. Probably nobody in the world had known it back in the summer and fall of 1942, but Guadalcanal had been the beginning of the end for the Japanese. They tried to defeat the raggedy-ass U.S. Marines on the Canal, and they couldn't do it.

LEAVING THE CANAL

It was on or about December 7, 1942. I no longer remember the exact date, or even the time of day, but we were assembled on the beach, and we knew we were finally getting the hell off Guadalcanal. A transport ship stood well out to sea, its boats coming toward us on their way in to pick us up. They were Higgins boats, the same type that had landed us ashore back in August, but this time they were taking us home. Well, not quite home, but to Australia, which was a good second choice. When they arrived at the beach, we climbed aboard, and as each boat filled with marines, it headed back out toward the ship. We were on our way to the USS *President Jackson*, a navy transport that would take us to Brisbane, a handsome city on Australia's east coast. Our Higgins boat plowed through the water, its diesel engine throbbing steadily, and like everyone around me, I was glad to be off the Canal. Some of the guys looked back. They got their last glimpse of what was truly a beautiful island, all green with its wide, white sand beaches. Some of them looked back all right, just long enough to thumb their noses at Guadalcanal before they said good-bye. I didn't look back; I looked straight out to sea, watching the *Jackson*, which seemed to grow larger as we approached. Its cargo nets had been dropped down the side of the hull, which was the standard way for troops to go aboard. Our Higgins boat came abreast of the *Jackson*, and like those around me, I reached out, grabbed the net, and started to scramble toward topside.

I'd been scrambling up the sides of ships since the days when those harder-to-climb Jacob's ladders were the most common way for a marine to board ship, but this day's climb was the toughest one of my life. That was true not only for me, but for all of us. Every last marine getting off Guadalcanal was weak after four energy-sapping months of combat, sickness, and too little food. I, for one, wasn't climbing that net with anything like the same speed that I'd always managed in the old days. Even so, I kept on going. Finally I made it to the top, feeling the *Jackson*'s deck solid beneath my feet.

One of the first things I did was look down along the side of the hull I'd just finished climbing. A few of our guys were on their way up directly behind me, many others were halfway up, and still others had made it maybe three-quarters of the way, but many of them had simply stopped moving. They had their arms wrapped in and around the nets, and they were hanging on for dear life, too weak to climb any further. A first burst of energy—or maybe it was just that powerful desire to get the hell off Guadalcanal—had been enough to take them partway up the net, but that was as far as they could go. It took me a minute or so to realize their trouble. They hadn't stopped for a second to catch their breath; they'd stopped because they'd run out of strength. I was taking my pack off my back when a sailor who stood near me said, "What's the matter with those goddamn marines? Look at them."

The matter with those goddamn marines was that they were half starved, suffering from any of several jungle diseases, and too weak to climb those nets without help. When I reflect back, I get angry at those navy brass sons of bitches. You would have thought they'd have told the sailors what condition we were in. They didn't tell their people we didn't have any food; that we were starving. Aboard ship, they were *only* getting two squares a day. They couldn't see that we were sick, that some guys who had been able to fight the Japs in hand-to-hand combat now could only wrap their arms around the ropes and hold on for dear life. They didn't realize we'd been climbing those damned cargo nets for three years and could run right up the side of the ship when we were healthy and fed. A couple of the *Jackson*'s sailors who were on duty topside and near the embarkation stations had a little more sense than that wiseguy who had made the remark. They saw what was happening, and realizing how weak our guys were, they started going down the nets to help them. They pushed and pulled and heaved our

November and Early December 1942

guys up and on deck. These many years later, I thank them sincerely for their help.

At least one of our guys had tears running down his face because he couldn't make it up that goddamned net. Another man who happened to be in my unit lost the trigger group out of his BAR while he was struggling up the net. Our BARs were relics from World War I. Two safety pins held the trigger group in place, and a combination of age and hard use on the battlefield eventually loosened those pins. The kid was hanging on to the cargo net for dear life, the BAR slung on his back, and with the ship's movement, the net kept swinging a little, making his climb that much harder. The trigger group on his weapon must have jostled loose, fallen out of the gun, and disappeared into the ocean, but the kid didn't realize it until he'd made it up on deck. Then, with the rest of us, he moved down below, where he had a few seconds to pull his gear together. He reported the loss of his trigger group to me. I had to report it to the gunny, who made a big issue out of it. You'd think it was the poor kid's fault.

What had sent us down below in the first place was the familiar wail of the air-raid siren, which meant a squadron of Japanese bombers was on its way to pay another one of its daily visits. With enemy bombers approaching, the ship's skipper had to get the *Jackson* under way in a hurry. The *Jackson* began to pick up speed, then started making the zigzag maneuvers that ships always make when an enemy attack is impending or in progress. Several more Higgins boats filled with marines were still on their way toward the *Jackson*. As they came abreast of the ship, I watched the kids in those Higgins boats struggle to grab the cargo net on the moving ship. Each man would wait his turn, then time himself and jump to grab hold of the swinging net and start his climb. That's how most of them got aboard the *Jackson*.

When my unit was ordered down below, we kept right on going, deeper and deeper, until we found ourselves in a compartment with no ventilation to speak of. We were a sorry crew, sick, dirty, stinking, half starved, and now we were stuck deep in the ship's bowels, where we choked on old, stale air while outside, bombs started coming down from Japanese planes. Like the others, I was in poor shape, my weight down from my then-normal 130 pounds to about 90 pounds. Even the biggest guys in our unit were as weak and underweight as the rest of us, with maybe the heaviest guy in the platoon weighing in at around 135 pounds. We couldn't even sit down comfortably on a bench, because the bones of our butts stuck out against our skin.

We were stuck deep down below in that stinking ship's compartment, listening to muffled explosions of Japanese bombs. The ship didn't take any hits, but we remained trapped in that compartment for a good half hour before they finally opened the hatch and led us up, directing us toward the ship's mess hall. At long last, we were served some decent food. I took that first delicious, warm bowl of thick macaroni soup, gobbled it up like a madman, and then proceeded to throw it up. I needed a second and then a third bowl before I finally managed to get food into my stomach and keep it down.

A little earlier, when they had finally let us out of that deep compartment where we waited out the Japanese air raid, I told myself, "If I'm going to die, there's nothing I can do about it. But from now on, there's one thing I'm *not* going to do: I'm not going to die deep down in the goddamned hold of some old rustbucket of a navy ship."

That was a promise I made to myself and kept. I never allowed anybody to get me deep down belowships like that again. A few years later, serving with a different outfit and on my way to and from a different bloody engagement—the battle of Iwo Jima—my unit was ordered down below on several occasions. Most of the others followed orders, but not me. I remember telling one sailor, "Hold it!"

"What's up?" he said.

I pointed at the hatch. "Open that son of a bitch, and let me up *now!*"

I meant it, and he knew I meant it. He opened the hatch and I went up on deck, where I could breathe good, fresh air.

CHAPTER 7

Three Guadalcanals

I spent thirty years in the corps, including a decade assigned to the Fleet Reserves, and when I officially retired from the Marine Corps in 1970—you never really sever the cord—it seemed like a lifetime had passed since I had gone through the Guadalcanal ordeal with so many good and longtime friends. It dawned on me years later, and only after I'd joined the Guadalcanal Campaign Veterans, that although it was but one island, three totally different Guadalcanals exist in the memories of the servicemen who were there during World War II.

That realization hit me slowly, and only after I started getting copies in the mail of the Guadalcanal Campaign Veterans' quarterly newspaper, *Guadalcanal Echoes*. I started seeing pictures and reading stories about the Canal, and nearly every time a new issue came into my home, I found myself opening the paper, then repeating to myself, "*This* can't be Guadalcanal! Where the hell did those guys get the cameras to take those pictures during the campaign?" At the time we fought the Japanese on that island, it was a court-martial offense for any of us to have cameras and take pictures. Obvious exceptions were made in the cases of war correspondents and certain personnel at command headquarters, but all combat marines were told explicitly that cameras were forbidden.

But in just about any issue of *Echoes*, I'd be likely to see, for instance, a photo taken back during the war showing a PX, or men in khaki uniforms eating chow in a nice, comfortable mess tent. Or a picture of a bakery. *A bakery!?* Another issue had a photo of a post office. *A post office?* "Do they have the right island?" I started asking myself. "Who in hell are these impostors, and where are these pictures coming from?" Recalling Guadalcanal in my mind's eye, it's very difficult for me to accept the fact that the photos and some of the stories that I've read in *Echoes* in recent years are about the *real* Guadalcanal.

Here's another oddity that came in the form of a query from one of the paper's readers: "Does anyone remember mules on Guadalcanal?" Many affirmative replies were sent in, and some had photos to back up their stories. *Mules?* I responded to *Echoes* with a short note of my own, saying that if mules had been on the Canal, we would have eaten them! It turns out that I was wrong about mules, and about other details, too.

Facts aside, I've discovered that sensory impressions also differ wildly from one veteran to another. Somebody once wrote a short piece to *Echoes* and mentioned the sweet, flowery smell of jasmine drifting out to sea. I recall the smell of jasmine, too, but only years after my Guadalcanal experience. When my wife, my son, and I lived in Sunland, California, we had night-blooming jasmine growing all around our home, but I never smelled jasmine on the Canal. The smells that remain as part of *my* Guadalcanal memories are rotted vegetation and the nauseating stink of dead, rotting bodies. But I've had to rearrange my memories and my thoughts. I've had to start putting a few things in perspective and draw a few new conclusions. I now realize that there were at least three different Guadalcanals, remembered by three different waves of troops who spent time there.

The first Guadalcanal is the one I know and remember, the Guadalcanal that existed from August to December 1942. That Guadalcanal consists of a small perimeter along the beach, starting just short of the Tenaru River, stretching westward to a point several hundred yards beyond the village of Kukum, and extending irregularly inland never more (and often much less) than a few thousand yards to the island's first line of high coral ridges. That first Guadalcanal was also an island of shortages. We were always short of rifle ammo, and always begging for a few precious rounds of supporting high-angle fire from our mortars and field guns. We were always short of food and water, and all we had to wear were the shoes and clothes we'd come ashore with. We were short of mosquito nets, quinine, and medical supplies. We saw very little incoming mail, and we had no paper or pencils to write letters home. I never saw a post office on *my* Guadalcanal, and I never saw anything that looked remotely like a PX. There were no movies, no mess tents, no bakery, no starched khaki uniforms, and in my experience, not one single goddamned mule. *We* were the island's animals, living on the ground and under the ground, and eating food that no mule would ever accept.

One thing we did have in large supply was incoming rounds of enemy fire. We were bombed and shelled day and night. Another thing we had in large supply was illness—mainly malaria, dysentery, and tropical ulcers. We went on patrol nearly every day, and we grew thinner every day from lack of food. Our wounded were evacuated only if and when a plane or a ship was able to come in and take them off the island, and that wasn't often. Sometimes they let us go swimming at night—but that was to push in barrels of aviation gas that the Yippee boats had dumped overboard for us to retrieve.

The first Guadalcanal, *my* Guadalcanal, was also the island that overwhelmed us with the feeling that we'd been abandoned. On too many occasions, the ships intended to bring in supplies and reinforcements would get shot up by the enemy, then would take off and disappear, and we would see no further sign of the U.S. Navy for several weeks. That was my Guadalcanal. One thing we did have was the constant threat of death, which was made palpable by the dirty, rotten stink of death that clung to our hair, our clothes, our teeth, and even the balls of our feet. Death was always with us.

After December 1942, and for the next four or five months, a second Guadalcanal came into being, but L-3-5 and the rest of the 1st Marines were no longer there to experience it. The second Guadalcanal was an island where the American perimeter moved outward in all directions. It was an island where the army mopped up pockets of Japanese resistance, and where American naval and air power grew stronger day by day. Luckily for the troops who had to be there, it was an island of better living conditions for all of them. Mail call became frequent, and ammunition and medical supplies grew plentiful. This possibly was the Guadalcanal that saw its first U.S. Post Office, and maybe even had something resembling its first PX and bakery. This second Guadalcanal was still a tough island to live on, but if you didn't get clobbered by enemy fire—and more often than not, you didn't—you were finding that the Canal was at least halfway livable.

The third Guadalcanal tells us a completely different story. After the last of the Japanese were either killed or driven off, the third Guadalcanal developed into an island with large airfields, large supply depots, huts, theaters, PXs, post offices, laundries, and a large marine training base. The 3rd and 6th Marine Divisions trained there in preparation for other battles that would be fought closer to the Japanese homeland. But the only Guadalcanal that I experienced was the first one.

Early in December 1942, what was left of the 5th Marine Regiment left *my* Guadalcanal on Higgins boats that took us to the transport ship USS *President Jackson*, which carried us the relatively short distance out of the combat zone to the handsome city of Brisbane, on Australia's east coast.

I want to say thanks to the men in the *Jackson*'s galley for serving those much-needed, good-tasting bowls of warm macaroni soup, once we'd managed to get belowdecks. The thing that struck me as strange about that soup was the fact that it didn't have any maggots in it.

Food with maggots in it: That was *my* Guadalcanal.

WEAPONS, TACTICS, AND METHODS OF SAVING OUR ASS

On the first of three Guadalcanals—*my* Guadalcanal—some of our weapons were good and others were bad. The Reising gun was a piece of junk that I soon learned was giving everybody else the same trouble it had given Wild Bill Kulchyki when we fought the first battle at the Matanikau. The marines' rifle during the Guadalcanal campaign was better. It was a leftover from World War I, the bolt-action Springfield '03, but in spite of its age, it was accurate and dependable. Many infantrymen would argue that the newer Garand .30-caliber semiautomatic rifle, better known as the M-1, was superior to the '03, but for better or worse, the marines on the Canal didn't get to use it. The M-1 hadn't been in production for very long back in '42, and it was still being distributed to the U.S. Army's combat units. The marines wouldn't get the M-1 until all army units received their full issue, and by that time, the Guadalcanal campaign was over. The Springfield '03 lacked the M-1's obvious advantage of being semiautomatic, which enabled it to be fired at a more rapid rate, but some good riflemen liked it better than the M-1.

One holdover weapon from World War I that nobody argues about is the famous BAR, the Browning automatic rifle. It was the most potent and dependable all-around semiautomatic and automatic weapon that the Marine infantryman took to Guadalcanal. The BAR, a .30-caliber weapon, first saw service in France during World War I, but old doesn't necessarily mean out-of-date. It was beautifully designed and built, it was rugged, and it remained a favorite weapon of American army and marine combat infantrymen in all theaters of World War II.

Prior to our leaving New River, North Carolina, in 1942, the 1st Marine Division held the BAR in such high esteem that Division Command decided to add a fourth squad to what previously had been our standard three-squad rifle platoons. The newly created squad was a BAR squad. It contained eight men, including the squad leader, who was a corporal, an assistant squad leader, three BAR men, and three assistant BAR men who doubled as ammunition carriers.

Addition of the BAR squad revolutionized the concept of the rifle platoon, because it gave the platoon leader three additional automatic small-arms weapons that could be used as weapons of opportunity once the platoon was committed to a specific course of action in a combat situation. At the same time, the BAR squad gave the company commander freedom to shift BAR teams within a platoon or lend an extra BAR team to a different platoon, according to the battle situation and plan.

Before the addition of the BAR squad, marine rifle platoons typically had one, or sometimes two, BARs to augment the '03 rifles in each of its three squads. In that older configuration, the strength of the squad and distribution of BARs was controlled by the varying number of men in a given company and within in the company's three platoons.

The addition of nine additional Browning automatic rifles to an infantry company made a dramatic difference in intensified firepower. From our standpoint, it seemed like giving the company commander free access to Fort Knox. And the most important factor in the effectiveness of this increased firepower was the excellence of the weapon itself. It's safe to say that the firepower, accuracy, and durability of the BAR played a very important part in the defeat of the Japanese Army.

In stories about L Company that I've been recalling here, as well as in many others that I wrote several years ago for *Guadalcanal Echoes*, I haven't always given full credit to the support elements from other units that accompanied us at times when we were in the middle of an offensive thrust or defending a position against enemy action.

For readers unfamiliar with the structure of a marine infantry battalion during World War II, let me explain that our 3rd Battalion was typical in that it consisted of three rifle companies, I, K, and L, plus a weapons company designated M Company. M Company's main weapons in 1942 were water-cooled .30-caliber heavy machine guns (HMGs) and eighty-one-millimeter mortars.

Each time L Company dug in at a defensive position, we were assigned a section of machine guns from M Company. The machine gun sections were rotated among the three rifle companies until, over the duration of our stay on the Canal, we came to know every one of the HMG crewmen almost as well as we knew our own squad members. When they were attached to L Company, members of a machine gun crew became part of our unit and we treated them as such.

Three Guadalcanals

And when it got down to the nitty-gritty, we could usually rely on a few mortar rounds from M Company's eighty-one-millimeter guns. Owing to chronic shortages of ammunition, a few rounds were usually as many as they could spare, but we were glad to get them. As the old song about mortars goes:

> They're over and under,
> If they're on, it's a wonder
> So cheer up, my Lads
> Bless them all.

Whenever Gunny Sergeant Borgeson could spare a round or two to aid us in our defense, those rounds were "on." Well, most of the time they were "on."

Early on during the Canal campaign, a thirty-seven-millimeter antitank gun was assigned to L Company's sector of the defense perimeter. That gun and its four-man crew were dug in with us in the coconut grove, adjacent to the rough unpaved road that went west along the shoreline to the Matanikau River, the area where the Japs were dug in. It's the same gun I referred to earlier when I described our defense of the western perimeter against Oka's unit on the morning of September 14. On that occasion, that thirty-seven-millimeter. fired about a dozen canister rounds into a mass assault that the Japanese were trying to mount, and those rounds, combined with our HMGs, our BARs, and our rifles, broke up that attack before it had a proper chance to get started. Those guys manning the thirty-seven-millimeter stayed in the grove with us for about a month. Both the men from M Company and the four-man antitank gun crew were vital components in L Company's successful defense of our sector of the perimeter. We owed a lot to Gunny Smallwood and Sgt. Harry Miller (after the war, Rev. Harry Miller) and their guys from M Company. We also owed thanks to Sergeant Davidson and his thirty-seven-millimeter crew that came to us from Regiment. They were all great marines and good friends.

During the early stages of World War II, communications equipment in a marine rifle company consisted of a couple of hand-cranked power phones and the two words *scarce* and *bad*. However, when a combat situation broke out at close hand, a couple of "sparks" from Regiment would join our company command post, and from there they were able to crank out an occasional message. The radioman, always informally known as Sparks, would become part of our outfit, as was the case when L Company went on that mid-August combat patrol to the Matanikau in search of the remains of the Goettge Patrol. Lord, what big, heavy, noisy radios they brought to our unit, but we needed them badly, noise and all. Thanks, guys!

Prior to the war, and continuing through the months of the Guadalcanal campaign, the corps remained a small organization. At one time or another, most of our NCOs knew personally, or served with, or at least knew by name, most of the officers and fellow NCOs in the marines. That's the main reason why, when I reflect on the different stories I've written about L-3-5 on Guadalcanal and realize that I haven't always given the names of outfits and warriors attached to our company, it's because to me, every one of us was a part of just one closely knit corps. We were as close as brothers.

After L Company's first month or so on the Canal, putting up with two-a-day bombings by Jap planes, sporadic shelling by the big land artillery piece we'd nicknamed Pistol Pete, and frequent shelling from Japanese warships out on the bay, we pretended to be blasé about the whole business. We treated those noisy interruptions as routine happenings—especially the runs made by the two-engine Japanese bombers.

To save our raggedy asses, we dug spider holes, and we sometimes pulled a cover of some kind over our heads after jumping in, such as bamboo matting that the Japanese airfield construction crew had left behind. Down in our spider holes, we were generally safe from anything short of a direct hit.

At the first wail of our air-raid siren, or at the first sound that signaled approaching enemy airplane engines, we would stop whatever we were doing and start easing our way toward our spider holes. Japanese aircraft engines had a distinct sound of their own, easy to recognize because they were different from our own familiar Grumman, Douglas, Bell, and Boeing warplanes.

As we strolled toward cover, our conversations consisted of casual banter, pretended nonchalance, and normal poking fun at each other. At the same time, we'd occasionally sneak an over-the-shoulder skyward glance to see which direction the planes were coming from. Usually it was from the west—from somewhere beyond the Point Cruz–Matanikau direction. We didn't know it at the time, and it wouldn't have meant anything to us anyway, but that westerly direction meant that the enemy planes were coming from the important Japanese naval and air base at Rabaul. Often we'd also look in the direction of our airstrip to see if any of our planes were going up after the Japs. If a couple of our Grumman F4Fs made it up, I liked to watch the sky for a few extra seconds, taking satisfaction in the way our fighters zoomed in like angry bees, disrupting the bomber formation and sometimes knocking a few of the Mitsubishis down before those suckers had the chance to drop their loads inside our perimeter.

Experience taught us a little bit about the trajectory of falling bombs. If the Jap planes were directly above us when they released their loads, we could play it cool and pretend to be casual about jumping into our holes. That's because we knew that by the time the bombs struck the ground, they'd explode a safe distance away from us, probably on or near the airfield. If we saw the bombs being released as the planes were approaching us, we knew we were in trouble. Those suckers were coming in on *us*! We'd hurry toward safety, hit our spider holes, hug the earthen sides and bottoms, and wait out the thumps and blasts.

For me, the screaming and whining of the downcoming bombs was more frightening than the actual explosions—the earth-shaking, knock-around rattle and roll that the blast and its concussion would hand us as our punishment from Tokyo. Whenever one of our fighter pilots got a good hit on a Jap bomber—and it happened quite often—the enemy plane would scream toward the ground in a power dive, nose first, trailing black smoke, sometimes with parts falling off. That was a sight I'll never forget. But it also spelled a new kind of danger, and we knew we had to hit that spider hole fast. Usually the screaming, smoking, burning plane had a bomb or two aboard. When it hit the ground, all hell jarred loose.

Once in a while, the normal whistling that accompanied falling bombs was joined by a new sound—the damnedest high-pitched *wooo-weee, weee-wooo* noise—a scream that was scary enough to shake the rice out of us. According to scuttlebutt that circulated after the first of those weird raids, the new noises were caused by empty sake bottles that the Japs would drop on us along with their bombs. More scuttlebutt had it that from time to time, our own pilots dropped empty Coke bottles on enemy positions along with their bombs as a way to retaliate. No matter who was on the receiving end, the shriek was scary—something a little extra to shake up the troops in an attempt to lower morale.

Another thing the Japanese planes did several times during the campaign's early days of August and September was to drop small sheets of foil down inside our perimeter. Anybody who'd been following the war in Europe knew that the tinfoil was supposed to disrupt our radar and confuse our radar operators. If that was the Japs' intention on the Canal, they were wasting their effort. There were plenty of supplies and a lot of equipment we marines simply didn't get during our four months on the Canal, and radar was one of them.

We didn't know for sure why the Japanese were dropping that foil, so it was natural to assume the worst. A couple of our old veteran China Hands warned us not to touch that damned foil. "It's probably dusted with chemicals that will burn holes in your flesh," one NCO said.

Then, in a move that's typical of military outfits everywhere, the order to keep away from the foil was directly reversed. We were told to pick up the sheets and turn them in. It was one more work detail to keep the troops busy between visits from the Japs. I'm sure that some of the guys who picked up that foil stashed a few sheets of it into a field pack or a pocket, to save as a souvenir. I'll also bet that a few of today's old grandpas have forgotten all about the foil that they once brought back from the Canal. Maybe they open an attic trunk or a half-forgotten footlocker, spot a couple of crumpled pieces of foil inside, and wonder what the hell they're looking at.

I can't prove it and I won't try, but I believe that between August and December 1942, the marines who were positioned inside that very small perimeter on Guadalcanal were bombed and shelled more than any other American unit in the Pacific theater. L Company took casualties in ground combat, but to the best of my recollection, not one of us was killed or wounded by the bombing and strafing of Japanese planes. What saved us is clear enough to me: our spider holes. The Canal survivors are proof that if you are properly dug in, it will take a direct hit to do you in. Whatever advantages and skills the Japanese military might have had in World War II, the accuracy of their bombers was definitely not one of them.

PISTOL PETE

Many years after the end of World War II, I started coming across a series of stories in *Guadalcanal Echoes* about veterans of the campaign who had been looking for, and had finally found, Mr. Akio Tani, a.k.a. Pistol Pete. For some of our guys, finding the onetime commander of that Japanese gun crew turned out to be a little bit like Stanley finding Livingstone. I never shared their enthusiasm. Finding Pistol Pete will never be a big deal for me, because he remains today as he was in 1942, a *persona non grata* in my life.

I am not a bitter person by nature. On the contrary, my World War II experiences have not controlled me or traumatized my life. In 1945, the war over, I started putting those experiences behind me, and I've gone on to live a largely happy, event-filled life. After the war was over, I served two tours of duty in Japan and became friends with a number of good Japanese people. On one occasion, I even took steps far beyond the call of duty to help a marine cut through miles of red tape and marry a fine and lovely Japanese girl. I did, however, perceive World War II as a very serious happening, and my visual memories of many dead, wounded, maimed, and crippled friends hit by enemy artillery fire just won't allow me to tell Mr. Tani that he and I are now good friends.

On Guadalcanal, Rifle Company L-3-5 spent most of its time in the coconut grove at the far western edge of the marines' perimeter, the part that faced toward the Matanikau River. Most of the rounds Pistol Pete fired at the airfield, or at our Kukum facilities, came from points far to our west, from somewhere across the Matanikau River. Most of them went safely over our heads. Occasionally, and maybe just to keep us honest, Pete threw a random round into our company area. On occasions when we happened to be involved in an activity that would be visible from a distance—like digging a well for drinking water or a bunker to climb into as a way of trying to save our hides—Pistol Pete might zero in on us. He'd send one round over a little long, a second round short, and a third round right on target. Zeroing in like that indicated that he had a forward observer watching us and helping him find his target.

In time, we became blasé about Pistol Pete, because the occasional rounds that he dropped into our defense area caused very little damage. But once in a while, Mr. Tani got lucky. Once one of our guys was sitting on the low stump of a coconut tree, just a few yards away from his foxhole, reading a small Bible that he always carried with him. He was a quiet, honest lad who really did read from his Bible when he had a moment to rest. Mr. Tani got the brass ring that day. The kid heard the incoming round at the very last second. He had time only to get up on his feet and was about to make a dash for his foxhole when the round landed right in front of him. It hit the ground right between his feet. There was a terrific explosion, and during the five to seven seconds it took his disemboweled torso to fly into the air then flop to the ground, a god-awful wail came out from his throat. I wish the Guadalcanal vets who were so happy to find Mr. Tani could have heard that dying kid's scream.

I understand that Mr. Tani, a.k.a. Pistol Pete, is now an elderly, quiet gentleman. He was a soldier who was just carrying out his orders in 1942, the same way that *we* were carrying out *our* orders. Fine. Mr. Tani and I wouldn't know each other if we were the last two people remaining on the face of the earth. That's the way I want it.

A LITTLE BIT OF LARCENY TO KEEP UP OUR MORALE

One day, as buck sergeant, I led a reconnaissance patrol. We were ordered to move out from the west end of our MLR, scout out the area through the coconut grove, keep moving as far as the Matanikau River, then circle back and report anything of military interest. We went all the way to the river that day, and except for the usual macaw and parrot squawking, we heard nothing out of the ordinary and saw nothing unusual. At the river, I signaled the men to turn and start heading back toward our perimeter.

We took a slightly different route on our way back, moving through a section of underbrush that we hadn't patrolled recently. We had gone some distance when the point man signaled, halting the patrol and catching my attention. I moved forward to see what had stopped him. As I approached, he pointed into an area of heavy foliage. Something was in there behind the foliage: a large camouflaged object that took the shape of something man-made. I signaled the rest of the patrol to move up and form a large semicircle around the object, then stand fast and cover it with our weapons in case one or more Japs were in there.

We remained in place for maybe three or four minutes, watching and listening. There was no sign of movement, no sign of life inside that thick patch of leaves and branches that somebody unknown to us had used to camouflage something.

But to camouflage what? My point man and I moved in a little closer and gradually made out that the object was a vehicle of some kind. We moved in closer yet. It was a flatbed truck, and clearly Japanese. "What's it doing here?" I asked myself. I didn't speak the words aloud. I didn't want to break the silence, but my mind was filled with questions: Why hadn't anybody seen it until now? How long had it been out here, and why? And the most important question of all: Was it booby-trapped?

I signaled back to a couple more men, moving them up to join us. While we covered the object with our rifles, they removed a few branches and a lot of loose foliage, and gradually the truck appeared beneath it all. One man crawled under the carriage, inspecting it for wires that might lead to explosives, or for anything else that might look suspicious. Another man carefully lifted the hood and gave the engine compartment a look-see. Carefully, I climbed into the truck's cab. I found that old-style ignition switch, with gas and spark handles, and the needle on the gasoline gauge showed plenty of gas. Everything indicated that this was no trap. Everything looked okay.

The rest of the patrol backed away to a safe distance, and I threw the switch that turned on the spark and gas. The engine kicked to life. It was as easy as that. With the engine idling, half of the patrol moved in and removed the rest of the camouflage. Then the entire patrol piled on, and we went chug-chugging and bouncing over the rough terrain and back through the coconut grove. I stopped the truck about fifty yards from our perimeter, parked our newly acquired vehicle, and we proceeded on foot back to our line of defense.

At that time, morale in our unit had hit pretty close to rock bottom. To make things worse, what little information we brought back from our various scouting patrols didn't seem to make much of an impression or have much value. We might report: "We heard noises in the distance that sounded like vehicles. Maybe like tanks."

"Well, okay. We'll check it out further," would be the answer.

Or maybe, after getting to a point where we could take a better look at Mount Austen, we'd say: "Looks like they're doing more cutting away at the foliage on that mountain."

"Yeah? Okay. Maybe we'll check it out."

So today it was: "We found a truck in the grove today."

"A truck? That's nice."

The apparent lack of interest on the part of our superiors didn't encourage us to elaborate. In fact, we decided that the best thing we could do was take matters into our own hands. I took my men back out to the coconut grove, and to our truck. Yes, by now it was *our* truck. We camouflaged the damned thing and decided that from now on, it would be strictly for our own use.

A few days later saw a U.S. Army unit arriving on the Canal to reinforce the marines. We watched them moving around at Kukum, unloading supplies, equipment, and food destined for their troops. It was about time we started seeing some decent supplies and equipment coming our way. To assist movement of all those goodies off the beach, the Corps Motor Transport had lined up a dozen or so trucks, both marine vehicles and trucks left behind by the Japanese. We in L Company decided to use a little of that famous Marine Corps initiative and help our army comrades.

Having been thoroughly trained in larceny back at New River—and adhering to the principle that "even if it's nailed down, you pry it loose and take it away"—I sauntered out to the beach and inspected the situation. I liked what I saw. Back at our position on the MLR, I rounded up plenty of volunteers. We proceeded to the nearby coconut grove, got our truck out from beneath its covering foliage, then moved ahead to join the line of vehicles that were transporting those many good things the army had brought ashore. We patiently waited our turn. When our Japanese truck finally moved up to become number-one in line, I announced to the supply people: "We're supposed to pick up foodstuff for the chow supply dump."

It worked.

It was as though we'd died and gone to heaven. The army was loading case after case of foodstuffs on our flatbed—peaches, canned hams, fruit juices, and other good things that we'd have been willing to kill or die for.

I cannot say that we drove our truck to the 1st Marine Division Supply Dump. That would be a lie. Instead, our truck made an abrupt left turn, which quickly took us back to the section of the MLR defended by L-3-5. As we arrived, others from our unit already were busy digging holes to bury the loot they knew we'd be bringing back with us. One practical-minded NCO was drawing a hasty sketch of the company area, a kind of map that showed the locations of the holes and listed the contents that were now disappearing into each of them: two cases of ham at one point, two cases of canned fruit at another. Before long, all evidence of our raid had disappeared, including the Japanese truck. Once again it was some fifty yards away in the coconut grove, safely camouflaged by a mound of fresh foliage.

Still another incident when a little bit of larceny kept L Company's morale from sinking to rock bottom took place after I'd moved up in the world, from corporal and squad leader to sergeant, probably in October. My men were holding our regular position on the MLR, but after being stuck operating from that spot for about a month, we were ordered to move a few yards to the rear, to what was called a reserve position. We were getting a short rest—assuming that rest or anything like it was possible inside our perimeter. Moving a platoon of guys from Company L-3-5 off the MLR at that time and place was comparable to a civilian family packing up and moving to a different part of town on an hour's notice. But we did it, and the Japanese didn't cause problems during the short time it took us to make the move.

My next instructions were to take my champions in small groups back to the relative safety of the Lunga River, where they could get themselves and the crummy clothes on their backs scrubbed up in fresh water. On my way back from one

Three Guadalcanals

trip, two enterprising marines (this is a polite way to describe a pair of expert, school-trained scroungers) got my permission to wander over to the village of Kukum, just to see how the other half was living. At Kukum, an MP parading around the ramshackle structure that passed for a warehouse attracted their attention. The scroungers could only wonder: What was in there worth the trouble to post a guard?

Being inquisitive young men, they wandered over to the building and started making small talk with the MP. What they learned struck them as information of great interest and momentous importance. The oversize shack, they were told, held a supply of Japanese chow and many cases of sake. But things that seem important at one moment can fade to insignificance the next, which is what happened as their conversation with the guard came to an abrupt halt. The air-raid siren had started wailing, and the drone of approaching Jap bombers filled the sky. Understandably, the MP was more interested in saving his skin than protecting captured stores.

"Good-bye, you guys!" he yelled, as he ducked out of sight and into a bunker that had been built for his protection.

Were my two buddies concerned about the approaching bombers? No way. What did concern them was the health and welfare of that large shack's contents. By now the bombers were in sight, and the thump of exploding bombs was shaking the very earth beneath their feet. The time had come for them to find an air-raid shelter, and the warehouse was the nearest shelter at hand.

They ducked inside and saw at a glance that what the MP had told them was true. All hell was breaking loose outside, but there in that haven, they beheld stacks of canned Japanese food and case after case of sake. It occurred to them, they told me later, that if a bomb ever scored a hit on this shack, everything would be lost forever. Better, they decided, to salvage a couple of precious items right now and run for it. Grabbing two large bottles of sake apiece, they burst out of the warehouse and ran for their lives as bombs fell and exploded all around them. Later, when they explained their protective attitude to me, I began to suspect that these scroungers had the makings of officer material in their souls. Anyhow, I understood their intentions and couldn't find it in my heart to disapprove of their action.

Back at our new reserve position, the scrounging duo told everybody their story while they shared the contents of those four magnum-size bottles with the rest of the platoon. Lubricated with sake, our imaginations began working double-time, and we started planning and plotting future action. What we needed was a surefire method to protect the rest of those fragile glass bottles in that Kukum shack. We all had ideas to volunteer, and after lengthy discussion, we worked out a solution. It required the use of a machine-gun cart, which our neighbors in the heavy machine gun section of M Company were eager to lend when hearing of our fortune. They were anxious to cooperate in the delicate tactical exercise we had concocted.

Our friends in the Japanese Air Force had become reliable visitors, making regular round-trips from Rabaul to say hello. We knew we could count on their appearance at nearly the same time every day. Next day, as the air-raid warning sounded, two future men of the cloth—alias our original pair of scroungers—took off on the double, making a dummy run in the direction of the warehouse. Just as they expected, they saw the MP do whatever he could to save his life by diving into his bunker and vanishing out of sight. So far, so good. The third day arrived, and so did the Japanese bombers, preceded as always by the siren's wail. Once again our scroungers took off like a pair of scalded geese, but this time the machine-gun cart went bouncing with them along the sun-baked road.

They arrived at the warehouse just as the bombs began falling. Taking a second to look around, they saw that the MP and everybody else in the area had ducked for cover. Everybody except them. Wasting no time, these brave men dashed into the shack and hauled the cart inside with them. Within moments, they loaded two cases of sake on the cart and covered their treasure with a poncho. Back outside again, and heedless of the bombs bursting in air, they made it all the way back to our reserve position. Bombs or no bombs, they traveled much slower now. The precious cargo merited maximum care.

The week that followed saw a total of four, maybe five, trips to that warehouse and back. Every time the Japanese bombers made their round-trip from Rabaul, our stout-hearted scroungers made their own round trip from Company L-3-5's reserve position. And by that time, every man in the company had a few goods to diminish hunger and thirst, not the least of those goods being a sake bottle, which he swore to guard and protect. The bottles' contents didn't need guarding. They were put to good use. A "pull" each morning, just before moving out on patrol, helped make our day—and our eyeballs—a little brighter and sharper. The sake's afterglow nearly made us overlook the miserable situation that we were in. Almost, but not quite.

But sooner or later, all good things must end. It wasn't long before the company was moved to a new position, and this time we were too far away from the warehouse to continue making those air-raid trips. But where there are scroungers with a will, there is a way, and by now every man in L-3-5 had learned to be an accomplished, academically trained scrounger. We'd been educated by a pair of PhDs in scrounging. Whenever rumors of liberated chow or liquid spirits drifted through the island's fetid jungle air, we had a full platoon of men who were equal to the task of salvaging their fair share of it.

MAIL CALL

When you've been sent off to war, mail call becomes a more important event than it is for most people in civilian life. At about the time the Guadalcanal campaign was heating up, one of the Hollywood studios released a move titled *From the Shores of Tripoli*. Its star was a new, handsome young actor named John Payne. Meanwhile, several thousand miles away in the South Pacific, it happened that L-3-5's ranks included a very young marine whose name was Pvt. John R. Payne. Back in 1942, a lot of movies were being made about the war, and American girls were going to their neighborhood theaters to see them. One of the favorites, largely thanks to actor John Payne, was *From the Shores of Tripoli*. Young ladies being what they were then, and still are (thank you, Lord!), many of them immediately fell madly in love with the sight of the actor.

Soon quite a few of those girls were writing fan mail to the movie star, telling him how handsome and sexy they thought he was, and often making intimate suggestions that they certainly would never talk about with their mothers, let alone their pastors. Far from any Hollywood film studio at the time, cut off from civilization and confined to the jungles of Guadalcanal, how could I possibly know about those passionate and torrid letters? Like many other marines in L-3-5, I know about those fan letters because several hundred love-struck young ladies addressed their letters, not to the actor's Hollywood studio, but to John Payne, U.S. Marine Corps. And many of those letters found their way to FPO, San Francisco, from which point they were forwarded to the Pacific theater. Eventually they found their way to Pvt. John R. Payne, L-3-5.

You have no idea of the entertainment those letters gave, not only to Pvt. John R. Payne, but to all the rest of us in the platoon. We read the juicier sentences aloud for the rest of the guys to hear. Sometimes we'd take turns, hamming it up, reading those passionate messages with orator-style diction and dramatic gestures. In a place like Guadalcanal, where entertainment ranged between scarce and nonexistent, those letters gave us a lot of laughs and were nearly as good as a visit from the USO.

A second mail-call incident was all my own.

From the time I was a kid, I would read anything that happened to be available. That habit came to a temporary halt during boot camp at Parris Island, when from the crack of dawn till the moment his head hit his pillow at night, no recruit had a moment to call his own. After boot camp, I found reading to be as good a pastime as any, cheap enough that even a marine private could afford it. Something from the Book-of-the-Month Club, something from the ship's library, anything. I was one of several guys in my squad who joined book clubs, and every month we'd each order a different book. When we finished whatever we were reading, we'd trade books, which gave each of us the most reading for the least amount of money spent. I was a pretty fast reader, but my good buddy Larry Gerkin was slow. "Don't memorize the damned book," I'd tell him. "Just read it."

"Marion, I'm going to bust your head," he'd answer, then he'd go on reading, very slowly.

In the summer of '42, we shipped out, first to New Zealand, and from there to war. That's when those bastards at the Book-of-the-Month Club dunned me. Late in our stay on the lovely island of Guadalcanal, when our planes were finally starting to get through with supplies, we had a mail call one day. "Marion," I heard, and I was handed a letter from the Book-of-the-Month Club. I opened it and found out that I owed them $2.50 and that I was past due by four months. It was polite enough, but it said something like pay up or they'd take care of me.

Well, I was just a little pissed. I'm out in the Pacific, eating rice and maggots and getting shot at by Japs, while some fat ass in a comfortable chair back in the States is trying to get two-fifty out of my hide. So I wrote right there, on their letter, and mailed it back to them. If they ever bothered to read it, they could have felt the venom. I wrote: "Dear sir: You're right. I owe you $2.50, and I ain't paying it. So if you don't like it, you just come out here and get me, and drag my ass back to some soft, comfortable jail at home. —Ore Marion"

I never did pay it. But years later, when I was living in California, my wife wanted to join the club, and I included with the form a note telling them that I had missed a payment when I was fighting in the Pacific. I got a brief letter back telling me that they no longer were collecting overdue bills from 1942.

YIPPEE BOATS

In the dog days of September and October '42, most of the ships that the U.S. Navy had in the South Pacific were either being repaired after engagements with the enemy or hiding in safe island harbors. No ships or planes were heading to the Canal to bring in badly needed supplies, and we were feeling the pain.

One evening just before dark, our platoon was ordered to Kukum Beach, where we were supposed to serve as a working party. Normally that meant a ship had arrived and we were being detailed to unload it. A few platoons from other units joined us, but when we looked out to sea, there wasn't a ship to be seen. There was nothing on the beach for us to move, either, so we had nothing to do but sit on the sand, skylark, trade scuttlebutt, generally shoot the shit, and wonder if and when a ship would come in that evening. Or ever.

The sun went down, and one more tropical night descended, sudden and pitch black as usual. Still there was nothing, no sign of any approaching ship. Then, about half an hour after dark, and from pretty far out over the water, we heard the first faint sound of an engine. At first we didn't know what to make of it. Its pitch was different from anything we were familiar with. Right away, somebody from the Marine Shore Party Unit showed up among us. I heard him tell our sergeant in charge that the boat we were hearing would probably make several passes parallel to the beach. At each pass, its crew would dump drums of aviation fuel overboard. My squad was assigned the detail of wading far enough out from the beach that the boat could approach us. We were instructed to grab hold of the gasoline drums as soon as they splashed overboard, and then push them ashore. The other men in our platoon would roll the drums up on the beach as far as the berm line, where they'd be out of the enemy's clear view when daylight arrived.

We waded into the dark sea. Our platoon had no sooner made it out to a point where the water was about waist-high when we heard that unfamiliar boat's motor approaching very close to us, sounding almost as though it were in idle. And now we could see the vessel, make it out as a blacker, more solid shape against the black sky. Its silhouette took shape as a small seagoing craft that moved very slowly, parallel to the shoreline.

A couple of voices sounded softly over the water from the boat's deck: "Heads up!"

With that came a series of loud splashes, heavy objects falling into the sea. And that turned out to be all we ever heard from that boat: the sound of its engine, the voices of its crew calling softly as a caution to us, "Heads up," and the succession of splashes. In ten minutes or less, that crew's work was done. Without a further signal or a by your leave, the engine's pitch changed, and that dark, shadowy boat disappeared into the night.

Our job of floating those fifteen or twenty barrels of fuel ashore was easy, but the guys on the beach had a more difficult time, rolling the drums up over the sand and into cover behind the berm line.

We had been visited that night by a Yippee boat. It was one of the many tuna boats that the navy had commissioned from our West Coast ports of San Diego, San Pedro, Monterey, and San Francisco. For quite a while, those mysterious nighttime boat visits were our only way of getting the supplies we needed in order to keep functioning as an effective military unit. The navy gave those boats the designation YP, followed by an ID number, hence Yippee. Where they took on the supplies they shipped to us, I don't know, but we were told that those West Coast fishermen reached us by dodging from island to island across the South Pacific, hiding in coves when they had to, making fast runs when they could, and timing their movements to approach Guadalcanal and arrive at Kukum Beach just after total darkness.

Months later, when I was off the Canal and recovering from a severe bout of malaria and malnutrition at a hospital in Melbourne, Australia, I met a sailor who told me that while he was assigned to the motor pool on Tulagi, he met an old high school friend from Point Loma, California. His friend told him how the Yippee boats came into being. The father of his buddy was a fisherman and the owner and captain of a tuna boat out of San Diego. The navy had taken the boat over, the way they were doing with many others like it. They commissioned the skipper and his eight-man crew after a week or so of indoctrination and had them sworn into the navy. There they were—as fast as that, they had become part of the U.S. Navy. Next they sailed across the South Pacific, snooping and drooping among the islands, doing whatever they could to keep us combat units supplied and operational.

It always has been the case at every naval station that you'll see many small, noncombatant boats—not ships, but small boats—each of them manned by a crew of not more than eight or ten men. You'll see these boats zipping around among the harbor's ships and docks, taking care of odds and ends, moving small items and equipment from dockside to vessels or from one ship to another.

The Yippee boats and their crews were among the many unsung heroes of the war in the Pacific. In total, they constituted a relatively few men who operated only a handful of boats, all of them taking care of those countless small details that were never foreseen by the navy's operational planners. Throughout the war, the Yippee boats went quietly about their work which, for the benefit of ten thousand marines on the Canal, turned out to be vitally important. Little or no mention has been made of the Yippee boats' visits to us. Too little credit is given for all the good work they did.

OUR VIEW OF NAVAL AND AIR COMBAT

In the years following World War II, I've often talked with Guadalcanal campaign veterans who'd been aboard ships and involved in sea battles on and near Ironbottom Sound. More recently, it occurred to me that many of the guys didn't realize that the marines on Guadalcanal had a ringside seat for most of those naval engagements.

Manning beach defense positions or being located on one of the high outer ridges near the defense perimeter, we usually had Savo and the Florida Island group in plain sight. Under most conditions when we were on a high ridge, we had a view of the Canal's coastline looking west nearly all the way to Cape Esperance, which is at the island's tip. When on patrol or in a defilade area—a spot where we had set up protective fortifications—our view of the sea would be temporarily hidden. But more often than not, we had a clear, unobstructed view of many miles of surrounding water.

Those now famous sea battles that gave Ironbottom Sound its name would start as a sudden disruption of a quiet, often moonless night. The Japanese had the habit of choosing the darkest nights to begin sea battles. From out of the silent blackness, there would come a shattering, often frightening *wham—bang!* We'd see flashes from big naval gun barrels, and then more flashes from their exploding shells. Searchlights would suddenly blink on from one ship and sweep another ship's outline—a favorite Japanese sea battle tactic—and illuminating flares would silhouette still another ship's superstructure. Somebody in our squad would usually say, "Man, we're giving them hell tonight!"

Maybe what was really happening was that *they* were giving *us* hell. But naturally, we always hoped for the best.

At first light of day following one of those terrific night battles, we would usually see some of our ships smoking and limping on the water or—like the heavy cruiser *Atlanta* on that November morning—being scuttled after their crews were forced to abandon ship. Maybe one or two other cruisers would limp slowly away, missing a stern, or a bow, or a part of the superstructure. The smaller destroyers seemed luckier somehow. We'd see them towing larger vessels, while open boats would be casting off from our dock at Kukum to pick up survivors. Looking down at the beach from one of our ridge positions, we'd see the shoreline cluttered with oil-soaked and blackened sailors who had abandoned their sinking ships and managed one way or another to make it to land. Many of them were wounded; all of them were tired.

We in the 1st Marine Division, well aware that we'd been abandoned earlier by our navy and were now witnessing American losses at sea, found the aftermath of those naval engagements doubly depressing. Luckily, most of us were young and naive, and it seldom took much to raise our spirits again and give us back our natural and customary optimism. We had very few sound reasons to believe we were going to win, but we were young enough and optimistic enough to assume against all odds that we would see the campaign to its end and defeat the enemy.

There were a few times when something tangible occurred to brighten our mood. On one occasion, we looked out to sea at daybreak and saw a very large warship that appeared beached on Savo Island. Two of our planes—probably all we could get into the air at the time—were making low-level, high-speed round-trips between Henderson Field and that big enemy ship. Each time they flew over it, they dropped a couple bombs, and the Japanese ship appeared too badly crippled to put up any resistance. A Japanese ship finally sunk!

On many a day, lying on the ground, or sometimes sitting against the base of a coconut tree, we had a very good view of air battles between the Japanese Zeros and our own Grumman F4F Wildcats. The Zero was faster and could outclimb our Grummans, but the Grummans could take a lot more punishment than any of the Japanese planes. At the sound of an air-raid siren, three or four of our Wildcats would come up off the fighter strip, and if they had enough advance warning, they'd climb as high as they could go. When the Jap bombers approached, our guys would zoom down on them, often knocking a couple of them down like duckpins. Anytime a smoking or partly crippled Japanese bomber fell out of formation, it was sure to be whacked by one of our guys who had been hanging out at a distance and waiting.

The situation changed when the bombers were escorted by Zeros—or when the Zeros came overhead by themselves to harass our own ground position and the positions of other companies, diving and strafing us while we scrambled for cover. We marines on the ground didn't take many casualties from the enemy planes, but they did keep us honest and humble. The Zero was as fast as that proverbial cat on a hot tin roof. Our Grumman Wildcats usually operated in pairs—sometimes one pair, other times two, which was usually as many as our air crews could get into the sky at any one time. Because the Zeros were much faster in a dogfight, they would often overshoot our Wildcats, but if the Zero swung around in a wide arc, it was shame on him! The Grumman would catch the Jap plane with a single machine-gun burst, which was usually enough to knock it out of the sky.

We watched our beaten-up but more rugged Wildcats fight the Zeros high, and we watched as they fought them low over the water. Sometimes we saw them fly between the island's tall palm trees, the Wildcats banked so steeply that they looked like they were standing on one wing. Planes and parts, both Japanese and American, showered down all around us.

Once in a while, when a Grumman was shot down, its pilot was able to bail out and make it to safety. One day we saw one of our guys bail out from his plane over the water. His parachute opened, and we figured he'd soon be rescued—until a Zero came zooming in, shooting him to pieces as he hung there helpless. That sight made our blood boil. Several other times, we watched a group of our SBD dive-bombers take off from Henderson Field and disappear over the horizon, probably chasing after part of the Japanese fleet. On many of those days, several of our planes would go out, but only one or two—or sometimes none—would come back. It was the same with our flights of Avenger torpedo bombers. Once a member of our Cactus Air Force came around, asking for volunteers as airplane gunners. Our reply was, "Get lost, Mac."

Anyway, whenever *Victory at Sea,* or *Air Battles in the Pacific,* or one of those other Pacific war documentaries appears on my television screen, I usually end up talking to myself, saying, "Hell, I watched 'em *make* that movie."

Whenever the Coast Watchers, friendly aircraft, submarines, ships, or whatever else spotted and reported a Japanese ship movement headed toward Guadalcanal in 1942, a platoon from Company L-3-5 would be moved from its primary position on the line to its secondary position, which was beach defense. Other companies along the entire length of the marine perimeter did the same thing. These movements were usually timed so that the unit being moved would take its position and be settled down just as the sun was setting. Fortunately the Japanese never attempted a landing on our beach during our entire stay on the Canal, but there was no way we could know that at the time. A night on the beach or at the berm line gave us ringside seats to those *slam-bang* sea battles—or sometimes to a shelling from a vessel that the enemy sailed within reach of our shoreline.

Our navy must have instructed our sailors to the effect that if forced to abandon ship near Guadalcanal, they should never attempt a night landing anywhere near the part of the beach occupied by the marines. To the best of my memory, no such landing ever occurred. The navy must have warned the crews: "Keep out of range of the beach at night, because those trigger-happy marines will dispatch you for sure." Even so, on several occasions after a night sea battle, we'd hear small boats moving about offshore, or maybe we'd hear a splash from an oar paddle that told us somebody was out on the water, trying to maneuver a raft. When dawn finally arrived, we'd see what we'd been hearing during the night: American ship survivors waiting for daylight so that they could safely come ashore, take care of their wounded, and organize themselves.

Tension was always high when an event like that happened, with every one of us on the alert. Whoever was making those sounds on the water might have been Americans, but they might just as easily have been Japanese. Word was passed to all in the beach defense unit: "Don't shoot till they hit the beach and you can see them."

One night I was looking out to sea, watching the flashes and hearing the booms of a rip-roaring naval battle. Then it was over. It was followed by a lull, the illusion of peace and quiet that always followed such slugfests. As I stared out in the direction of the now pitch-black ocean, I gradually heard a small boat's motor, its sound getting louder. Then no sound at all. The engine had shut off. It started up again, remained in idle, then its pitch changed as it slowly approached the beach. We couldn't see it. We could only hear it as it approached our beach, seeming to be making directly for our position. All my senses were on the alert. Every man in the platoon was on the alert. We had no way of knowing if this was one of our guys—or one of the Japanese.

The sound came closer, telling us that the boat was practically at the shoreline. Again the engine was shut off. More silence. Then a voice came to us from across the water, in plain, ordinary, American-sounding English: "Back off. I think we're too close to the beach."

A different voice replied, but it was muffled, and we couldn't make out the words.

The first voice answered, loud and clear, "Back off, damn it! We get any closer and those crazy bastards will open up on us."

The way he was talking, we figured this boatload had to be our guys. We whispered among ourselves—and that's when we started to have our doubts. Our Japanese friends had used several tricks on us before, and some of them spoke better English than we did. Was this another one of their tricks?

Anyhow, the boat stayed out there for the rest of the night. We could hear it drifting in, moving out, back and forth, but that was all we could hear. And we couldn't see a damn thing. At long last there came the first gray light of dawn, the moment when dim shapes first start emerging out of the darkness.

"Holy Christ, look at that!" one of our guys shouted.

By now we all could see it. Out there on the water's surface, maybe a hundred yards or so in front of us, was a small boat of a type that none of us could identify. That wasn't important. What we couldn't miss was the fact that it was loaded to the gunwales with guys standing shoulder to shoulder, many of them holding a regulation-size American flag that they'd unfurled so that it stretched from bow to stern for all to see. Even under those circumstances, it was a damn good sight for our tired eyes.

As we watched, one of our NCOs moved away from his position, yelled, got the survivors' attention, and directed them to move a few hundred yards to where they'd find the Kukum boat landing. Away they went, and away went another night on the Guadalcanal beach defense. I never found out what ship they'd been on. Funny, but that didn't seem important at the time. The important thing was that they'd made it ashore.

TORPEDOES AND THE USS *ALCHIBA*

During the Guadalcanal campaign, nearly everybody on the island knew of and spoke about the supply ship USS *Alchiba*. It was one of the precious and all-too-few transport vessels that brought us our much-needed supplies. One thing a little unusual about the *Alchiba* is the fact that it was bombed, torpedoed, and nearly sunk by the Japanese while unloading our supplies—not once, which wouldn't have been unusual, but on two separate occasions. The *Alchiba* was repaired at the spot where it was first hit, and then it was hit again, right after the first repairs were completed. The Japs seemed to have some special gripe against the *Alchiba*, but they never did sink her. The story of that gallant ship and its brave crew was told and retold many times by the men of the 1st Marines, until it took on the quality of a legend. All the newly arriving troops heard stories about how the *Alchiba*'s crew stayed aboard, made repairs, refloated their ship, and proudly sailed away. It passed among the men through word of mouth, and later it was written about by several different authors and reporters.

The first torpedo that struck the *Alchiba*'s hull was a personal insult to every rifleman in the 1st Marine Division, because so many of us had worked on that ship—in its hold, on its deck, or at the dock. We'd taken part in loading or unloading the supplies and equipment it carried. The *Alchiba* began to seem like an old buddy, and it hurts when a buddy gets zapped. Back in '42, it was the men from marine rifle companies who did most of the loading and unloading whenever supply ships came in. That was an unquestioned part of staff and command thinking: "Keep your troops razor-sharp by subjecting them to hurry up and wait, or by making them load and unload ships."

Fred Harris, a member of M-3-5, was on a work detail near the *Alchiba* the second time it was hit. Here's his story:

A tug assists in fighting the fires on the USS *Alchiba*, which had been torpedoed by a Japanese submarine. UNITED STATES MARINE CORPS

Marines on the beach at Lunga Point watch as the *Alchiba* burns.
UNITED STATES MARINE CORPS

There were about half a dozen of us, and we had been on the *Alchiba* that morning cleaning up the mess from the fire and firefighter's efforts after the torpedo that nearly sank her the first time. We were told the *Alchiba* had been struck by a torpedo the night before, but there was not even a wisp of smoke coming out of the ship by the time my group climbed aboard, which was about midmorning. We were detailed to finish the work started by the just-departed cleanup team.

We were dismissed from the *Alchiba* about noon and assigned to complete the unloading of a flat barge that was moored nearby. It had been loaded with red-painted barrels of aviation gas, but by the time we got on board, that cargo had been reduced to a dozen or so barrels, stacked two high on the barge's ocean end. No activity was visible aboard the *Alchiba*. On the barge where we were working, we stood about three feet above the water's surface while we tossed off barrels of aviation gas. That was when a Japanese sub's conning tower suddenly rose some two feet above the water's surface and just a few feet out from our barge, close enough that we could have touched it.

Later the general consensus was that the sub had torpedoed the *Alchiba* the night before, then remained motionless underwater at the same location while our gasoline barge moved in and came to rest directly over it. But as we worked on the barge, the sub moved out from under us, then surfaced, its bow pointed straight at the *Alchiba*. We saw a puff of vapor, and water mist that rose about twelve or fourteen feet from the sub's bow, on the side facing the ocean. That would have been the torpedo being released. Next thing I noticed was a sailor up on the *Alchiba*'s deck being led off with blood running down his face.

No sign of a periscope was ever visible. From where I stood, I was able to see down into the empty space of the conning tower for about three feet beneath the water's surface. It was painted a glossy black. There was not a single visible paint scrape, weld, rivet, opening, ladder, gun, or evidence that one had ever been mounted. No A-frame, rope, or blemish on the forward deck or port side of the conning tower. The outside of the sub was painted a glossy light tan. We were looking at the sub from the top and port side, and from the conning tower forward. The remaining gasoline barrels blocked our view of its entire after end.

Then the sub made its getaway. A bow gunner on one nearby U.S. ship got off a burst of twenty-millimeter and probably would have fired for effect had he not noticed us marines among the gas barrels. Some of our ships with depth-charge capability finally got the message and tried to turn the bay upside down a full mile away from where the sub was resubmerging as silently as it had surfaced.

I sure would like to read the navy's action report of that event. The navy sent me a picture of a Japanese sub designated the *I 16*, which they said was the one that did the number on the *Alchiba*. They never responded when I told them that if this was really the sub that fired the torpedo, then it picked up the bow gun pictured after it left the Guadalcanal waters. There was no bow gun on the sub I saw, and I was close enough to jump on it.

Many years have passed since that summer and fall of 1942, and many different events have blurred together in the minds of the marines who were on the Canal back then. Some of my own memories have blurred, so today I can't be certain whether another story I want to tell here is about the *Alchiba* or some other transport ship that the Japanese tried to torpedo. In his book *Guadalcanal Remembered*, Herb Merilat, an officer assigned to General Vandegrift's command post, recalls the day when a Japanese torpedo missed one of our ships and came up on the beach at Kukum. Merilat's torpedo and mine could very well be the same one. If it is, the target was not the *Alchiba*, because the date Merilat gives is well before the *Alchiba* was hit.

But this isn't so much a story about the ship as it is about a Japanese torpedo that missed its target. Was the intended target the *Alchiba*? Maybe yes and maybe no. Maybe it doesn't matter, because what's most important about this particular Japanese torpedo is not its target, but that it came all the way up on the beach. Not on just any old beach. It came up on *our* beach!

During most of the Guadalcanal campaign, the waters off the coast at Kukum village were infested with Japanese submarines, every one of those subs looking to pick off whatever American or Australian shipping happened to come into its periscope sights. The *Alchiba* was just one among many targets. Some of the torpedoes hit our ships, and some of them missed. One of them didn't just miss, it kept right on going until it reached dry land.

My torpedo story occurred when I was a corporal and a squad leader, returning from a daily patrol with my men. No sooner were we back when our exec officer came up to me with a brand-new order: "Corporal, I need you and four of your men to get your gear back on and go down to the beach at Kukum. You'll report to navy Lieutenant So-and-so."

"To the beach, sir? How will I recognize this navy Lieutenant So-and-so?"

"No problem, corporal," the exec officer told me. "He'll be standing near a Jap torpedo that came up on the beach. It's about twenty yards up from the waterline at Kukum."

"Sir? *What* torpedo on the beach, sir?"

"Never mind the questions, corporal. Just round up your men and report to Lieutenant So-and-so."

"Yes, sir."

But I couldn't believe what I'd just heard. Report to a navy officer? Report to a Japanese torpedo? Sometimes I found myself thinking that our command liked to keep the troops off balance. Keep us confused, hungry, and generally deprived, and we'll be ready for the glory and thrill of battle, for cold steel, and even for torpedoes on the beach.

There were five of us on that torpedo detail: Larry Gerkin, Hap Poloshian, Stanley Zega, Yogi Milana, and yours truly. It turned out that we had no trouble finding the lieutenant. We moved down to the beach, and as we neared a big, shiny, totally alien object in the distance, we saw exactly one man standing next to it. Nobody else went close. Nobody *wanted* to go close. The object was a torpedo, all right, and nobody else was dumb enough to be within several hundred yards of it. Just that one navy officer. The closer we got to his torpedo, the bigger it seemed to grow. But I won't exaggerate the facts. It was about twenty feet long, maybe three to four feet in diameter, and it looked very, very lethal.

When we were about fifty feet from the monster, I told my men to stand by while I went forward to speak with the navy lieutenant. We weren't happy about being there, but the lieutenant was very glad to see us. No, he was *overjoyed* to see us. He was most cordial, and most anxious for us to get started on our detail. I could only ask him what in hell it was that we were supposed to do with a torpedo. He told me that we were to fill sandbags and stack them around its big, ugly nose. While stacking those sandbags, he told us to take special care that we didn't disturb a wheel that stood out on the left side of the cone.

"If you touch it, it will blow us all to hell," the lieutenant told me. His words were a reminder of where we'd all eventually go, but now our trip to hell was going to have us riding there on a Jap torpedo.

The men didn't like this detail for beans, and who could blame them. I didn't like it any better than they did. Anyway, we started shoveling sand—Gerkin, Poloshian, Zega, Yogi, and me. Among the five of us, we had two entrenching tools and three pickaxes. Back in those days, we didn't have many entrenching tools, and for that matter, we didn't have any other types of shovel, either. Riflemen didn't rate them. Maybe the decision makers back stateside thought such tools would have made our lives too easy. We'd been taught how to dig

This lethal Japanese torpedo missed its target—perhaps the *Alchiba*—and came up on the beach near Kukum. Marion's squad was detailed to stack sandbags around the live torpedo. UNKNOWN

positions with pickaxes, helmets, and even our hands, so who needed shovels?

Soon my men were preparing sandbags, two men filling while the other two carried the bags to that god-awful torpedo, which was still carefully guarded and protected by the very nervous lieutenant. It was the fastest we ever worked on any detail.

I nagged that navy lieutenant about the sandbags. "Where did you get them, lieutenant? They're the first sandbags we've *seen* on this island. Do you suppose we could have a few leftovers when we get through? All we have are Japanese straw-woven bags, and they're all rotted and smelly."

Finishing the detail seemed to take forever, though we actually finished in a little less than two hours. By that time, the nose cone of the torpedo and an area that extended back about seven feet were surrounded to a height of about three or four bags higher than the level of the torpedo itself. The lieutenant decided that he was satisfied with our work. Mainly, I think he was happy that he was still alive and could now move away fast. For our own part, we were very happy to be leaving that awful thing so that we could get back to the more familiar comforts of small-arms fire, aerial bombing, and artillery and naval gunfire. After all that, the navy lieutenant refused to let us take any of his goddamned sandbags. You'd think he'd have been more grateful.

Several days later, my squad and I were dug in at one of our regular positions, just west of Kukum and along the jungle side of the MLR. All of a sudden we heard a single loud boom—one very large explosion that punctuated the more peaceful jungle sounds of an otherwise quiet day. Soon after that big bang, we heard, via L Company's field phone, that the torpedo had been blown up. The only thing left on the beach was a hole in the ground decorated with fragments of those precious sandbags. I hated to think of those valuable sandbags, now lost to us forever—but it could have been worse. It could have been fragments of us.

A VISIT FROM HOME

One afternoon during the worst of our days on Guadalcanal, we watched an airplane come in, heading for a landing at Henderson Field. Being gravel crunchers, most of us didn't know one type of plane from another, but this one was unusual because it wasn't a combat plane. It was a transport.

At that time, we hadn't seen a friendly ship in the bay for several weeks. The only friendly airplanes we'd seen lately were the patched-up jobs our flyboys were able to get airborne to harass the Jap Zeros and destroy some of the bombers that came over the island nearly every day.

Our ammunition was low, our medical supplies were lower, and our food rations were at rock bottom. The little food on hand was what remained of the Japanese rice and canned goods they'd left in the Kukum warehouse when they'd fled the area back in early August. We had no mosquito nets, practically no quinine or atabrine to treat the malaria cases, no tincture of violet to swab the skin ulcers caused by jungle rot, and very few bandages to cover wounds from battle. By this time, we didn't have many more than two or three remaining hand grenades per rifle company. All we had left was our youth, our stupidity, and our will to do or die, coupled with a ton of loyalty.

In the midst of that adversity, down came a transport plane on Henderson Field. As we watched it descend, then disappear behind jungle foliage before touching down on the runway, our first thought was that we hadn't seen one of those suckers in too long a time. The warriors of our platoon—L-3-5's 1st Platoon—were more than a little excited about what that airplane might be bringing in. After we conducted a short powwow, Lieutenant Flaherty decided that as platoon leader, he was appointing himself to ease out of our area, hike to the airfield, and get a firsthand, hawkeye view of what that plane had brought to the island for us.

Off went Flaherty, and we waited, hoping for good things to come our way. After a while we saw our lieutenant strolling back in our direction, puffing on what looked to be a fresh, factory-made cigarette. He was grinning with pleasure, and as he got nearer, we saw that he had a carton of genuine stateside cigarettes tucked under one arm—a sight previously unseen at that time and place. We asked the obvious questions.

"The plane's loaded with smokes, pipe tobacco, shaving gear, soap, toothbrushes, and a lot more good things," Flaherty told us. Then he told us the rest of the story.

A well-known charitable organization had flown these supplies to the Canal as morale boosters for the marines. That same organization, which normally got these and other things for free from their various manufacturers, was now selling their goodies, Flaherty told us. Representatives of the charitable organization had arrived on this godforsaken island with the single purpose in mind of *selling* a planeload of stuff that we hadn't seen since we'd climbed down the nets of the USS *Fuller*.

"Cigarettes are going for a dollar a carton," Flaherty told us.

Back in '42, assuming you were not in a combat zone but somewhere near a PX, a sailor or a marine could buy a carton of name-brand cigarettes tax-free for sixty cents, or we could walk away with some of the offbrands like Sensations for a mere thirty cents. But the winners who had come in on the transport plane were charging a buck, and Lord knows how much for toilet articles and other good things. To top it all off, they'd had their merchandise flown in for free on a military transport.

We told Lieutenant Flaherty that in case he had a chance to make contact with anybody connected with that organization, he could feel free to pass on our opinion of their operation. We delivered that opinion in a long series of four-letter words. The following day, a squad from our platoon came back from patrol after running into a couple of stray Japanese, now deceased. Our guys returned with two packs of Singapore cigarettes issued to Japanese troops. The cigarettes had small paper holders and were known among our guys as the best-tasting and most satisfying smokes this side of a manure pile. Even so, we preferred them to the cigarettes that had come in on the transport plane. We figured that anybody who bought anything from that charitable organization under those conditions was a traitor.

CHAPTER 8

The Cobbers

We picked up the word *cobbers* from the New Zealanders during our stay there just before we invaded Guadalcanal. Most of us liked New Zealand. The people were friendly, the beer was good, and the girls were friendlier yet. Cobber was, and probably still is, a common word in Australia and New Zealand for a very good and loyal friend. A cobber is somebody you can always depend on. Just about everybody in our outfit was, and remains to this day, a good cobber.

Those of us who were in L-3-5 on Guadalcanal in 1942 had never heard of the term *bonding*, whether among cobbers or riflemen or anybody else. When we finally heard that word, well after the end of World War II, no one seemed able to explain exactly what *bonding* meant, or how and why it occurred. I couldn't explain it either, nor do I have any clues about it now.

On the Canal, we marines were abandoned several times, by the leadership in Washington, D.C., and on down the line to include the American generals and admirals in Brisbane, Wellington-Aukland, and Pearl Harbor. We became sick from the effects of long periods of rain, heat, insects, dysentery, and malaria. We were short of ammunition, medical supplies, and food. During those four months on Guadalcanal, we all lost weight, twenty or thirty pounds. Meanwhile, of course, the Japanese were trying to kill us. For a long time, there were no ships or airplanes to help us. We were expendable and, it seemed, we were doomed.

The only things we had in the world were each other. We were in it together, day and night, come hell or high water.

After Guadalcanal, I was in combat again on Iwo Jima, but I can't remember many faces or names of the men in my outfit. Memory also remains largely blank in the aftermath of several later "police actions." But the names and faces of those young warriors I fought beside on Guadalcanal are as clear to me as though I'd seen them only last week instead of half a century ago.

A few years ago, several old cobbers persuaded me to attend a reunion of Guadalcanal Campaign Veterans. Most of the L-3-5 guys hadn't seen each other in more than fifty years. We weren't teenagers anymore, but we recognized each other on sight. It was "Hi-ya, Knucklehead! How's it been?" "Ok, Ma-Keki, how about you?" (Ma-Keki was the nickname given to me for some reason when I was on the Canal with L-3-5.) "Good," I said. "Have you seen Hap?" "He's around somewhere, talking with the Yogi-man."

I now believe that in our subconscious minds, we had always been together, from Guadalcanal to that day of our belated reunion. And I believe we were destined to remain together for as long as the last man among us stays alive. I enjoyed every minute of our reunion, glad that I broke down and reluctantly decided to attend.

One of the guys talked on, mentioning somebody my old mind had half forgotten, and then he said: "He was one of our guys. Go out to the bar and you'll recognize that meathead. He hasn't changed a bit. Hell, how could he? He's one of *our* guys." I did recognize him, as well as the others who were with him at the bar. They were all *our* guys.

I stayed in the corps after World War II, retired from active duty after twenty years, then twenty-six more years went by before I made contact with more than one or two of my old Canal cobbers from L-3-5. I seldom had anyone to speak with about those terrible experiences, no one with whom to share my memories of those days back in 1942. So I just didn't talk

L-3-5 veterans at a 1994 reunion in Richmond, Virginia: (left to right) Ernest Snowden, Jesse Broderson, Curtis "Speedy" Spach, Willie Shoemaker, Don Prewitt, Ore Marion, and Henry Klemicki. ERNEST SNOWDEN

about them. Not with anybody. Then, out of the blue one day, an old cobber phoned and asked if I remembered a certain incident that had occurred on the Canal. Gradually a few more cobbers began calling and asking how I'd been getting along in civilian life. At that point, a sort of floodgate opened. Our guys began calling each other regularly, and I kept getting calls that I came to welcome, calls asking me how things were going. I called many of them, too, and wrote to many others, asking about their families, their children and their grandchildren. It made me happy when I heard that *they* were happy. It saddened me when I heard of their misfortunes. It hurt a little when I heard that one or another of the old cobbers had passed away.

A few years back, I had to undergo major surgery. Right away, I began receiving phone calls and letters from our guys all around the country: Was everything all right? Did I need any help? Why didn't I let some of the guys know about my health problems?

There aren't many of our old cobbers left today, but those of us that are are as close as ever. I have given this "bonding" idea a lot of thought over the past few years, but I still don't know what happens to bring it about, or how it really comes to be. Modern-day management schools try to instruct young trainees to bond with their workforce. Good luck, say I. It's too bad that most of my raggedy-ass, magnificent bastards who had to eat Japanese rice spiced with maggots aren't around any longer. Possibly they could teach the professors of management exactly how bonding comes about. Some of the cobbers might have an answer. I never did, and I still don't have one.

There is no way that I can name all of my old Guadalcanal mates in this account, or tell stories about the lives they've lived over the many years since the end of World War II. I have only enough knowledge to talk about just a few of them in the short remembrances that follow, but that's not to say that I've forgotten the others, or that I think they are any less important. I love every damned one of them—those still living and the many others now gone.

BEN SELVITELLE

I first knew Ben Selvitelle when we were stationed at Guantánamo, Cuba. Unlike many of the kids in the corps back then, Ben had a high school diploma. He was a New Yorker, I believe from Brooklyn, and a very intelligent guy. If the first sergeant needed extra clerical help, he always knew enough to pick Selvitelle. Ben had joined the corps about a year before I enlisted, and when I first knew him he was a buck sergeant. He was about five-foot-nine, and a good-looking guy of medium build with Italian features.

Our unit was the first to be transferred up to New River, North Carolina, from Guantánamo, when that camp—now Camp Lejeune—first came into existence. Our job was to put up the camp's original tents and to unload the lumber trucks when they started building the permanent structures, mess hall, showers, and other buildings. It was during our stay in North Carolina that Ben met the girl he would eventually marry.

We had been at New River for about two weeks when the people from the neighboring town of Kinston made the goodwill gesture of inviting the marines to come into town for a visit. We were taken into various homes for dinner. Later that day, I was with Larry Gerkin and a few others on Kinston's main street when we ran into Ben and another marine, each with a pretty girl on his arm. The girl with Ben was Jackie, whose father was postmaster in the nearby town of Moorehead City. Ben dated her during all the time we were at New River and never looked at another girl, so it was pretty clear that he and Jackie were serious. They eventually married, and as time passed, I came to know her as one very fine woman.

When L-3-5 landed on Guadalcanal, Ben was a buck sergeant in charge of L Company's LMG, or light machine-gun section. Every marine rifle company had a section that consisted of three light machine guns, normally in the charge of a buck sergeant. In August, at the first Matanikau battle, Ben and his LMGs were on my platoon's flank and firing steadily, playing a valuable part in our victory that day. Then in mid-September, during our defense of L Company Ridge, our first sergeant was wounded in action, and Ben became acting first sergeant. At the end of that month, he was promoted to platoon sergeant, which was the same occasion when I was promoted to buck sergeant. When we were evacuated from the Canal and sent to Australia, Ben was promoted to gunnery sergeant while still remaining acting first sergeant. It couldn't have been more than another four or five months before he was promoted again, this time to first sergeant, which made him the youngest first sergeant in the entire 1st Marine Division. He was twenty-one years old at that time.

In 1943, while I was stateside and in the hospital, Ben was in New Guinea, where units of the 5th Marine Regiment were sent to Milne Bay and spread out where they could be used if needed as replacements for MacArthur's Army. That was shortly before L-3-5 went into combat at Cape Gloucester, where they took too many casualties and lost too many good marines, including Stinky Denham. Ben made it safely though Gloucester, and by the time L Company was finally shipped back to the States, he'd risen to the rank of sergeant major and NCO in charge of the company. I saw him again at Camp Pendleton, California. From there, Ben crossed the country to North Carolina to marry Jackie.

Ben's next assignment was at Quantico, Virginia, where the commanding general's aide made it a point to take Ben in to see the post's commanding general. By that time, General Vandegrift was marine commandant and was also at Quantico. The next thing Ben knew, he was shaking both generals' hands and talking with them about old campaigns. As Ben later told me the story, Vandegrift turned to the post commanding general at one point and remarked, "We're commissioning kids off the street, for Christ's sake. See what you can do for the first sergeant."

Ben was commissioned that day. The marines sent him to school, and he got both a bachelor's and a master's degree. By the time the war was over, Ben was a captain. Shortly after the war, Ben spent some time in China, then later served two tours as an infantry battalion commander in Vietnam, where he was awarded the Legion of Merit on two occasions.

When Gen. Charles C. Krulak took command of General Fleet Marine Force, Pacific, he had Ben transferred to his command, and Ben became his chief of staff. Later General Krulak formed the first counterinsurgency unit at the Pentagon, and Ben went with him, again as chief of staff. In 1962, during the Bay of Pigs incident, Ben was sent to Guantánamo and placed in command of a marine defense garrison in the event that Cuba decided to attack our naval base there. I visited Ben at his home after his retirement, and on his den wall was a photograph showing him briefing the Joint Chiefs of Staff and President John F. Kennedy.

Ben retired from the corps in 1975, and he and Jackie returned to her hometown of Moorehead City, North Carolina, where they bought a home and settled down. Their long and happy marriage gave them three children, a daughter and two sons. One son graduated from West Point, the other from Annapolis, from where, like his dad, he went into the marines. Ben taught school for a while after his retirement, but the last time I saw him, it was clear that his health was failing. He died a few years ago. Ben and I remained good cobbers to the last.

LT. COL. FREDERICK C. BIEBUSH AND CPL. RALEIGH BRIGHT

It might seem strange to be pairing a lieutenant colonel with a corporal, but Biebush and Bright had at least one thing in common: They both loved a good time on the town. Lt. Col. Frederick C. Biebush commanded the 3rd Battalion, 5th Marine Division, on Guadalcanal in 1942. He was a competent leader on the battlefield, and a colorful hell-raiser, typical of the Old Breed, the rest of the time. He was a lover of wine and John Barleycorn in any order that those good things presented themselves to him. His career in the marines dated back to the Nicaragua campaign in the late 1920s.

I got into trouble with Biebush on a few occasions but have to admit that it was usually my fault. He got into trouble with me on still another occasion, and since he had rank on me, that could have been more trouble for me than it was for him. But Biebush wasn't a man to hold a grudge, and all our troubles were resolved amicably.

In July 1942, we were in Wellington, New Zealand, billeted on the transport ship *Fuller*, which would soon take us into combat. General Vandegrift's 1st Marine Division, where I was then just a lowly corporal, was preparing to depart for what turned out to be amphibious landing exercises in the Fiji Islands. From there we knew that we were going on to a location unknown, which turned out to be Guadalcanal. Raleigh Bright and I had girlfriends in Petone, a suburb of Wellington, and on many an evening, after a hard day's duty loading supplies on our ship, we would violate regulations and sneak ashore to meet our dates. Everybody was aware that the marines' departure from Wellington was imminent, which is why we were officially restricted to the ship after duty hours.

Bright and I weren't about to let that minor detail prevent us from going into town. We had no real problems until we happened to choose one particularly ill-advised evening to do our partying. We didn't know exactly how bad it was going to be for us until the wee hours of morning, when we returned to the dock.

Our ship was gone! The whole damn fleet was gone from the docks of Aotea Quay. The ships had moved far out, then anchored in the middle of the bay. We'd been left behind. In other words, we were in deep shit. *Rocks and Shoals* (our unofficial name for the Marine Corps book of regulations) read that anyone missing a movement during wartime was subject to a life term at hard labor or hanging.

"What do we do now?" Bright asked me, as we stood on that otherwise deserted and dismal quay.

"Hell, I don't know. They'll have us breaking rocks for this violation, so we'd damn well better figure out something!"

Hope was rapidly fading but not entirely lost. In the dim, early dawn light, we could look far out on the bay and make out distant silhouettes of the fleet at anchor. The problem was, how in hell were we going to reach our ship? As dawn's gray light began to brighten into a desolate morning, a large mail truck came out to the dock area and parked. Guessing why it had arrived, we hurried to meet it.

"Bringing mail to the fleet?" I called.

"That I am," the lone driver answered. "Last mail call before the fleet moves out."

"When is the fleet supposed to pick up the mail?" I asked.

"Right soon," the driver answered. "As a matter of fact, out yonder it looks like a boat heading this way to get these bags."

Sure enough, we could make out a motor launch from the fleet, heading toward our dock. Flapping on its stern was the small flag indicating that it was an official U.S. Navy mail carrier. Our savior was in sight. *Thank you, oh Jesus!*

As the launch eased up to the dock, Bright and I offered a hand and helped secure the boat to the pier. Then without a word or a signal to anyone, we jumped down and into that beautiful motor launch, knowing that somehow it was going to save us. It was manned by a coxswain and an engineer, both of them carrying sidearms. They told us loudly to get out and off this boat because it was an official navy mail boat. What's more, we weren't authorized to board, and we were violating *blah blah blah* . . . They went on and on, and for a while we just let them yell. We had nothing to gain by arguing, but there was no way we intended to get off that launch. The launch was our one and only hope.

Finally, when the sailors stopped for a second to catch their breath, I told them that we belonged on the *Fuller*. I also insisted that we were *not* getting off their boat until they took us to the fleet. By that time, the mailman had his truck opened and was ready to pass the mailbags down to the launch. Doing our best to become friendly hitch-hikers and maybe change the coxswain's mind, we helped stack and load the bags on the deck of the launch, and when the mailman freed its lines, we hauled them in. As the launch pulled away from the dock, we found ourselves comfortable seats on top of what must have been close to fifty mailbags.

Halfway out on the bay, the coxswain told us he could not under any circumstances take us to the *Fuller* without permission from the Flag—the fleet's flagship. "Very simple," I said. "Ask the Flag what you're supposed to do with us." I knew that he wouldn't dare toss us overboard.

He didn't argue. One way or another, he had to get rid of us. The engineer began to semaphore the Flag, and the ship signaled back the location of our transport, which was anchored somewhere among that huge assembly of ships, along with permission to take us to the *Fuller*. As we approached our familiar old ship, a Jacob's ladder appeared as if by magic from the deck and unrolled down the side of the hull. I was the first to grab it. I started climbing up fast, with Raleigh Bright moving directly behind me. As I glanced up toward the ship's rail, I saw what seemed to be every officer in the 3rd Battalion glaring down at us. Leading the pack was our battalion commander, none other than Lt. Col. Frederick Biebush. With him was the battalion exec officer, our company commander, the battalion sergeant major, and our company's first sergeant. The moment my feet touched the deck, First Sergeant McMullen spoke two stern and simple words: "Follow us."

Bright and I were led to Colonel Biebush's tiny cabin amidships. With the colonel, Bright, and me squeezed inside, that cabin was overcrowded. It was a very bad moment to be standing so close to the colonel, but Raleigh and I just didn't have a choice in the matter. Old Biebush really tore into us, chewing us out at length with four-letter words, some of which even *I* had never heard before. He promised to have us shot at sunrise, walk the plank, and at very least, be put on "piss and punk" for the duration of the war.

"Lucky for both of you," he bellowed, "that you're competent squad leaders. I can't afford to lose any one of my squad leaders at this time. Now get the hell out of my sight, and don't make one false goddamn move as long as you're in my battalion. Furthermore, officially, you are both on restriction for ninety days. *Now get the hell out of my sight!*"

Colonel Biebush put on a good act that morning—pure fire and brimstone with piss and punk added. But my guess is that as he was chewing us out, he was probably thinking of similar stunts he had pulled earlier in his own career.

It might have been ten days or so before our "missed-boat" near catastrophe that I'd been assigned sergeant of the guard at Wellington's Aotea Quay. The quay took in our entire dock area, which could be entered through two gates. I was only a corporal at the time, but it wasn't unusual for us to be assigned to a duty or detail that normally should have gone to somebody with a higher rating. During daylight hours, a gate corporal and a private or PFC were assigned as sentries at each of the two gates. One of the many orders that the sentries had to enforce was that no alcoholic beverages were to be allowed inside the quay area or taken aboard the ships. This was a tough order to enforce, because every other marine or sailor coming off liberty would do his best to pass through the gate with a bottle taped to his ankle, or under his arm, or maybe in his hat, or god knows where else. More often than not, the bottles were discovered. The offenders were told they could go across the street and drink what they had, or we would confiscate the bottle and destroy its contents the next morning.

On my second or third evening as sergeant of the guard, I was called to Gate Number 2, where the gate corporal was speaking with none other than our battalion commander, Colonel Biebush. Biebush was clutching a box to his chest, and a glance inside the box revealed two gallon jugs of a red liquid that anybody could see was wine. Colonel Biebush smiled as he spotted me. "Ah! Corporal Marion. Just the man I want to see." He indicated his cache. "I have these two jugs that I would like to take up to my stateroom."

"Sir," I said, "if those jugs contain alcoholic beverage, we can't allow them to go past this point."

"Now, corporal, you don't have to be chicken-shit about this small matter," the colonel replied.

"Sir, I'm not chicken-shit, because it wasn't me who wrote those orders. The chicken-shit admiral who signed them is the guilty party."

The colonel's reply was restricted to a couple of snorts and mutterings to himself. Then he turned and began heading along the sidewalk toward Gate Number 1. As he continued walking along his side of the green-painted fence, I, on the inner side, walked along slowly, keeping pace with him. After some distance, Colonel Biebush stopped, and I heard scraping sounds coming from his side. The next thing I saw was his two hands, spread apart and gripping the fence's top. Following that, his hat, his head, and then his face appeared. As he saw me, he muttered, "Chicken-shit," then dropped back to the sidewalk. He proceeded a little farther and I continued to follow. The same scene was repeated, complete with the same muttering, "Chicken-shit." As he continued toward the other gate, I could hear him mumbling curses to himself. I grinned, but I didn't say anything.

Finally we both arrived at Gate Number 1, by which time its corporal had been called and forewarned by the corporal at Gate Number 2. By now that box with its two jugs must have gotten pretty heavy, because the colonel put it down on the sidewalk. Then he looked at me. "I'll make a deal with you, corporal. If I leave this box here in your care for tonight, can I be sure it will be here in the morning?"

"You can, sir."

"Good. At that time, I'll reclaim the box and take it elsewhere."

"That's a deal, colonel."

With that, the colonel passed through the gate and went down the dock to the *Fuller*. He wasn't staggering, mind you. He might have been just a little unsteady on his feet, probably because of New Zealand's misty, rainy winter season—weather that would aggravate nearly anyone suffering from lameness coupled with chilblains.

Next morning before breakfast, I was aboard ship. I managed to find the battalion adjutant, and returning to the gate, we stuffed each jug into a double gunnysack. Then, as we boarded the *Fuller*, the adjutant called out to the officer of the deck, "Coming aboard with training equipment!" We had no problem.

The next time I saw our battalion commander, he showed signs that he'd taken good care of his chilblains and lameness.

Years later, back at Camp Pendleton, I was present at the ceremony marking Lt. Col. Frederick C. Biebush's retirement from the corps. There was the usual fanfare and endless ritual, the afternoon was hot, and it was clear to me that the sooner the ceremony was finished, the happier the colonel would be. When the formalities finally ended, he spotted me, broke away from several glad-handers, came up to me, and clapped an arm around my shoulder. "Sergeant," he told me, "my *real* pleasure serving all these years in the corps was working with men like you."

"Including all the trouble I gave you?" I asked.

"Goddamn it, yes! *Especially* all the trouble you gave me, Marion. That was half the fun! You have any cigarettes on you? I need a smoke pretty bad."

SGT. WILLIAM STEEN AND SGT. JOHN BRANIC

I want to remember two fine marines I knew well, Sgt. William Steen and Sgt. John Branic, whose bodies we had to leave behind on Guadalcanal.

Steen joined L Company when we were at New River, at about the time that the United States entered World War II. He came from Maine, and he had served four years with the corps in the 1930s, and then went into the Marine Reserve. At about the time of Pearl Harbor, when he returned to active duty, he joined L Company, 3rd Battalion, 5th Marines. In June 1942, just before the 5th Marine Regiment left the States for duty in the South Pacific, Steen, Walt Sincek, and Don Mallory were all promoted to the rank of platoon sergeant. Steen was a friendly guy by nature, but that took nothing away from the fact that he was also very competent. He was in his mid to late twenties at the time, about five-foot-ten, with light hair and light complexion. He always had a smile on his face.

After the accident that took Steen's life, during our bivouac in the high grass on our first night on the Canal, nobody ever talked about it. The way he was killed was the kind of thing you never want to happen, and when it *did* happen we just did not want to talk about it. On the night he was killed, I was dug in a few feet away from my own platoon sergeant, Quentin Shumate; our platoon leader, Lt. Flash Flaherty; and Sgt. Bill Kulchycki. Steen's unit was dug in to our right, not much more than twenty or twenty-five yards from us. It was too dark to see anything, but I heard the *bang* of a rifle shot, and a yell, then somebody hollering, "Get the corpsman!" Soon I heard the corpsman's voice: "We gotta get him out of here right away." But Steen was dead by the time they started to move him. He was buried in the marines' cemetery on Guadalcanal. We were lucky to have a man like Bill Steen in our unit, and his death was a tragedy.

Sgt. John Branic was the platoon sergeant in Lt. George Mead's platoon, and both he and Mead were killed in action at the first battle of the Matanikau. Branic, who came from Pittsburgh, was about six feet tall or maybe a little more, with dark hair and complexion. Like Steen, it didn't take much to put a grin on his face. Though affable, Branic was more quiet by nature, and extremely sensible. Both Steen and Branic were a credit to the corps, and had they survived the Guadalcanal campaign, their personalities and good sense were sure to have earned them commissions.

The marines always make a special effort to evacuate the bodies of their KIAs, but the confusion at the first Matanikau was extraordinary, and John Branic's body remained where he fell. This bothered us all, but Ben Selvitelle took it the hardest. Even years later, he often said to me, "I can't understand why we left John up there." I had to dismiss Branic's death from my mind, but Ben couldn't forget it, couldn't stop feeling bad about it. We all saw too much of death during the big war.

LARRY "HARDROCK" GERKIN

Larry Gerkin, my squad's dependable BAR man on the Canal and my assistant squad leader, was a peaceable guy, but also a person to whom things always happened. Those unfortunate things ranged from having that Japanese naval artillery shell land on his spider hole to his griping about the corps to General Vandegrift while thinking he was trading scuttlebutt with just another gravel cruncher. For the most part, Gerk was soft-spoken, a man of relatively few words, even gentle in temperament. But if angered or deeply grieved, he could suddenly become a wild man.

Gerk was a year or two older than I. When he and I first became friends, he told me that his earliest recollections of life were traveling across America's southwestern desert country as a very young child with his mother, his father, and a burro. His parents were prospectors, and when he grew up, he also did some mining for a living, which is how he got tagged with his Marine Corps nickname, Hardrock. As a child, he never knew a permanent home. When he became old enough to start grammar school, his parents left him with friends in a small Arizona town, then went off to do more prospecting. While he was still in his teens, he worked for a couple different mining companies out west. Later, hearing about good-paying job opportunities with a tunnel-digging crew in the East, he moved to New York City and helped dig a tunnel under one of the rivers surrounding Manhattan Island.

Gerk was a man of great physical strength, who didn't mind hard labor. He joined the marines at the end of 1940, about a year before the Pearl Harbor attack. By then he'd been working and living in the Washington, D.C., area, and it was there that he met the girl he truly believed he was going to marry.

When Gerkin joined the corps out of Washington, D.C., he'd told that special girlfriend that circumstances were forcing him to leave her behind, but that he would certainly marry her some day. Everybody who ever knew Larry Gerkin knew him as a man of his word, so that girlfriend of his certainly knew that he would keep his promise. Before our four months

Lawrence "Hardrock" Gerkin and his BAR "smokepole" at New River, North Carolina, during the winter of 1941–42.

ESTATE OF ORE J. MARION

on Guadalcanal, he'd written to this young lady faithfully and as often as he could, and she regularly answered his letters. As a man who always kept his word, he assumed that everybody else did the same.

Not one man in our company received a "Dear John" letter while we were on Guadalcanal. That was probably due to the infrequency of incoming mail deliveries, because shortly after we left the Canal and arrived in Mount Balcombe, outside of Melbourne, "Dear John" letters picked up a bit, coming in at a slow but steady pace. We were stationed at a military post about an hour by train from Brisbane when Hardrock received the granddaddy of all "Dear John" letters.

During World War II, "Dear John" letters caused as much mayhem among some of the guys as enemy troops and Tokyo Rose combined. I knew several men in combat who, after receiving such letters, threw all caution to the winds and in short order became battle statistics. Maybe it was a stroke of good luck that when Larry Gerkin got his "Dear John," we were off the Canal and safely away from any combat zone.

One quiet and otherwise uneventful morning, mail call sounded at our post. Mail call was far from the most important thing on Gerkin's mind that day. He was sitting on the edge of his bunk, holding his head in his hands, which was the best he could do to nurse a massive headache brought on the night before by many long pulls from several of those tall imperial quarts of that beloved and frothy Aussie brew, Foster's ale. Shortly after mail call, one of the men came into the platoon barracks and distracted Gerk from his hangover just long enough to hand him a letter. His hangover forgotten, Larry eagerly opened the envelope and read the letter, but as his eyes scanned the pages, the eager look on his face gradually dissolved into an expression of deep unhappiness. He dropped the letter on the floor and let out a half sob, half growl from the deepest part of his chest. That deep growl was a sound to be heard only on those rare occasions when Gerk became deeply, inconsolably upset.

Those of us in the barracks who were old hands, and who had heard the Gerkin growl on a couple of isolated past occasions, now knew enough to make a quick, quiet exit from the platoon bay. But at least half of the lads now in our unit were replacements, young and inexperienced men who were not yet acquainted with the dark side of this normally calm, businesslike, combat-tested corporal. Not having the good sense to take off, they continued about their business.

I can't vouch for what followed because, no longer being on the scene, I had to accept reports from those who remained. They told me that Gerkin slowly rose from his bunk, sobbing and growling, then picked up his metal bunk and threw it against the barracks wall. Next, he picked up the cast-iron potbelly stove, which by good fortune was cold, and threw it out the front door. The new replacements were moving fast by now, exiting the premises through windows and doors, ass over elbow, with Gerkin assisting many of them in their rapid departures.

Heading toward the barracks' back door, Gerkin met an unsuspecting replacement who was coming out of the showers, dressed only in a towel. It is said that Gerk picked the poor guy up and threw him at least ten feet. With that, he left the barracks, sobbing.

The barracks were situated on a hilly knoll that sloped down toward the sea. Hardrock staggered down that hill, kicking rocks, picking up boulders half the size of GI barrels and throwing them eight or ten feet in random directions. Many sapling trees were just starting to grow on that hill, and Gerk stopped once in a while to pull several of them up by their roots. He disappeared from sight beyond a stand of trees that grew near the water. No one went after him. We were worried, but the time had clearly come to leave the man alone. When you've been in combat with a man, you get to know his every ache and pain, just as he gets to know yours. We knew that Gerk was in deep pain, and we hated that woman from far away. We'd never seen her and we would never know her, but she had wounded our good buddy worse than the Japs ever could.

Gerkin disappeared into the stand of trees near the shore, but that was just the beginning of his departure. Compelled by loyalty, we NCOs could only suspect the worst and knew we had to start a cover-up to protect him. We made sure he wasn't reported absent after twenty-four hours, and we kept the cover-up going into the middle of the second day. At that time, a phone call came into the camp from a constable in a small village five or six miles up the coast. He was detaining one Cpl. Lawrence Gerkin. No charges had been placed against him, but "would somebody come and get the poor bugger?"

A jeep was quickly dispatched in the direction of the village. We returned with our "Dear John" buddy, who was now sober, recovered, and wearing a sheepish grin.

"Hi, Gerk!" somebody called.

"How's it going, buddy?" another guy said.

Nobody mentioned his letter and nobody mentioned the incident. It was back to work for all of us, and it was business as usual. We had closed ranks and protected him because we knew that the next "Dear John" might be addressed to any one of us.

Gerk survived the big war, and by 1945 he was a platoon sergeant. Back in the States, he married a wonderful, caring woman, and in the mid-1950s, after suffering a medical problem, he retired from the corps at Camp Pendleton, California, with the rank of gunnery sergeant. He and his wife went on to spend many active and happy retirement years in Oceanside, California. Larry died in 1981, many, many years too early.

RICHARD "YOGI" MILANA

Richard Milana, known as Yogi to everyone in L-3-5, stayed with L Company after Guadalcanal and saw action at Cape Gloucester and Peleliu. He was well liked by his fellow marines but was sometimes a little less popular with several of the officers—mainly those who didn't appreciate being shown up by a mere private who was quicker and more accurate at reading map coordinates or doing practical math calculations than they were. Yogi has always had a good brain in his head. He also was an excellent rifle shot and had natural athletic ability, the latter skill much appreciated by the rest of us that morning when he swam from a Guadalcanal beach to a navy destroyer, then swam back toting breakfast supplies for a bunch of underfed and starving marines. Yogi is a good-natured guy with an opinion about everything you can imagine, and he has never been shy about expressing those opinions. To this day, he'll see something in the newspaper or on TV news that doesn't sit well with him, and his normal reaction is to write a letter to his congressman, the president, or any other public figure he thinks needs to be set straight.

Yogi grew up in Brooklyn. He had quite a bit more formal education than most of L-3-5's gravel crunchers, having put in a year or two at Brooklyn College before heeding his country's call and joining the corps soon after Pearl Harbor. During the years between the two world wars, his father made a good living in show business as a performer, playing in New York theaters and traveling the vaudeville circuit. Among other things, the senior Milana had a successful act as a sword swallower. Among his friends were many entertainers who later went on to the big time in radio, the movies, and television.

After World War II was over and Yogi had received his honorable discharge from the corps, he took advantage of the GI Bill, got a degree from Columbia University and another from Cornell, and then enjoyed a long, successful career as an engineer until his retirement in the 1980s. Meanwhile, he had married, settled down, bought a home in one of Brooklyn's better neighborhoods, and raised a family. After his retirement, Yogi sold his Brooklyn brownstone, trading it for an attractive ranch-style home in Hernando, Florida. He and his wife live there to this day, and from time to time I get a phone call or a letter from Yogi, urging me to come down to Florida for a visit. He's a good man who deserves all the good things that life has given him.

ERNEST SNOWDEN
Ernest Snowden joined the corps from the Louisville, Kentucky, recruitment office, trained at Parris Island, and then

came with us to Guadalcanal. Ernie remained with L-3-5 for about two more years. After Australia, he spent time on New Guinea, then saw action at Cape Gloucester at the end of 1943. He was slightly wounded in action at Cape Gloucester but was back with L-3-5 after nine short days of recuperation. He was wounded a second time on Peleliu in 1944.

> We hit Peleliu on September 15. We used alligator tanks for landing. The one I was on made it all the way up to dry land, but a lot of them got hung up in the coral, which meant the boys had to get out and walk. From our position, we could see them wading toward the beach in water that was about waist-deep while the Japs sprayed the water with bullets. The Japs were shooting from out of a hole where they were dug in. They killed a number of our boys, until one of our marines carrying a flamethrower said, "Cover me for a minute." Some of our boys kept the Japs busy by shooting at the hole where they were dug in. That gave him the chance to slip up next to the hole and shoot the flamethrower into it. I imagine he cooked the Japanese, because that was the end of their shooting at us. I didn't go in there to see.
>
> I was there for only three days, then was hit on the morning of September 18. Our company was on the move, and I was on the tail end of it when a Japanese mortar shell came down within a few feet of me. It went off, and after all the dust cleared, I felt something warm running down my leg. I'd caught a piece of Japanese shrapnel in the butt. A corpsman patched me up temporarily, and they put me on a stretcher and carried me back to the beach. I told the guys at the beach that I thought I could walk, but they wouldn't let me. Instead, they put me on an alligator that took me out to a hospital ship.
>
> I came back to the States in December 1944, arriving in San Diego. I served the rest of my duty in the States,

though they were getting ready to send us overseas again, this time to invade Japan, when the atomic bombs hit Hiroshima and then Nagasaki in August 1945. I felt relieved about that, because when the Japanese surrendered, I knew I wouldn't have to go back overseas again.

After his honorable discharge from the Marine Corps, Ernie returned home to Clay City, Kentucky, married, settled down, raised a daughter, and lives there to this day.

SGT. WALTER SINCEK
When L-3-5 was on the Canal, Walter Sincek was a platoon sergeant, leading the 3rd Platoon damn near to hell and back. With men of the likes of Speedy Spach and Art Boston, Walter's 3rd Platoon fought like demons at the crest of L Company Ridge during the big mid-September battle. They refused in the face of several intensive attacks to fall back and abandon our ridge. Again during all the Matanikau River battles between late September and late October, Walter and the 3rd Platoon were in the thick of the fighting. To this day, when Speedy Spach talks about his old platoon sergeant, he nearly always ends his story saying something like "In L Company, Walter Sincek was a legend."

Walter was a big, strong man, well over six feet tall, with a big, deep, booming voice and a dry sense of humor. He grew up in Pittsburgh, joined the corps in the mid-1930s, did a four-year hitch, and then returned to civilian life until Pearl Harbor put him back in uniform. When he reenlisted, his prior experience earned him the rank of corporal, and it wasn't long before he took the next step up to sergeant.

Walter stayed with L Company after Guadalcanal, then went to Cape Gloucester, where he was shot up pretty bad. L Company took more combat casualties at Gloucester than at any of its other World War II engagements, so it's possible that the serious bout of malaria that finally separated me from the company might also have saved my life. Most of L Company's

KIAs at Cape Gloucester resulted from a single battle, when Col. William MacDougal ordered the men to cross a creek defended by at least one, and possibly two, Japanese machine-gun emplacements. Every time they took a step off the creek's bank, machine-gun fire would open up and knock a couple of them down.

Walter was one of the NCOs who protested to MacDougal, telling him that he was getting too many of our men killed. MacDougal told him, "Go out there and get your men across that creek or don't come back."

Walter went out with the intention of following orders and crossing that creek, and in the process, he was hit by three or four bullets. Not long after that, Colonel MacDougal was himself shot up by the Japs. Sincek and MacDougal were among the many seriously wounded who were somehow evacuated from the battle zone that day. Walter told me that it must have been hours later when he regained consciousness. By that time, he was on a hospital ship, tied down to a top bunk for safety. He was slipping in and out of consciousness, and at one point he came out of sedation just long enough to hear somebody groaning directly below him. Then Walter made out Colonel MacDougal's weak voice coming from the bunk beneath his: "Sincek, you awake?"

"Yeah," Walter managed to gasp.

"Can you move a little?" MacDougal asked. "You're bleeding, and it's dripping down on top of me."

Walter couldn't move. Not only was he strapped to his bunk, but he was just too weak to move, even had the straps been loosened. He told me that he passed out again, and hours later, when he regained consciousness, he asked a corpsman how Colonel MacDougal was making out.

"The colonel didn't make it," the corpsman told him. "He was buried at sea."

Walter did make it, but that was the end of combat for him. After the war ended, he went to Ordnance School at Quantico, where he met Virginia, who also happened to be a marine sergeant. Walter and Virginia hit it off and were soon married.

They later settled down in Oceanside, California, where they raised two strong boys. Walter and I had always been good friends, and at this stage in our lives, we also became neighbors. Walter, Virginia, my wife, Melva, and I spent many happy social occasions together, they with their two fine boys, and us with our good son, Richie. Walter and Virginia had a wonderful marriage, but it was much too short. I was on my second postwar tour in the Far East when I heard the bad new that Virginia had died.

Walter Sincek, the L Company legend, eventually settled in Washington State with one of his sons and lived on until the early 1990s. He and I kept in frequent touch until his death.

CURTIS A. "SPEEDY" SPACH

Curtis Allen Spach landed on Guadalcanal with the first wave of marines on August 7, 1942, and stayed on the front lines for the full 110 days until December 9, when L-3-5 was relieved and evacuated to Australia. He was in L Company's 3rd Platoon, and he was on top of L Company Ridge helping to defend it during the big September battle when we took quite a few casualties. Speedy wasn't among the casualties, though he was also in the thick of the several battles we fought at the Matanikau River. Spach survived the war, and as of 2003, he and his wife live happily in his hometown of Lexington, North Carolina. He keeps in touch regularly with his marine cobbers who survived Guadalcanal. Curtis Allen Spach wrote the following letter to his father in February 1943.

> Dear Dad,
> I think you will find this letter quite different than the others which you've received from me. My health is well as could be expected, as most of us boys in the original outfit that left the States together, only about [CENSORED] of us are still here. The others are replacements. The missing have either been killed, wounded or out from other various sources, mainly malaria fever.

On May 16 '42 we left New River, N.C., and went to the docks at Norfolk. On the 20th at midnight we hit the high seas with 7,000 Marines aboard the USS *Wakefield*. We went down through the Panama Canal and past Cuba. On the 29th we crossed the international date line, latitude 0°, 0', 0", longitude 85°, 45', 30". Was continually harassed by [Japanese] submarines as we had no convoy whatsoever.

We landed in New Zealand 28 days later and they were wonderful to us as we were the first Americans to arrive there. We lived aboard ship at the dock for about a month, loading equipment on incoming ships getting ready for *"The Day."* After working day and night, we left and went to one of the Fiji Islands for four days. I was aboard the USS *Fuller* picked up in New Zealand. In our convoy were about 100 ships including 3 aircraft carriers and the battleship *North Carolina*. We also had air protection from Flying Fortresses coming from Australia. On August 6 we had our last dinner aboard ship and they gave us all we wanted with ice cream and a pack of cigarettes. Just like a man doomed for the electric chair, he got any kind of food for this his last meal. That was our last for a while. Each one of us received a letter from our commanding officer, the last sentence reading "Good luck, god Bless You and to hell with the Japs." On the morning of the 7th, I went over the side with the first wave of troops as Rifle Grenadier, just another chicken in the infantry. With naval bombardment and supreme control of the air, we hit the beach at 9:47. All hell broke loose. Two days later, our ships left, taking our aircraft with them, [so that we were] never to have any sea and air protection for the next two [CENSORED]. In the meantime the Japanese Navy and Air Force took advantage and gave us hell from sea and air. I won't say what the ground troops had to offer us yet. I can say we never once retreated but kept rushing forward, taking the airport first thing.

Left to do or die, we fought hard with one purpose in mind to do: kill every slant-eyed bastard within range of rifle fire or the bayonet, which was the only thing left to stop their charge. We were on the front lines 110 days before we could drop back for a shave, and wash up. Don't many people know it but we were the first Allied troops to be on the lines that long, either in this war or the last. We had to face artillery, both naval and field, mortar bombings, sometimes three or four times a day, also at night, flame throwers, hand grenades, tanks, booby traps, land mines, everything I guess except gas. The most common headache was caused by machinegun fire, snipers, rifle fire, and facing sabers, bayonet fighting, the last most feared by all. I was in five offensive drives and also in defense of our own lines. I've had buddies shot down on both sides of me, my own closest call being a shot through the top of my helmet by a sniper. Once, I had to swim a river [the Matanikau] when we were trapped by the enemy.

With no supplies coming in we had to eat coconuts, captured rice, crab meat, fish heads. We also smoked their [the Japanese'] dopey cigarettes. We also captured a warehouse full of good Saba Beer, made in Tokyo. Didn't shave or have a haircut for nearly four months, looked rather funny too. Wore Jap clothing such as underwear, socks, shoes. Had plenty of thrills watching our boys in the airplanes dog-fighting after they sent us some planes to go on the newly finished field that they had built. We found field pieces and pictures of American girls and mothers on Japs that we killed. They were taken off the Marines at Wake Island. They used explosive and dum-dum bullets in their long rifles so we cut the ends of our own bullets off with bayonets so that when they [the Japanese] were hit, the bullet would spread, making a hell of a hole in them. You had to beat them at their own tricks. What few of the old fellows [are] still here, many of them are scarred by various wounds, and 90% of them have malaria. I've been down with it several times but I dose heavy with quinine till I feel drunk. It gets you so that you feel as if your eyes are popping out, and [leaves you feeling] very weak and lousy. We want to come home for a while before seeing action again, which we are told is in the very near future, but they won't [let us] do it, even though the doctors want us to. We were continually bombed and strafed but we took it pretty good. The average age of the boys was 21, and most were around 18 to 20. When we were finally relieved by the Army, who were all larger and older men, they were surprised to find us kids who had done such a good job. My best buddy at the time was caught in the face by a full blast of machinegun fire, and when the hole we were lying in became swamped by flies gathering about him, and [he] being already dead, I had to roll him out of the small hole to the top and open ground, and the dirty SOBs kept shooting him full of holes. Well anyway, God spared my life and I am thankful for it. I know that you and dear Mama's prayers helped bring me safely through the long months of it. I hope that you will forgive me of my misdoings, as it had to take this war to bring me to my senses. Only then did I realize how much you both had done for me, and Dear God, maybe I can come through the next [battle] to see you and my friends again.

God bless the whole world, and I'm looking forward to the days when Italy and Germany are licked so that the whole might of the Allied nations can be thrown in to crush Japan and the swine that are her sons, fighting to rule the white race. I heard an English-speaking Nip say that if he didn't die fighting, that is, if he didn't win or if he was captured, and later went back to Japan, he would be put in prison for 17 years and that all his property would be taken over by the government. That's his point of view. Wherever we go, us boys will do our best always and till the end, when we don't have the strength to press a trigger.

Please understand that I didn't write this so as to worry you any more than I already have, but I wanted you to know I am doing my best for your Uncle Sam. Maybe some day I will be able to sleep in that thing called a bed and eat from a table. Just simple everyday things, but they mean a lot when you have to live in jungles and lay in filthy, stinking surroundings day after day. If you let the folks over there see this, cut out the names of the ships and certain countries which I mentioned, for they shouldn't be discussed. Wishing you all health and happiness, will say goodbye for now. Give Mother and the kids my love.

> Love always, Your son,
> Allen

EPILOGUE

A Note on Iwo Jima

In February 1945, just a little more than two years after saying good-bye to Guadalcanal, I went into combat again, this time on Iwo Jima. It was a very different experience from Guadalcanal, and while my memories of the Canal remain vivid after sixty years, my recollection of Iwo has faded into a nasty lethal blur. Guadalcanal had been four slow months of misery and deprivation; Iwo Jima was a short, violent burst of pure hell. We lost many marines killed and wounded on Iwo Jima, but the campaign was over in something like four weeks. Back on the Canal, we lost relatively few men, but we subsisted on practically no supplies at all. We damn near starved to death. On Iwo Jima, we had all the supplies we needed, and more. Our problem was avoiding a quick, violent death.

Landing on Iwo Jima, we went in on LCVPs, which were landing craft with front ramps, big enough that we could fit a jeep on them with us. For that landing, I was a company gunnery sergeant with the 5th Pioneer Battalion, and also was head of the demolitions section. I'd trained our company—made up mostly of recruits—in infantry tactics back at Camp Pendleton, but we went ashore as a demolitions section with the 26th Regiment. After Suribachi was secured, we reverted to being a rifle company and remained so for the rest of our time on Iwo. The 26th Regiment was a part of the 5th Marine Division, which hadn't existed back when I was on Guadalcanal with L-3-5. Iwo Jima was bad. Anyplace you went, whatever you were doing, you were facing enemy fire. And you couldn't see the enemy because they were all dug in underground.

The day we landed, we went to the island, approaching it two boats at a time, zigging and zagging because the Japanese were firing at us as we came in. I believe my boat was in the second or third wave. Instructions were, as always, to keep our heads down, but I was peeking because I always wanted to see where I was going. I was looking toward the island, but except for incoming fire, there wasn't much to see. No buildings—nothing.

One thing I did see was the boat on our right getting hit when it was about a hundred feet from the beach. It was swamped in no time, but because it wasn't too far out, most of the guys made it in. I already was moving when our boat hit the beach, and I was halfway along the ramp as it was being lowered. Well before we landed, I'd told my guys, "When I hit the beach, I'm going to run. And you SOBs had better be right behind me."

When our ramp went down, it hit a kid from an earlier wave lying dead in the sand. The Japs had let the first few waves land and had let them come in just so far. Gen. Holland M. Smith, in his book *Coral and Brass*, says that the Japanese let our men advance inland to a distance of about 350 yards, which in my estimation seems correct. Then they cut off our waves and opened up with everything they had, clobbering each ensuing wave as it came in. We were instructed to go in just so far and dig in. I don't recall the distance, but it wasn't far. I carried a .50-caliber machine gun's receiver on my shoulder and a carbine slung across my back. For demolition, I had a pack of twelve blocks of TNT strapped to my chest, each block with a cap in its center. If I'd gotten hit by enemy fire, I wouldn't have been just killed—I'd have been blown up into a lot of tiny pieces. I also carried markers with red flags attached to them, for sticking in the ground and identifying the locations of land mines.

With my first step on the beach, I sank into the island's goddamned black sand, my feet going in a couple inches above my ankles with every step I took. I ran like hell anyway, my men right behind me. The first thing we reached was a berm, a steep embankment made by the heavy surf where it hit the shoreline at high tide. The surf nearly always came in from one direction, always hitting the same side of the island. It was the side where we were making our landing. We soon found out that the other side of the island had a halfway decent beach, which many of us believed we should have used for landing in the first place. On the second day of landings, the LSTs could hardly make it in because of the rough surf. It got so damned rough that even a seagoing tug was breached sideways, getting washed back and forth in the surf. Nobody—absolutely nobody in command—had the initiative to say, "Let's land on the island's other side." By that time they could have used the beach on the other side, because by the second day our troops had made it across that very small island. Not only was it important to get our equipment ashore, but most important of all was getting the wounded off the island. And there were plenty of wounded.

On one occasion on the beach, I ran for cover and made it to a shell hole. A doctor was in the hole, just sitting there, tears running down his face. I said, "What's wrong, doc?"

"I can't get these kids off the beach," he said "They're dying, and I can't get them off. The small boats that try to come in just get crushed."

It wasn't until halfway through the Iwo Jima operation that they started using the beach on the other side of the island. They were slow about it because of the way the operation order had been written. That order said that the beach they'd selected for the initial landing was perfect, so that was the order we had to follow.

Regarding the now-famous marine assault on Mount Suribachi, we were far from having the enemy cleaned up off the beach, but my unit was ordered to pick up our .50-caliber machine guns and move ahead to an area closer to Suribachi. I was told to fire into a cave that we knew held Japanese. The idea was to give them sporadic fire and keep them busy trying to fight us while another of our units climbed Suribachi from the opposite side. We could see our guys occasionally as they made their way up that small volcanic mountain—I think they were from the 26th Marines. They got to the top, which is when the first flag went up, but it came down pretty fast—I'd judge after seven minutes or so—because there was still ferocious fighting going on up there. You don't read much about it, but there was still plenty of fighting up on Suribachi. It was maybe an hour later that we saw the other flag go up, the big one you see in the famous news photo.

MANILA JOHN

"Manila" John Basilone was one of the marines who died on Iwo Jima. He also had been on the Canal in C Company, 1st Battalion 7th Marines, at the same time that we in L-3-5 had held up our end of the MLR against the Japanese. I want to include Manila John in this recollection because he was a personal friend. He was also a fine marine who played a big part in fighting off the Japanese land attack aimed at capturing Henderson Field in October '42. On that day, we in L-3-5 had our hands full fighting the Japanese in the area around the Matanikau River.

John didn't begin his military career as a marine. He did a hitch in the army before World War II and was stationed for most of that time in the Philippines. He boxed there and developed a reputation as a better-than-average fighter in the ring. For his matches, he used the name Manila John, which stayed with him for the rest of his too short life. After his army hitch, he returned to civilian life, but it wasn't long before war broke out in Europe. John decided to reenlist, this time joining the marines. He received an immediate NCO rating because of his army experience.

I first met John in New River, North Carolina, shortly before the Pearl Harbor attack. When the 7th Marine Regiment was reactivated soon after Pearl Harbor, he and a number of other NCOs from my outfit were absorbed into it and given priority in staffing. As soon as the 7th Regiment had a full complement, it shipped out from New River to American Samoa, which was then being harassed by the Japanese Navy's southern fleet.

The 7th Regiment arrived on Guadalcanal about a month after our original D-Day landing on that island, among the first of our badly needed reinforcement units. The Canal had to have been a rude shock for them after their Samoa duty. Back there, just about all of the 7th Regiment's action had taken place among the local female population and at several of Samoa's drinking spots.

On the Canal, John Basilone's C Company was a machine-gun unit of Chesty Puller's 1st Battalion. John distinguished himself in combat when a Japanese company attacked Puller's position south of Henderson Field during the night of October 24–25 and was recommended for the Medal of Honor. He was awarded the medal after we left the island and arrived in Australia. After that, he was sent stateside, where he joined several other medal winners on a U.S. War Bond tour. As he later told me, he put up with that hokum for a while, and then told the big wheels that he'd had enough. He told them he'd feel better about himself if he could go back into combat with his machine-gun company.

The next time I saw John was back in California, at Camp Pendleton. This was long after the Guadalcanal campaign, and a short time before we both shipped back out again to the Pacific, this time headed for Iwo Jima. During the months between my combat experiences on Guadalcanal and Iwo Jima, I'd married Melva, the mother of my son and my good companion of many years until her recent death. It turned out that John had gotten married at about the same time as Melva and I.

I'd just come off liberty on a Sunday evening, and as I checked in at Pendleton, the duty NCO mentioned to me that a party was going on at a tent a short distance down the company road. The boys were celebrating because one of them had just gotten married, and the NCO thought I probably knew the new bridegroom. The just-married marine turned out to be none other than Manila John Basilone.

"Hi-ya, Ore, join the party!"

It was long-time-no-see, and since we were both newly married, we drank to our mutual good fortune.

The next stop for us both turned out to be Iwo Jima. On that godforsaken island, the Japanese mortar units developed a

Ore Marion after the Guadalcanal campaign but before Iwo Jima.
ESTATE OF ORE J. MARION

tactic that cost many American lives. They would register their mortars on an especially prominent bomb crater, and wait until they spotted several marines dive or crawl into that crater for shelter. At that point, the Japs would drop a mortar shell into the crater—*Bam!*—and God help the men who thought they'd found a safe spot on the battlefield.

It was still my platoon's first day on Iwo Jima, and I was lucky enough to be in a smaller crater that the nearby Jap mortar crews either didn't see or hadn't thought worth targeting. They'd been too busy zeroing in on a large crater nearby. One of the guys in my platoon dove into my crater and said to me, "Jesus, stay put! Everyone is dead around here." His words came to me against the crackle of rifle fire, machine-gun fire, and blasts from mortar bursts that were breaking loose in every direction around us.

I stayed put for about ten minutes, then took off for what I naively believed was a safer spot. I rushed toward the big crater, which wasn't more than ten yards away, then stopped when I reached its edge. What I saw there was bad. John Basilone was in there and he was dead. So was a lieutenant I didn't know. A third man was down there with them, and I recognized him as Gunnery Sgt. George Barnyak. At first I thought he was dead, too, but a corpsman got to him in time, and George survived.

That awful day was the last time I saw John Basilone. I prefer to remember him on that earlier, happier evening back at Pendleton, when we drank together to celebrate our recent marriages.

Postscript by Thomas Cuddihy

Ore J. Marion died on March 3, 2003, a little more than four months before his eighty-second birthday. Though diagnosed with lymphoma, and having undergone a couple of major operations several years earlier, he was always cheerful, outgoing, and physically active. He refused to be bedridden until the final week of his life.

I saw him for the last time during Christmas week of 2002, little more than two months before his death. In fact, on Christmas Day, Ore and I drove together on snowy Buffalo streets to enjoy Christmas dinner together with his sister Doris and several other close relatives. I am just one among Ore's several nephews. We all exchanged gifts and enjoyed the day, but Ore was clearly fatigued by early evening when I drove him home. In the car, he mentioned this book. "It seems to me we've got it nearly finished," he remarked.

"You're right," I said. "All that's left for me is to check the spellings of some names. Make sure we have them right. Then we'll print the whole thing out and go looking for a publisher."

"That's good," he said. "It really *is* done, then. And we got it down just the way I wanted it."

Ore and I spoke of other things over the following day or two, before I returned home to Long Island, but except for a few brief phone calls in the weeks that followed, that was the last time we spoke together about the book.

Ore Marion lived a long and mainly happy life, but of course there were sad times, too. He outlived his wife, Melva, by many years, then outlived his only son, Richard, who died far too young in 1988. Richard, called Richie by many friends and relatives, followed in his dad's footsteps, serving a hitch in the

Marine Corps and acquitting himself honorably in Vietnam. He returned to civilian life and settled down in the Buffalo area, where he married a fine hometown girl, Kathleen O'Connor. They raised a son, Jeffrey, who currently practices law in Williamsville, New York, a Buffalo suburb. Ore's grandson Jeff is now happily married. He and his wife, Kelly, have a son of their own—Ore's great-grandson—a bright, healthy, cheerful little boy named Gregory. Ore was the first person, other than his mother and father, to hold little Greg in his arms.

On May 14, 2003, with Jeffrey and Kelly in attendance, Ore Marion's ashes were interred at Arlington National Cemetery in a formal ceremony that did honor both to him and to the United States Marine Corps, which he truly loved. To Ore J. Marion, *Semper Fi* was more than just a motto. It was a way of life.

Thomas Cuddihy
September 2003
Farmingdale, New York

A Guadalcanal Glossary

Words or terms marked with an asterisk (*) are cross-referenced.

Alligator Creek. The marines' nickname for the Ilu River, a small and for the most part shallow river located east of Henderson Field and flowing into the sea. It was a natural habitat for man-eating alligators, which killed a few incautious marines during the course of the Guadalcanal campaign. In September 1942, it was also the site of the so-called battle of the Tenaru River, a marine victory. On some of the first Guadalcanal maps available to the marines, the Ilu River was mislabeled as the nearby Tenaru River, which added further to the confusion of names.

BAR, or Browning automatic rifle. This potent and very dependable weapon saw service in the U.S. Army and Marine Corps during both world wars and in Korea. It is a .30-caliber gun mounted on a retractable bipod and having firepower comparable to a light machine gun. Although heavier than a standard rifle, it is far more portable than any reliable machine gun of the World War II era.

Berm line. A strip of land situated inland from a beach and running parallel to the shoreline. It takes the form of a rise in the terrain where the beach ends and gives way to inland formations and vegetation. Also, any shelflike rise in relatively flat terrain.

Cactus Air Force. The nickname given to the makeshift squadron of U.S. Navy and Marine pilots who began using Henderson Field as their air base following the marine invasion of Guadalcanal.

Cobber. An Australian colloquial term that means the same thing as *pal* or *buddy* in the United States, or *mate* in England. Marines who fought in the Solomon Islands during World War II spent considerable time in Australia and New Zealand, where they picked up many local phrases. Many American veterans of Guadalcanal used (and still use) the word *cobber* exclusively to signify those special buddies with whom they shared battle hardships and experiences.

Corpsman. The marines' equivalent of an army medic. A doctor's assistant.

CP. Command post.

D-1. Division Personnel Section.

D-2. Division Intelligence Section.

D-3. Division Operations Section.

D-4. Division Supply Section.

Digger. An Australian infantryman, the equivalent of our raggedy-ass marine*.

Entrenching tool. This small shovel with a folding handle is part of an infantryman's standard field equipment, used mainly to dig foxholes or spider holes*.

Expeditionary cans. Metal containers designed and used by the U.S. military to carry approximately five liquid gallons of anything from gasoline or motor oil to drinking water or hot coffee. These containers later became better known as "jerry cans," because they were originally designed and used by the German military, called the Jerries by Americans and Brits during World War II.

Fieldstrip. To take a weapon apart to the extent of separating its main components, as a first step in cleaning it, lubricating it, and when necessary, making minor repairs.

Fighter Strips One and Two. Henderson Field was initially a single airstrip designed to accommodate both larger planes and fighters. Subsequently during the course of the Guadalcanal campaign, a second smaller airstrip, called Fighter Strip One, was constructed east of the main airfield and used for fighter planes. Still later, a third airstrip, Fighter

Strip Two, was cleared on an area of flat land across the Lunga River from the main airfield and northwest of it. Fighter Strip Two was little more than a leveled grass field, but it was adequate to accommodate Grumman F4F Wildcats and other U.S. fighter planes. Oddly, Fighter Strip Two fails to appear on many maps included in battle histories of Guadalcanal, though there are many textual references to it.

Gunny. Marine slang for gunnery sergeant.

Higgins boat. Any one of several types of diesel-powered craft used for military operations, designed by the engineer and boat builder Andrew Jackson Higgins. The Higgins boats used for marine landings and subsequent operations at Guadalcanal were open boats that accommodated a marine-size platoon, or approximately thirty to forty men. The Higgins boats used at Guadalcanal were not the well-known barge-type landing craft with a bow that lowers to become a ramp, such as the kind used to land troops at Normandy in 1944, but were considerably smaller. The marines who landed on Guadalcanal disembarked from their Higgins boats by climbing over the gunwale when the boat's bottom touched the beach.

Ironbottom Sound. Nickname for a stretch of ocean located between Guadalcanal and Savo Island. It is so named because of the large number of U.S., Australian, and Japanese ships that went to the bottom in the course of many fierce naval engagements from August 1942 to January 1943. Today that underwater wreckage is covered with coral and is home to a huge variety of marine fish and other life forms, which makes it a favorite haunt for sport divers.

Jungle rot. The informal name for a common medical problem suffered by combatants in jungle terrain during World War II. Because of the tropical humidity, the lack of basic sanitation, the scarcity of antiseptic medications and bandages, and an environment filled with harmful bacteria, flies, and general decay, any untreated skin lesion was likely to become infected, and the infection nearly always spread and worsened for as long as it was left untreated. The result was jungle rot—painful and debilitating skin ulcers suffered by the majority of both American and Japanese frontline fighters on Guadalcanal.

Kanai grass. Typical ground covering on grassy plains areas of tropical islands throughout much of the South Pacific. Kanai grass is tough and fibrous and grows in thick clusters, often to a height of five or six feet. In appearance, it is similar to Johnson grass or sorghum, common in the American Midwest. When a marine was situated in a thicket of tall kanai grass, he could often hear the thrashing of somebody moving just a few feet away from him, though each man seldom could see the other.

KIA. Killed in action.

Lewis gun. An air-cooled .30-caliber light machine gun, first used by the marines in France during World War I. Two Lewis guns were mounted in turrets located forward on Higgins boats* used by the marines for the Guadalcanal campaign.

LMG. Light machine gun.

M-1 rifle, or Garand. The standard U.S. Army infantryman's rifle during World War II and for many years after was this .30-caliber, semiautomatic, gas-operated weapon with an effective range of several hundred yards. Being gas-operated was what made the M-1 semiautomatic, a technical improvement over older, manually operated bolt-action rifles like the earlier Springfield '03*. The rifleman manually operated the M-1 rifle's bolt only once, as he inserted a new clip of ammunition into the magazine. Slamming the bolt shut served to position the clip's first bullet into the firing chamber. When that round was fired, the explosion's trapped gas activated a piston in the rifle's mechanism that automatically operated the rifle's bolt, ejecting the spent cartridge and moving the next round of ammo from its clip and into the firing chamber. Thus to fire subsequent shots from the M-1, the rifleman needed only to squeeze the trigger. The marines didn't have the M-1 during the Guadalcanal campaign, though the army's Americal Division brought it to the island when they relieved the marines during the later part of the campaign. The M-1 is a rugged, sturdy, and accurate weapon that remained the standard American infantryman's rifle until it was replaced by more advanced rifles at about the time of the Vietnam War.

MIA. Missing in action.

Military crest. A point on the topography as one approaches the summit of a hill, ridge, or other high land formation. A military crest's position in relation to the summit is determined entirely by the land formation's shape. A military crest exists when, from the hill's summit, the land's curve or slope is such that a person or object located just below the military crest is out of the line of sight of any observer who is at the summit. Advancing to a land formation's military crest in combat is a preliminary step toward advancing to the summit, taking it, and thus commanding the entire hill or ridge.

MLR. Main line of resistance, or the string of defense positions located along the perimeter of any territory being held and defended.

Nambu. A light Japanese automatic rifle or submachine gun that was used extensively on Guadalcanal. The Japanese also used a Nambu automatic sidearm, or pistol.

Navy jargon. Because they are a branch of the U.S. Navy, the marines use many sailors' terms, which often differ not only from civilian jargon, but also from jargon used in the U.S. Army. Here are just a few of the more common navy/marine terms: *deck*, to indicate not only a ship's deck, but also the floor or the ground; *bulkhead*, to indicate a wall; *sack* to indicate a bed or cot; *boot camp*, the eight-week-long equivalent of basic training in the army; *brig* for a military prison (equivalent to the army's *stockade*); and *bay*, to indicate a large room on land or a ship's compartment.

New River. The World War II–era marine base located in North Carolina, today much enlarged and renamed Fort Lejeune.

Nicknames. It would appear that virtually every marine who served during World War II soon picked up a nickname from his buddies, and the nickname stayed with him forever, sometimes becoming better known than the name on his birth certificate. Everybody from privates to generals picked up a nickname. For instance, everyone who has ever been in the U.S. Marine Corps knows the name "Chesty" Puller, though not everyone is aware that Puller's first name was Lewis. Mysteriously, though a second-generation Italian-American, I picked up the Polish nickname "Makeki," from one of my Polish-American buddies. I have no idea what "Makeki" means, or if it means anything. Nicknames of some of my fellow cobbers* include "Yogi" Milana; "Hardrock" Gerkin; "Manila" John Basilone; "Stinky" Denham; "Speedy" Spach; "Brute" Krulak; "No-Clothes" Trabendus; and "Beebee-Eyes" Parnelli. Many new nicknames were assigned to cobbers during the Guadalcanal campaign, often as unofficial badges of honor, but because of their triple-X rating, they are best omitted from this glossary.

Ninety-day wonder. World War II nickname for college graduates who, because of the manpower shortage, were commissioned as army or marine second lieutenants or navy ensigns immediately after a very brief ninety-day officer-training course. These fresh-out-of-college kids were often underestimated and sometimes sneered at by the military's regulars because of their inexperience. Even so, the majority of "ninety-day wonders" served their country well, and several of them earned my respect and friendship, including the young officer who was my platoon leader on the Canal, Lt. John "Flash" Flaherty.

Old Man. Informal name for the CO, or commanding officer, of any military unit, whether a company commander with the rank of captain or a general who commands an entire division.

One-Log Bridge. The name given by the Americans to a crude wooden bridge used at various times by both the Japanese and Americans to cross Guadalcanal's Matanikau River.

A Guadalcanal Glossary

The bridge was located in jungle highlands, roughly a mile upstream from the river's mouth.

Piss and punk. Marine slang of the World War II era for being jailed in the brig and restricted to a diet of bread and water for any serious violation of regulations. Most of the time, the bread was improved by a mess sergeant who felt some compassion for the man who'd been put on piss and punk. Normally, the jailed man's buddies would work a deal with the mess sergeant (maybe a bottle of booze allegedly for medicinal purposes), who would proceed to "load" the loaf of bread before it went into the oven. A loaf with a circle marked on the crust would indicate a hard-boiled egg inside. A loaf marked with a straight line would contain cold cuts (usually referred to as "horse cock"). An X on the loaf sometimes indicated fried chicken baked into the loaf. Marine regulations dictated that before a man could be put on piss and punk, he had to be given a cursory physical exam and weighed. After five to ten days on piss and punk, he would often gain weight. The medics could never figure out why.

Pistol Pete. The marines' nickname for a long-range Japanese field artillery piece that lobbed random shells into the marine-held sector of Guadalcanal throughout the campaign. Pistol Pete's targets varied from day to day and probably were selected at random by Japanese spotters, many of them situated on Mount Austen, the combat sector's highest point. Pistol Pete inflicted relatively light damage during the campaign and served mainly as a Japanese effort to lower the Marines' morale.

Raggedy-ass marines. The World War II nickname for the 1st Marine Division—one of the most famous and most highly decorated of all American fighting outfits from the time it first distinguished itself in France during World War I. The description "raggedy-ass" was based on the fact that during the 1920s, '30s, and '40s, the 1st Marines' field uniform was an odd mixture of army and navy apparel. When it came to supplies and equipment, the marines of that era nearly always had to settle for the leftovers and hand-me-downs from the army and navy.

Scuttlebutt. Gossip and/or rumors. A scuttlebutt is literally a water fountain either ashore or on a ship, similar to a civilian water cooler, where employees congregate to take a break and trade gossip.

Seabees. The popular name given to U.S. Navy construction engineers and their work crews. The Seabees built many valuable military installations during World War II, one of their better-known operations being the construction of Guadalcanal's Henderson Field following the marines' occupation of that partly built Japanese landing strip.

Shelter half. A component in an infantryman's field pack that consists of a piece of canvas and comes with pegs and rope. Two shelter halves can be combined to make a small, two-man pup tent—a sleeping shelter for times when infantrymen set up a bivouac, or a temporary campsite.

Spider hole. A variation on the well-known foxhole, the spider hole was a marine's common way of "digging in" when situated in battle terrain. It tended to be both deeper and smaller than a standard foxhole, and accommodated only one man, while a foxhole might sometimes be wide enough for two or more men. During a bombardment, a marine often took advantage of the spider hole's small opening by crawling inside and covering it over with any solid material that was handy. Use of the spider hole was a major reason why the marines suffered light casualties during severe air and sea bombardments. The enemy needed to score a direct hit on a spider hole to inflict a casualty, and direct hits fortunately were rare occurrences.

Springfield M1903. Also known more simply as the Springfield '03, or the '03, this .30-caliber bolt-action rifle was the marine infantryman's standard weapon throughout the Guadalcanal campaign. The designation M1903 stands for the year when this rifle first came into use. It was a standard weapon for both the U.S. Army and Marine Corps in France during World War I. By 1942, it was being replaced throughout the U.S. Army by the M-1 rifle*. However, the marines were not issued the M-1 until after the army had been fully supplied, by which time the Guadalcanal campaign had ended. The new M-1, being semiautomatic, had the advantage of a more rapid rate of fire than the '03, although many experienced riflemen, myself included, found the '03 to be somewhat more accurate than the M-1.

Washing Machine Charlie. The marines' term for one particular slow-flying Japanese airplane that circled over the marine-held sector of Guadalcanal nearly every night during the entire campaign and dropped one or two bombs at random. Washing Machine Charlie got its name because the distinctive chugging sound of the plane's engine reminded the marines of a washing machine motor. The plane's bombings caused very few casualties and served the Japanese mainly as a rudimentary form of psychological warfare.

WIA. Wounded in action.

YP Boats. Nicknamed Yippee boats by the marines, and also sometimes called "tuna boats" by the sailors who manned them, these were originally civilian vessels of several types, relatively small in size but oceangoing, and adapted for use by the navy to ferry supplies to Guadalcanal.

Index

Page numbers in italics indicate illustrations.

Air Battles in the Pacific (film), 247
air combat, 246–47
  bombing raids, 223, 228–33
  support, 137, 147–49
aircraft
  Avenger torpedo bombers, 247
  Flying Fortresses, 147–49
  Grumman F4F Wildcats, 246–47
  Japanese Zeros, 173–77, 246–47
  mystery, incident, 177–83
Alchiba, USS, 250–54
  marines watching burning of, *252*
  tug fighting fires on, *251*
  unloading heavy equipment from, *27*
Aldridge, Clarence, 130, 131
  wounding of, 132–33
Americal Division of the U.S. Army, 14
Anderson, Sergeant, 184
antitank guns, 227
Arndt, Ernest "Monk," 79, 93, 94
Arnold, Pharmacist Mate, 87
Astoria, sinking of, 71
Atlanta, USS, 14, 195–204, *200*
Avenger torpedo bombers, 247

B Company, 3rd Battalion, 5th Marines, 81
Ballentine, Eugene, 82
BAR squad, 225–26
Barbey, Major, 134
Barnes, Joe, 64
Barnyak, George, 295
Basilone, John "Manila," 292–95
bayonets
  accident, 129–30
  fix, 190

beach defense, 247–50
  examples of inept leadership on, 101–7
Biebush, Frederick C., 121, 131, 134, 267–73
Blake, Bobby, 62–64
  speech, 65–66
Bloody Ridge, battle of, 11–13, 121, 136
Bloody Ridge: The Battle That Saved Guadalcanal (Smith), 128
Blue Manual, The. See Fighting on Guadalcanal
boats, Yippee, 241–44
bombing raids, 223, 228–31
  Pistol Pete, 231–33
bonding, 261, 264
Book-of-the-Month Club incident, 240–41
Borgeson, Gunny Sergeant, 227
Boston, Arthur J., 2, 64, 67, 126, 160, 282
  on Goettge Patrol massacre, 79–80
  on L Company Ridge, 122–25, 127–28
Bowen, Robert O., 171–73
Branic, John, 82, 84, 273, 274
  first marine killed in Matanikau engagement, 92–93
breakfast incident, 116–20
Bright, Raleigh, 140, 267–73
Broderson, Jesse, *263*
Browning automatic rifles (BARs), 225–26
Buffalo Evening News, quotes from, 23, 39, 42, 80–81, 95, 136, 154, 174, 177, 183, 204
bunkers, 151–54
Byrne, Red, 208

Cactus Air Force, 137
cameras, 221
Camp Cable, catching malaria at, 189
Canberra, sinking of, 71
Cape Gloucester engagement, 282–83
caribou, 115–16
Carter, Fred, 212
Carver, Corporal, 82
Case, John, 88, 104
Chicago, 199–201
China, Japanese invasion of, 214–15
cobbers, 75–77, 261–64
  Biebush, 267–73
  Branic, 273
  Bright, 267–73
  Gerkin, 275–79
  meaning of, 75
  Milana, 279–80
  Selvitelle, 265–67
  Sincek, 282–84
  Snowden, 280–82
  Spach, 284–88
  Steen, 273–74
Colhoun, USS, *105*
  sinking of, 104–7
communication systems, 45, 228
Coral and Brass (Smith), 290
Coral Sea, battle of the, 216
crabs, land, 36
crossing the T, 197, 199
Cuddihy, Thomas
  introduction by, 1–14
  postscript by, 297–98
cutting a field of fire, 140–42

Dahlgren, Virginia, 59
Davidson, Sergeant, 227
Davis, H. M., 211
D-Day, 24–39, *25*
  landing craft heading toward shore on, *29*
Dear John letters, 277–78
defense positions, delay, 195–96
Denham, Harry "Stinky," 28, 61, 64, 266
Diedrick, Sergeant, 191
Division Intelligence Section (G-2), at Matanikau River, 7–8
dogs, encounter with, 168–69

Edson, Merritt A., 11–12, 121, 158, 210
  Raider Company, 155, 159–60
Edwards, Billy, 199

Farmer, Edward, 122, 126, 128, 140
Feagin, C. M., 211–12
Few, Frank, 79, 80, 93
5th Marines
  detachment of, at Matanikau River, 7–8
  rifle companies, 64
  See also individual battalions; individual companies
5th Pioneer Battalion, 289
Fighting on Guadalcanal (booklet), 208–14
  excerpts from, 211–13
1st Battalion, 5th Marines, 155
1st Battalion, 1st Marines, at Tenaru River, 8–9
1st Parachute Battalion, 12
1st Platoon, at first battle at the Matanikau, 83–84
flags, raising the colors on Guadalcanal, 74
Flaherty, John "Flash," 26, 30, 47, 48, 49, 72, 102, 113, 122, 128, 129–30, 140, 149, 156, 173, 196, 259–60, 274
Fleet Marines, 59–60
Fletcher, Frank J., 7
Flying Fortresses, 147–49
food
  larceny of, 235–36
  shortages of, 77–79
  special breakfast incident, 116–20
Ford, Henry, 2
Frank, Richard B., 107, 131
friendly fire incident, 131–33
From the Shores of Tripoli (film), 239

George Elliot, attack on, 32–34
Gerkin, Lawrence E. "Hardrock," 44, 64, 88, 89–90, 91–92, 94, 104, 106, 142, 152, 153, 201, 241, 256, 275–79, 276
  Japanese Navy Zeros and, 174–77
  Rhodes and, 162–65
  Vandegrift encounter, 204–8
Ghormley, Admiral, 76, 107

Index 311

Goettge, Frank, 7–8, 93
Goettge Patrol
 massacre, 79–80, 93
 remains, discovery of, 93–94
Grumman F4F Wildcats, 246–47
Guadalcanal
 approaching, 23–24
 D-Day on, 24–39, *25, 29*
 the first, 222–23, 224
 leaving, 217–20
 marines on, *135*
 raising the colors on, *74*
 the second, 223–24
 smell of air on, 31–32
 strategic importance of, 5–6
 terrain of, 4–5
 the third, 224
Guadalcanal Campaign, 216
 battle of Bloody Ridge, 11–13, 121, 136
 battle of Savo Island, 7, 47
 battle of the Tenaru River, 8–9, 32, 94–95, 215
 in brief, 6–14
 D-Day, 24–39, *25, 29*
 environmental caused casualties during, 11
 examples of inept leadership during, 101–7
 first battle of the Matanikau, 10, 79–88, 92–93
 goal of Japanese during, 10
 Iwo Jima operation comparison, 289
 Manchester on, 71–72
 map of, *16*
 massacre at Matanikau River, 7–8
 naval engagements, 11, 14
 overview and background of, 3–4
 second battle of the Matanikau, 13, 154–67
 third battle of the Matanikau, 13, 167–73
Guadalcanal Campaign Veterans, reunion, 262, *263*
Guadalcanal: The Definitive Account of the Landmark Battle (Frank), 107, 131
Guadalcanal Echoes, 1, 211, 213, 221, 226, 231
Guadalcanal Remembered (Merilat), 254

Guadalcanal Veteran's Museum, 213
Guffin, Tom, 144–45, 201

Haberle, Frank, 130, 131
 wounding of, 132–33
Halsey, William, 107, 194
hand-to-hand battle, 191
Harris, Fred, on *Alchiba*, 250–54
Hawkins, William, 81
Hayes, USS, *29*
Henderson Airfield, *40*
 capture of, 39–42
Honiara, 187, 188
howitzer incident, 149–51
Hunt, Leroy P., 45, 97–101

I Company, 3rd Battalion, 5th Marines, 81, 155, 160, 189
Ichiki, Kiyoano, 8, 32, 94, 214, 215
 death of, 9
Illich, Ivan, 2
illnesses, 11, 223
Ilu River, 95
Infantryman's Journal, The, 210
Ironbottom Sound, 11
Iwo Jima operation, 289–98
 Guadalcanal Campaign comparison, 289
 Japanese mortar units tactics during, 293–95
 Mount Suribachi assault, 291–92

Japanese Army, 214–17
Japanese "Betty" bombers, attacking U.S. ships, *33*
Japanese landing craft, 113–14
Japanese mortar units, tactics of, 293–95
Japanese Navy Zeros, 173–77, 246–47
Japanese sword, marines displaying captured, *170*
Japanese tanks, at Matanikau River, 183–85
jasmine, 222

K Company, 3rd Battalion, 5th Marines, 155, 160, 189
Kawaguchi, Kayotaki, 12, 13, 214, 215
Kelly, Carl, 130–31

Klemicki, Henry, 64, 116, 130, 131, 263
  wounding of, 132–33
Kokumbona, examples in inept leadership at, 96–101
Koro Island
  fiasco, 17–23
  terrain, 17–18
Krulak, Charles C., 267
Kukum Village, 42–47
  submarine incident at, 44–46
Kulchycki, "Wild Bill," 26, 30, 34–35, 43, 73, 91, 274

L Company, 3rd Battalion, 5th Marines, 60
  company street at New River, 63
  general situation on Guadalcanal, 49–52
  getting ready for war, 61–65
  on Koro Island, 17–23
  leaving Guadalcanal, 217–20
  men of, 1–3, 64, 66–69
  veterans at reunion, 263
L Company Ridge, attack on, 121–36
L-3-5. *See* L Company, 3rd Battalion, 5th Marines
landing craft, Japanese, 113–14
larceny incidents
  flatbed truck, 233–35
  food, 235–36
  sake, 236–39
leadership, inept, 95–96
  on Guadalcanal, 101–7
  at Kokumbona, 96–101
Little, "Doc," 82
  death of, 83
Los Angeles Evening Herald and Express, 85

M Company, 3rd Battalion, 5th Marines, 189, 226–27
  antitank gun crew, 227
  machine-gun near disaster, 101–4
McAllan, Francis R. "Chink," 24, 39, 64, 208
MacArthur, Douglas, 71
MacDougal, William, 283
machine guns, heavy (HMGs), 226
McMillan, George, on Matanikau River Engagement, 159–60
McMullen, William, 126
maggots, 78
mail call incidents, 239–41
  "Dear John" letters, 277–78
Mallory, Don, 273
Manchester, William, on Guadalcanal Campaign, 71–72
Manchuria, Japanese invasion of, 214
"Manchurian Nights" (song), 214
maps, Guadalcanal Campaign, *16*
Marine Corps, 55–57
  boot camp, 57
  examples of inept leadership in, 95–107
  1st Division, 4
  infantry battalion structure, 226–27
  joining the, 55–57
  "Old Breed," 60
  prewar years in, 57–61
  rifleman's training, 109
  self-reliance of, 208–14
  silent contempt offense, 56
  warriors, 52
  See also 5th Marines; *and individual battalions; individual companies*
Marine Raider Battalion, 12
Marion, Gregory, 298
Marion, Jeffrey, 298
Marion, Kathleen O'Connor, 298
Marion, Kelly, 298
Marion, Melva, 293, 297
Marion, Ore J., 1–2, 10, *58*, 212–13, *263*, *294*
  death of, 297–98
  family and childhood of, 53–55
  first duty station, 59
  joining L-3-5, 60
  joining the Marines, 55–57
  nickname, 262
  prewar years in Marine Corps, 57–61
Marion, Richard, 297–98
Matanikau, first battle of the, 10, 79–83
  entering village of Matanikau, 85–88

Index

first marine killed at, 92–93
1st Platoon experience at, 83–84
objective, 79
2nd Platoon experience at, 81–83
Matanikau, second battle of the, 13, 154–67
casualties, 161–62
Japanese charge, 159–60
Matanikau, third battle of the, 13, 167–73
Matanikau, village of, 187–88
Matanikau-Point Cruz engagement. *See* Point Cruz engagement
Matanikau River
Japanese tanks at, 183–85
massacre at, 7–8
Maxwell, William E., 96–101
Mead, George, 81, 82, 84, 140, 274
death of, 83
Merilat, Herb, on torpedo coming ashore, 254–55
Midway, battle of, 216
Miglen, Charlie, 82, 85
death of, 83
Milana, Richard E. "Yogi," 2, 44, 54, 67–68, 90, 94, 104, 256, 279–80
experience with 1st Platoon at Matanikau, 83–84
special breakfast incident, 116–20
on submarine incident at Kukum Village, 46
Miller, George, 90
Miller, Harry D., 95, 227
missed-boat incident, 268–71
Morris, Paul, 140
mortars, song about, 227
Motsinger, Jim, 128
Mount Austen, 147, 195
Mount Suribachi, assault on, 291–92
Muck, Timothy E., 82
mules, 222

Nasu, Yumio, 13
death of, 14
naval engagements, 11, 14, 195–204, 244–46
"Betty" bombers attacking U.S. ships, *33*

crossing the T tactic used during, 197, 199
Japanese tactics during, 199
Naval Powder Factory, 59
Navy, example of inept leadership in, 104–7
New York Times, 71
New Zealand, 261

O'Dell, George, 64
Oka, Colonel, 13–14, 214, 215–16
Old Breed, 60
Old Breed, The (McMillan), 159
O'Neal, Thomas, 184

Parker, Joe, 157
parrot incident, 111–12
Patch, Alexander, 4, 14, 193
Payne, John (actor), 239
Payne, John R., 239–30
Pazofsky, Harold, 128
Peleliu, 281–82
photographs, 221
Pigeon, Roger, 199, 201, 203
Pistol Pete. *See* Tani, Akio
Point Cruz engagement, 187–95
Poloshian, Hap, 41, 90, 94, 104, 106, 114, 129, 130, 158, 256
President Jackson, USS, 208
on board, 219–20
getting aboard, 217–19
Prewitt, Don, *263*
promotions, 140–46
Puller, Lewis "Chesty," 13, 155, 165–67

Quincy, sinking of, 71

Reising submachine guns, 91, 224
Rhodes, Luther L. "Dusty," Gerkin and, 162–65
rifle grenade, 47–49
rifleman's training, 109
rifles
Browning automatic, 225–26
Springfield '03, 209–10, 225
Rivera, Ralph, 144
Rogers, Pete, 64
Rumbley, T. E., 212
Rust, Bill, 79
Rust, Edward, 84

sake, larceny of, 236–39
Savo Island, battle of, 7, 47
scouting patrol, 109–13
   parrot incident, 111–12
2nd Battalion, 1st Marines, at Tenaru River, 8–9
2nd Platoon, at first battle at the Matanikau, 81–83
Selvitelle, Ben, 64, 90, 91, 93, 126, 144, 145–46, 201, 265–67, 274
semaphore messages, 118
senses, heightening of, 198
Shambo, 197
Shoemaker, Willie C., 64, 83, *263*
shortages, 222–23
   food, 77–79
Shumate, Quentin, 30, 82, 274
silent contempt offense, 56
Sileo, Nick, on platoon entering village of Matanikau, 85–88
Simon, Thomas F., 82
Sincek, Walter "Chum," 140, 194–95, 273, 282–84
Smallwood, Gunny, 227
Smith, Holland M., 290
Smith, J. W., 82
Smith, Jerry, 104
Smith, John, 171
Smith, Michael S., 128
Smith, Milton H. "Smitty," 123
snapping in, 137–39
Snowden, Ernest, 2, 54, 69, 137, *263*, 280–82
   on discovery of Goettge Patrol remains, 94
   experience with 2nd Platoon at Mantanikau, 81–83
   on Japanese tanks, 183–84
   on Peleliu experience, 281–82
Somick, Boris C., 83
Spach, Curtis A. "Speedy," 2, 54, 64, 160, *263*, 282, 284–88
   on Japanese tanks, 184
Spaulding, Joseph, 93
spider holes, 151–52, 228
Springfield '03 rifles, 209–10, 225
Spurlock, Lyman D., 26, 72, 79, 156
Steen, William, 24, 273–74
   death of, 38–39
submarine incident, at Kukum Village, 44–46

supplies incident, 259–60
sword, Japanese, marines displaying captured, *170*

Tani, Akio (Pistol Pete), 11, 231–33
tanks, Japanese, at Mataikau River, 183–85
Tenaru River, battle of the, 8–9, 32, 94–95, 215
3rd Battalion, 5th Marines, structure of, 226–27
3rd Battalion, 2nd Marines, 155
Tokyo Express, 8
Tora Ridge. *See* L Company Ridge
torpedo incident, 254–58, *257*
truck, larceny of, 233–35
26th Regiment, 5th Marines, 289

Vandegrift, Alexander A., 4, 71, 97, 100, 147–48, 165–67, 192–93, 266
   Gerkin encounter, 207–8
victory fever, 9
Victory at Sea (film), 247
Vincennes, sinking of, 71

Walt, Lou, 158
warriors, main ingredients that make good, 52
weapons, 56, 61, 224–28
   antitank guns, 227
   Browning automatic rifles (BARs), 225–26
   heavy machine guns (HMGs), 226
   howitzer incident, 149–51
   Reising submachine guns, 91, 224
   Springfield '03 rifles, 209–10, 225
Wellington's Aotea Quay, 271
Whaling, William J., 79
wine incident, 271–73
Woods, Eddie "Curly," 41, 83, 104

Yippee boats, 241–44
yoga, 118

Zega, Stanley "Stash," 41, 104, 256
Zeros, Japanese Navy, 173–77, 246–47